Mentoring While White

Mentoring While White

Culturally Responsive Practices for Sustaining the Lives of Black College Students

Edited by Bettie Ray Butler,
Abiola Farinde-Wu, and Melissa Winchell

LEXINGTON BOOKS
Lanham • Boulder • New York • London

Published by Lexington Books
An imprint of The Rowman & Littlefield Publishing Group, Inc.
4501 Forbes Boulevard, Suite 200, Lanham, Maryland 20706
www.rowman.com

86-90 Paul Street, London EC2A 4NE

British Library Cataloguing in Publication Information Available

Library of Congress Cataloging-in-Publication Data

Names: Butler, Bettie Ray, 1981- editor. | Farinde-Wu, Abiola, editor. | Winchell, Melissa, 1976- editor.
  Title: Mentoring while white : culturally responsive practices for sustaining the lives of Black college students / edited by Bettie Ray Butler, Abiola Farinde-Wu, and Melissa Winchell.
  Description: Lanham, Maryland : Lexington Books, [2022] | Includes bibliographical references and index.
  Identifiers: LCCN 2022006374 (print) | LCCN 2022006375 (ebook) | ISBN 9781793629913 (Cloth : acid-free paper) | ISBN 9781793629920 (ePub)
  Subjects: LCSH: Mentoring in education--Social aspects. | African American college students--Social conditions--Case studies. | College teachers--United States--Attitudes. | United States--Race relations.
  Classification: LCC LB1731.4 .M66 2022 (print) | LCC LB1731.4 (ebook) | DDC 371.102--dc23/eng/20220215
  LC record available at https://lccn.loc.gov/2022006374
  LC ebook record available at https://lccn.loc.gov/2022006375

To JESUS CHRIST my Lord and Savior; because apart from Him I can do nothing.

I dedicate this book to my husband Jeremy. Your constant prayers, support, and encouragement kept me during one of the lowest points in my graduate school process and it continues to sustain me daily. For this, I am forever indebted to you. To my son, Jeremy Jr. (dissertation baby), and my daughter, Joie Simone (reappointment baby); you are my why. Seeing your smiles everyday gives me strength for the journey. To my parents, Walter and Sharon Ray, I am but a product of your love and many sacrifices. To Bishop Bertram Hinton Jr. and First Lady Nickie Hinton your FAITH and prayers reached heaven on my behalf and I am forever thankful for your both. To my fellow Bethelites, you bear witness that this book is all for His glory, and by His grace. Last, to my family and friends that continue to run this race with me. I am deeply grateful for you all.

In memory of Fannie Mae Weatherly.

—Bettie Ray Butler

I dedicate this book to Ayoka and Iyanu, my joy and miracle. I pray that when they attend postsecondary schooling that there will be more faculty and staff of color who look like them—teaching them, nurturing them, and inspiring them. However, if systemic and structural barriers limit people of color in higher education, I am hopeful that this book will serve as a testament to what must be done to sustain the souls of my children and all Black college students.

—Abiola Farinde-Wu

I dedicate this book to every one of my BIPOC students, especially my first students at Classical High School in Lynn, Massachusetts. I owe my entire career—including the publication of this book—to you. Thank you for sharing your lives—your families, your communities, your histories, your excellence, your struggles, your joys, your achievements, and especially, your resistance and activism. Your lives transformed my own. I remain your student and, I hope, a co-conspirator with you for humanity's collective freedom.

—Melissa Winchell

Contents

Foreword

Christine Sleeter

About three decades ago, as an early career professor attending conferences, I often started conversations with the prompt: "Tell me about what you are working on." Rather quickly, I noticed a pattern in how people responded. Almost without exception, the white men launched into descriptions of research projects in which they were collaborating with, or being mentored by, one or more senior faculty members, either in their current institution of employment or the institution of their doctoral studies. Conversely, almost without exception, the women of color began by describing their current research, but then shifted into their frustrations with professional isolation. Unlike their white male colleagues, most of the women of color I talked with were not plugged into research networks with senior scholars, nor were they being actively mentored by anyone where they worked or where they had earned their doctorates. White women's responses were somewhere in between.

At the time, I was editing a book series, "The Social Context of Education," for the State University of New York Press. As I listened to these researchers describe their work, I was drawn mainly to the work of the scholars of color who were writing about issues such as schooling of Mexican Americans, the political context of bilingual education, curriculum planning for American Indian education, and teaching diverse populations. All that many of them needed was for someone to understand and take their work seriously, hold open a door to publishing, and encourage them through it (and, in one case, stand up for them when the publisher thought the book might be "too Black"). Others needed not only that, but also mentoring and coaching through the writing process, something I had been well-prepared to do by my own mentor, Carl Grant. Over a twelve-year period, the series produced thirty books, eleven authored by women of color, nine by white women, and five by men of color.

It is now 2022, and I would like to think that much has changed since those early career conference conversations. But, as Butler, Farinde-Wu, and Winchell show clearly in *Mentoring While White*, people of color are still positioned as "perpetual outsiders" within academia (Shavers & Moore, 2019). White faculty, who occupy a clear majority on most campuses, tend to be oblivious to racial inequalities, unquestioning of white norms of the university, and accustomed to the institutional position of power they occupy (Louis, Louis, Michel, & Deranek, 2018). As a result, students and faculty of color are still subject to what Butler, Farinde-Wu, and Winchell refer to as "reckless mentoring" rather than mentoring rooted in what Jackson, Sealey-Ruiz, and Watson (2014) call "reciprocal love and an ethos of care" (p. 399).

Student demographics have shifted markedly, but university faculty, particularly at predominantly White institutions, are still overwhelmingly White. In 2017, while 14 percent of undergraduate students were Black, only 6 percent of professors shared their racial background (Flaherty, 2019). While racial matching in mentoring might be preferable to cross-racial mentoring (Blake-Beard, Bayne, Crosby, & Muller, 2011), the demographics preclude it. As one of my African American colleagues put it, White faculty need to learn to "share the joy" of mentoring Black students.

Mentoring While White is the book we need. Written for all who desire to positively mentor Black students but for White faculty in particular, this book situates mentoring within an assets-based understanding of Black students that frames the purpose of mentoring as not just retaining students, but also enabling them to thrive. At its best, mentoring benefits both mentee and mentor—it is based in reciprocal relations in which each party brings something to the table, rather than one-way relations in which the mentor dispenses advice to passive mentees. Chapters offer rich descriptions of Black university students' experiences with mentoring, illuminating barriers students confront as well as the positive impact of supportive mentoring. While this book does not offer a "to do" list—indeed, there is no such list since every student and every relationship is unique—it is designed to equip White faculty members with insights, frameworks, questions, and plenty of Black student voices, that will enable readers to learn to become the mentors that students want and need.

But mentoring is about more than including Black students in White academic spaces. Calabrese and Tan (2020) critique the concept of inclusion for its inherent limits. Writing about classroom practice, they maintain that, "Reform efforts focused on inclusion do little to disrupt systemic inequities" (p. 434). Inclusion in classrooms refers to the extension of rights, in a context in which teachers have the power to decide which rights students will have access to. The language of inclusion does not disrupt the hierarchy between teacher (or faculty member) and students, nor the majoritarian ethos into which students are being mentored for inclusion. In contrast, the idea of "rightful presence" assumes the right of everyone to bring their whole selves into a context that enables the political process of reauthoring the rights themselves. Students are no longer passive recipients of rights someone else has determined, but rather active and knowledgeable agents who have a voice in shaping the context into which they are being included. The notion of rightful presence suggests that in mentoring relationships, Black students are positioned as knowledgeable agents who have as much to give to, as to gain from, the mentoring relationship. Mentoring requires reciprocal dialog in which both mentee and mentor listen and learn.

"Rightful presence" supports the idea of mentoring for racial justice, which implicitly is at the heart of this book. As mentoring that is framed as rightful presence opens up space to identify and challenge Eurocentrism in higher education, it necessarily disrupts White supremacy, including the dominance of Eurocentric knowledge and White people's power to define the world. Walters and colleagues (2016) point out that, rather than treating race of the prospective mentees as a problem to be addressed, we should instead be focusing on the "structural and interpersonal aspects of discriminatory practices that perpetuate inequities" (p. 289). The authors offer cultural humility and cultural safety as stances for mentoring that transcend inclusion. Cultural humility involves a process of self-reflection and self-critique, and relinquishing the role of knowledgeable expert to the mentee, who knows what he or she needs. Cultural safety acknowledges and confronts the context of institutional racism and/or colonialism and attendant unequal power relationships between mentor and mentee, for the purpose of addressing these.

As White faculty learn cultural humility, and learn to recognize ways in which racism and colonialism permeate the university and its wider context, and as White faculty learn to share power with rather than hold power over Black students, then White faculty members can begin to take on the crucial work of disrupting and dismantling White supremacy that is right around them. The essays in *Mentoring While White* offer a fabulous set of resources for this work.

REFERENCES

Blake-Beard, S., Bayne, M. L., Crosby, F. J., & Muller, C. B. (2011). Matching by race and gender in mentoring: Keeping our eyes on the prize. *Journal of Social Issues, 67*(3), 622–643.

Calabrese Barton, A., Tan, E. (2020). Beyond equity as inclusion: A framework of "rightful presence" for guiding justice-oriented studies in teaching and learning. *Educational Researcher, 49*(6), 433–440.

Flaherty, C. (2019, August 1). Professors still more likely than students to be white. *Inside Higher Education*. www.insidehighered.com/quicktakes/2019/08/01/professors-still-more-likely-students-be-white.

Jackson, I., Sealey-Ruiz, Y., & Watson, W. (2014). Reciprocal love: Mentoring Black and Latino males through an ethos of care. *Urban Education, 49*(4), 394–417.

Louis, D. A., Louis, S. L., Michel, S. D., & Deranek, J. E. (2018). Reflection, realization, and reaffirmation: Voices of Black and White faculty members engaged in cross-racial mentoring. *Multicultural Perspectives, 20*(4), 205–215.

Shavers, M. C., & Moore, J. L., III (2019). The perpetual outsider: Voices of Black women pursuing doctoral degrees at predominantly white institutions. *Journal of Multicultural Counseling and Development, 47*(4), 210–226.

Walters, K. L., Simoni, J. M., Evans-Campbell, T., Udell, W., Johnson-Jennings, M., Pearson, C. R., MacDonald, M. M., Duran, B., Cargill, V. A., & Stoff, D. M. (2016). Mentoring the mentors of underrepresented minorities who are conducting HIV research: Beyond cultural competency. *AIDS and Behavior, 20*(S2), 288–293.

PART I

Mentoring and Lived Experiences

Chapter One

Beyond Reckless Mentoring

(Re)Imagining Cross-racial Mentor-Mentee Relationships

Abiola Farinde-Wu, Melissa Winchell,
and Bettie Ray Butler

MENTORING AS RECIPROCAL LOVE

The act of mentoring is a form of reciprocal love (Jackson et al., 2014), a cyclical co-exchange of mutual enrichment to ensure the individual and collective prosperity of mentor and mentee. This type of radical mentoring is needed in higher education for Black students now more than ever. As we write this chapter, mass protests are occurring both nationally and abroad in response to the modern-day lynching and senseless killing of Black women and men. Breonna Taylor, Ahmaud Arbery, Rayshard Brooks, and George Floyd, these are the names of the most recent victims of either anti-Black racism, white supremacy, and/or police brutality. Their Black bodies were struck down due to the color of their skin. Their deaths engendered global outrage and incited action in support of the Black Lives Matter movement (founded by Alicia Garza, Opal Tometi, and Patrisse Cullors, all Black women).

Aligning with this action, Love (2019) contends Black folks need more than white allies, they need co-conspirators, people willing to use their privilege and leverage their power for the advancement of marginalized groups. Unfortunately, even in educational spaces, Black students are less likely to experience such co-conspirators (Reddick & Pritchett, 2015). With this hard truth in mind, we offer this book, *Mentoring While White: Culturally*

3

Responsive Practices for Sustaining the Lives of Black College Students, in acknowledgment of those who have lost their lives driving while Black, jogging while Black, sleeping while Black, yelling while Black, parking while Black, babysitting while Black, sitting in a van while Black, selling CDs while Black, opening the door while Black, walking and wearing a hoodie at night while Black, holding a toy gun while Black, being in a dark stairwell while Black, holding a cell phone while Black, shopping while Black, and eating ice cream while Black. It is our hope that by centering the lived mentoring experiences of Black college students, white[1] faculty and others will acknowledge that their inaction is a form of complicity. That said, we urge white faculty in particular, who comprise the majority of higher education faculty (National Center for Education Statistics, 2017), to become co-conspirators by mentoring Black college students with intentionality.

Further, we detail our own respective mentoring stories as examples of both reckless mentoring[2] and reciprocal love mentoring. To that end, the purpose of this chapter is to examine the doctoral mentoring experiences of three women—Nigerian American, African American, and white. Through the lens of intersectionality (Crenshaw, 1991), our respective autoethnographies are offered to ground and introduce the varying themes presented in this book. In this chapter we first interrogate the current literature on efforts to recruit, retain, and sustain Black college students. We then situate our theoretical framework as a lens used to examine our narratives. In reconciling our experiences, we provide a cogent discussion that addresses larger systemic and structural issues that influence mentoring in higher education, while also recommending effective mentoring practices in our conclusion. We argue that the mentoring of Black students in higher education must be purposeful, moving beyond *do no harm* rhetoric and instead, sustaining the lives, bodies, and spirits of Black college students.

LITERATURE REVIEW

Black Experiences in the University

Despite the desegregation of schools via *Brown v. Board of Education* (1954) and the landmark Civil Rights Act of 1964, despite the promises of legislators to close opportunity gaps via iterations of the Elementary and Secondary Education Act (ESEA) of 1965 (including the No Child Left Behind Act of 2002 and more recently, the Every Student Succeeds Act of 2015), persistent inequities remain for Black college students. As a result, Black students are less likely to be prepared for, attend, and complete college. The grade point averages of Black college students are often lower than their white peers; as a consequence, many Black students are underrepresented and underachieving at universities (Dahlvig, 2010; Green et al., 2017; Harris & Lee, 2019; Reddick & Young, 2012).

Worse, Black college students experience their higher education as discriminatory, especially at predominantly white institutions (PWIs) (Reddick & Young, 2012). Despite the diversity of the Black population on university and college campuses, Black students report experiences of homogenization in which they are perceived as being more similar than different (Green et al., 2017). Within this flattening of Black identities at the university, Black students are saddled with the academy's deficit narrative of their inability to perform (Green et al., 2017). From feelings of disconnectedness and isolation to a persistent lack of relationships with white faculty, to a lack of culturally sustaining curriculum in their programs of study, Black students face enormous structural barriers to achievement while in undergraduate and graduate programs (Brittain et al., 2009; Green et al., 2017; Harris & Lee, 2019). Although there is not an abundance of research on Black transgender women and men in higher education, they too face pervasive discrimination and oppression—some might even suggest at higher rates than their cisgender counterparts.

In addition, intersections of Black identities create varied experiences of powerlessness in the ivory towers of the academy. Black women, for example, report feelings of marginalization and social isolation (Allen & Butler, 2014; Grant & Ghee, 2015). While Black women are more represented at the university than ever, their experiences are of invisibility, voicelessness, and "outsider within status" (Howard-Hamilton, 2003, as cited in Grant & Ghee, 2015, p. 762). The effects are equally damaging for Black men, who are more underrepresented in the university than Black women and who also experience isolation (Brittain et al., 2009; Harris, 2012).

MENTORING BLACK STUDENTS IN THE UNIVERSITY

Given the opportunity gaps for Black students in higher education and their racial experiences in universities, multiple studies have examined whether the mentoring of Black students by faculty can have a positive effect (Campbell & Campbell, 2007). However, "mentoring" is a highly contested term in the education literature. Beginning with Levinson's seminal work in 1978, the term has been defined and categorized in dozens of ways (Harris, 2012; Reddick & Young, 2012). Green et al. (2017) described mentorship as both a verb and a noun, a process and a relationship. Generally, scholars agree that within the academy, mentoring is a relationship between an advanced career academic and less advanced career academic or beginning student, and that this relationship varies in its form, scope, and effect (Campbell & Campbell, 2007). In highlighting those forms, however, binaries of mentoring—formal versus informal, academic versus affective, career versus psychosocial, instructional versus developmental—persist in the literature (Ishiyama, 2007; Reddick & Young, 2012; Sutton, 2006). Given the use of binaries within academic institutions to reify white power and supremacy, reciprocal love mentoring can move mentoring beyond this kind of reckless positivism and towards a praxis of mentoring that liberates and sustains Black lives in the university.

Studies on mentoring demonstrate mixed results in terms of the impact of faculty mentorship for Black students in the university. Early studies of mentoring established a positive correlation between mentoring and Black student retention, persistence, and satisfaction with their higher education experience (Blackwell, 1989; Strayhorn & Terrell, 2007). Other studies, however, found that Black students in mentoring programs had lower GPAs than those not in a program, and that mentored students showed no benefits in terms of their mental health (Brittain et al., 2009). Campbell and Campbell's (2007) study also found that gains in GPA for mentored students dissipated over time, though mentored students did complete more credits than non-mentored students. In sum, even studies that struggle in measurable positive effects of mentoring for Black students highlight the need for their mentorship (Brittain et al., 2009). This recommendation is due to evidence suggesting that mentoring for Black students has positive effects (Harris, 2012). For example, Strayhorn and Terrell (2007) found that formal, research-focused mentoring relationships positively impact Black students' satisfaction with their university experience.

Yet, these findings in support of formal, academic-focused mentorship contradict with other findings and recommendations in the literature. Some studies support a positive correlation between unstructured interactions between Black students and faculty and increased academic achievement (Defreitas & Bravo, 2012; Lundberg & Schreiner, 2004). In their autoethnography, Grant and Ghee (2015) recommended the use of informal mentoring relationships to better the outcomes of African American female faculty and doctoral students. Similarly, Reddick and Young (2012) argued that psychosocial mentoring is and should be the primary concern for Black students who are targets of campus racism, including microaggressions. Ishiyama (2007) found that Black college students are more likely to seek out personalized mentoring and to describe a mentor as "someone who is personally supportive," especially at PWIs (Ishiyama, 2007, p. 547).

Thus, it is not surprising that numerous studies find that Black college students prefer and benefit from a Black faculty mentor, given their experiences of racism and discrimination at the university and beyond (Allen & Butler,

2014; Grant-Thompson & Atkinson, 1997; Guiffrida, 2005; Jackson et al., 1996; Milner et al., 2002). However, the results of coethnic mentorships are mixed, with some studies reporting no effect on retention or achievement (Campbell & Campbell, 2007; Harris, 2012). More to the point, even as increasing numbers of Black college students become undergraduates, graduate students, and doctoral candidates, the numbers of Black faculty are not following suit (Harris & Lee, 2019; Reddick & Young, 2012). The representation of Black faculty lags behind the representation of Black students. As a result, Black professors find themselves paying a "cultural taxation" (Padilla, 1994, as cited in Reddick & Pritchett, 2015, p. 55) by attending to issues and relationships that the university perceives as needing the teaching, scholarship, or service of Black faculty. Both the overburdening and disproportionate numbers of Black faculty result in a lack of Black mentorship for Black university students.

WHITE FACULTY AS MENTORS TO BLACK UNIVERSITY STUDENTS: DOING HARM

As a result, the literature highlights the need for white faculty to mentor Black college students (Harris & Lee, 2019; Reddick & Pritchett, 2015). As Reddick and Young (2012) argued, mentoring Black students is every faculty member's responsibility. Yet traditional models and conceptualizations of mentorship do great harm to minoritized students by propping up the white systems of oppression and dominance—including the practices of competition, elitism, and subordination—within the academy (McCormick, 1997).

In fact, white faculty are often ill-equipped to serve as allies/co-conspirators to Black students. Their biases interfere, sometimes even explicitly (Davis, 2007). And when not explicit, white faculty veil their biases behind their academic agendas and the busyness of their work lives (Guiffrida, 2005), accepted academic discourse (Davis, 2007), and colorblind insensitivities (Guiffrida, 2005). In addition, the historical legacy of racism in the United States "is a one-sided scenario of mistrust" (Johnson-Bailey & Cervero, 2004, p. 18), in which Black students have few, if any, reasons to trust white faculty:

> . . . in cross-cultural mentoring what should be a simple matter of negotiation between two persons becomes an arbitration between historical legacies, contemporary racial tensions, and societal protocols. A cross-cultural mentoring relationship is an affiliation between unequals who are conducting their relationship on a hostile American stage, with a societal script contrived to undermine the success of the partnership. (Johnson-Bailey & Cervero, 2002, p. 18)

This historic hostility and racism has implications for mentorship; Black students report a lack of trust in their white mentors (Dhalvig, 2010). Students of color "express feeling disconnected from white faculty members . . . [and] having to continuously prove themselves, defend their intellectual interests, and vie for opportunities to serve as graduate assistants or publish with advisors" (Harris & Lee, 2019, p. 104). Black students are both invisible to faculty (passed over for opportunities) and hypervisible (perceived as representatives of Black culture and community) (Reddick & Young, 2012). Many Black students find white faculty to be culturally and racially insensitive; further, Black students believe that white faculty are unrealistic role models (Guiffrida, 2005).

In fact, Black students often experience their white professors negatively. They describe experiences in which faculty belittled them by "giving them inordinate praise for things like 'speaking well,' 'being smart' or, in the case of one student who was a dance major, getting her 'hips into it' more than the other, mostly White students" (Guiffrida, 2005, p. 712). Black students understand these effusive incidents of unmerited compliments as evidence of white faculty's stereotyping of them and white faculty's low expectations for Black students' intellect and abilities. As a result, many Black students perceive white professors to be less willing to "go above and beyond by actually supporting and advocating for students" (Guiffrida, 2005, p. 711). And, this is true even when Black students have more interactions with faculty outside of class than their white peers; Black students are less likely to find the interactions rewarding than their white classmates do (Guiffrida, 2005; Lundberg & Schreiner, 2004).

WHITE FACULTY AS MENTORS
TO BLACK UNIVERSITY STUDENTS:
MOVING BEYOND DOING NO HARM

Yet according to the literature, white faculty can learn to be effective as mentors to Black students in higher education. White faculty must be race-conscious and empathetic to the racial experiences of their students, even when those experiences contradict their own (Johnson-Bailey & Cervero, 2002). Reddick and Young (2012) defined eight competencies for white faculty who mentor students of color. Some of these competencies include: race consciousness, caring for the mentee, making explicit the cultural norms of the university, developing supportive structures, including the mentee in their networking, and staying current with epistemologies and methodologies of interest to Black students.

In addition, the literature makes clear that white faculty have a responsibility beyond individual cross-racial mentor relationships; they must learn and resist politics in their institutions that are racist. Johnson-Bailey and Cervero (2002) suggested that white faculty can support initiatives that further the careers of faculty and students of color; in addition, they indicated that white faculty should endorse and attend antiracist workshops that educate white faculty and students.

While some researchers positively describe the necessary role of a white faculty member to educate the Black protégé about the cultural norms of the institution or department (Green et al., 2017; Reddick & Young, 2012), there is little literature about the role of the white faculty member as an ally or co-conspirator (Love, 2019) in resisting these (white supremacist) norms. In fact, the binaries of mentoring previously described in this chapter (formal versus informal, academic versus affective, career versus psychosocial, instructional versus developmental) strengthen the status quo of the academy. These binaries mirror the positivist, scientific epistemologies and ontologies most valued within the university (Kincheloe & Tobin, 2015). Thus, business-as-usual in institutions of higher education include a separation of academic life from personal life and a preference for the brain over the body (Reddick & Young, 2012), a disembodiment particularly harmful for minoritized students who value multiple ways of being and knowing. In addition, institutions of higher education are marked by academic formality, patriarchy, tradition, competition, subordination, exclusion, hierarchy, and a dependence of minoritized students on late-career faculty who are largely white, male, and middle-class (Grant & Ghee, 2015; Green et al., 2017; Johnson-Bailey & Cervero, 2004). These cultural qualities are assumed to be cultural and reproduced by the dichotomous constructs of mentorship used in the literature and in institutions to supposedly benefit Black students.

Within current research on cross-cultural mentoring, the call is for studies that enumerate the qualities of successful relationships between white faculty and Black students (Guiffrida, 2005; Reddick & Young, 2012). What is needed, especially in light of white people's growing concern for Black lives, is a theory of mentorship that moves beyond binaries, encompasses multiple possibilities, and resists white supremacy within the individual mentor and mentee and the institution. This chapter—and this book—provide multiple re-imaginings of what cross-racial mentorship can be.

THEORETICAL FRAMEWORK

This personal narrative autoethnography employs intersectionality (Crenshaw, 1989, 1991) as a theoretical framework. Collins and Bilge (2016) remind us that the concept of intersectionality existed prior to the work of Kimberlé Crenshaw; however, Crenshaw both coined the term and advanced the theory. In clarifying intersectionality, Carbado et al. (2013) affirm, "Rooted in Black feminism and Critical Race Theory, intersectionality is a method and a disposition, a heuristic and analytic tool" (p. 303). As such, for the purpose of this analysis, we focus on the intersectionality of race, gender, and class. An examination of these interlocking social categories is appropriate because the use of one identity marker does not accurately capture an analysis of our collective narratives (Crenshaw, 1989).

As cisgender women, Abiola, Bettie Ray, and Melissa share the same gender. However, acknowledging our complex identities, Melissa self-identifies as a white woman from a low-socioeconomic background, while Abiola and Bettie Ray identify as Black women from lower-middle class backgrounds. More specifically, Bettie Ray is an African American woman, whereas Abiola is an immigrant, a Nigerian American woman. Hence, our social identities, class, and locations engender shared and divergent experiences within systems of oppression (Crenshaw, 1991). With a focus on intersectionality, different identity combinations reveal hierarchies of power, privilege, advantages, disadvantages, marginalization, and discrimination when engaging with white faculty in higher education.

AUTOETHNOGRAPHY

In capturing our respective experiences, we view ourselves as the phenomenon and employ a personal narrative autoethnography (Ellis et al., 2011). Autoenthnography (see Ellis, 2004, 2009) as a method is appropriate for this examination because it "seeks to describe and systematically analyze (graphy) personal experience (auto) in order to understand cultural experience (ethno)" (Ellis, 2004; Holman Jones, 2005, as cited in Ellis et al., 2011, p. 273), connecting these personal experiences to larger cultural, social, and political issues in hopes of initiating action and change. More specifically,

> personal narratives propose to understand a self or some aspect of a life as it intersects with a cultural context, connect to other participants as co-researchers, and invite readers to enter the author's world and to use what they learn there to reflect on, understand, and cope with their lives. (Ellis, 2004, as cited in Ellis et al., 2011, p. 279–280)

Through our personal narratives, we detail our memories, recollections, interactions, and conversations with others in higher education and analyze our shared and divergent experiences as we converse with each other and write collaboratively. Although we use our real names, pseudonyms are used for people and locations throughout this chapter.

POSITIONALITY

Considering that "autoethnography acknowledges and accommodates subjectivity, emotionality, and the researchers' influence on research . . . " (Ellis et al., 2011, p. 274), we detail our positionalities and their relevance in critically conducting this examination. As mentioned, we are three women academics—Nigerian American, African American, and white. The first author is a first-generation immigrant who began her doctoral training at a PWI in the south but completed her degree in the southeastern region of the country. The second author is a white first-generation, low-income cisgender woman who completed her doctoral program at a state university in the northeast while working full-time as an urban high school teacher. The third author is a first-generation college student who was the first Black woman to be admitted into her doctoral program in political science at a PWI in the south. After four years, she transitioned to a different program at the same institution, where she received her doctorate in urban education.

At present, we all are faculty members at state public universities where we either mentor undergraduate or graduate students. In disclosing our race and place (our racial identities and place of training), gender, and current professional positions, we acknowledge the interconnectedness of our personhood to our current research examination. Aware of our complex positionalities (Milner, 2007), we engage in kitchen table reflexivity, "where through informal conversations, researchers critically and reflexively engage with the fluidity of their positionalities throughout the research process" (Kohl & McCutcheon, 2015). Through this iterative reflexive process with each other and ourselves, we are mindful of how bringing our whole selves to this examination influences our analysis, and we aim to critically unpack our identities through stories of our experiences to illuminate our *truth*.

FINDINGS: THE POWER OF TELLING YOUR STORY

Through an intersectional lens (Crenshaw, 1989), the personal narratives detailed below are from the lived mentoring experiences of three women academics during their progression in higher education. Below, we offer same-race and cross-race mentor-mentee relationships encompassing both reckless and reciprocal love mentoring examples we experienced throughout our journeys in academia. We offer both these contrasting descriptions in hopes of positively informing white faculty mentoring actions and behaviors toward Black college students. While many of the stories we present capture intentional and effective mentoring, others detail spirit murdering[3] and missed opportunities for faculty.

ABIOLA'S STORY

Being a graduate student is difficult. Attempting to successfully navigate the implicit systems and structures within academia while trying to progress through one's graduate program can be physically, psychologically, and emotionally taxing. Now, couple these stressors with the embodiment of race and gender, being Black and a woman in a historically white and male-dominated space. As a Black, immigrant, cisgender woman, those who have truly mentored me during my graduate and postgraduate training were Black men. In all honesty, I am unsure why these two Black men invested so much of their time and energy into my success, but I am grateful and sure that the reasons for their actions are complex, fluid, and layered. While I do not attribute all of my success to these Black men, I do acknowledge their intentional actions in my journey as an act of reciprocal love mentoring. Their mentoring encompassed more than informal, bi-weekly meetings about how academia operates and how best to proceed; rather, they, in their respective methods, provided access, opportunities, sponsorship, modeled success, and most importantly, they were co-conspirators (Love, 2019), leveraging their power and privilege for my professional advancement. To illustrate their acts of intentionality, below I offer two examples of such mentoring.

Black Male Faculty Mentoring

In 2010, I began my graduate journey at Bluebonnet University (BBU), my alma mater. At the time, I was a full-time, inservice high school English teacher who taught at the same high school I graduated from. Initially, I did not apply for the PhD program at BBU, I simply started taking classes to see if the program was a good fit. Upon entering this program, I met Dr. Livingston, a confident and driven Black man who held the title of associate professor of Urban Education. In his class, I learned a great deal about race, equity, and social justice. Many of his teachings shape my perspective today. Fast forward to the completion of my first year, Dr. Livingston received a promotion at BBU and was offered a distinguished professor position at the University of Queen City (UQC). In accordance with his UQC contract, he could bring two graduate students with him to the university. Perhaps Dr. Livingston saw in me what I was not yet able to see in myself, but in an act of intentional mentoring, I believe he made sure that my BBU admission application was approved and also offered me the opportunity to accompany him to UQC as a funded graduate student. Essentially, I had two options: 1) continue my PhD at BBU, or 2) begin a new PhD journey at UQC, under the mentorship of Dr. Livingston. I chose the latter and am better for it.

My second example is from my 2014 postdoctoral experience. When I accepted my postdoctoral position at Steel University, I had already secured a tenure-track position at a public-state university. I decided to forgo this job opportunity because I knew the mentorship I would receive as a postdoctoral student under Dr. Richards, a distinguished professor of Urban Education, would far exceed the knowledge I would gain in my first year as a new faculty member. My postdoctoral fellowship contract specified a two-year appointment. I stayed at the university for three years, which speaks to the mentoring I received. When I learned that Dr. Richards was leaving Steel University for another position, I knew it was time for me to also leave because as the director of a major center at the university, Dr. Richards provided safety from institutional racism, a community, a commitment to the work of racial justice, and continual guidance.

Upon meeting Dr. Richards, one can tell he is a kindhearted, hardworking intellectual. For me, during my three years as his mentee, I worked. I worked real hard. However, I was fully funded, receiving a paycheck for my role as a project manager and an additional start-up stipend that covered travel and other expenses. For instance, the American Educational Research Association (AERA) conference was financially supported every year. Also in my position, I received my own office, and was given the time and space to conduct research. In addition, when I married my partner, Dr. Richards celebrated us by hosting a gathering in his home in our honor. My last year with Dr. Richards, I was advanced to the position of visiting assistant professor, which was accompanied by a sizable pay increase.

I do not share these accounts to illustrate my good fortune because as we all know, no one progresses though academia unscathed. I share these experiences to capture intentional, reciprocal love mentoring in action and inform the mentoring practices of white faculty. My relationship with these two Black men was/is indeed, a cyclical co-exchange of mutual enrichment that ensured our individual and collective prosperity. As I stand on the shoulders of these two giants, I am mindful to contribute to their continued success and am equally intentional in paying their contributions forward to the next generation of Black scholars.

When Mentoring Goes Wrong

My mentoring experiences with Black men in academia has not always been pleasant. Before Tarana Burke (a Black woman) founded the Me Too Movement, before I could recognize sexual harassment, I was a twenty-something-year-old graduate student working diligently to graduate and secure employment upon graduation. As an emerging scholar, on more than one occasion, I was sexually solicited by seasoned and respected Black male scholars in my field. To be specific, although these men were married with children, one scholar offered to fly me to visit him on one of his professional engagements. Another scholar sent inappropriate and unrequited messages that possessed an informal air of familiarity. In reflecting on these disturbing experiences, these scholars' blatant abuse of their power and privilege is shameful and alarming, especially as leaders in a field that espouses equity and rejects the oppression of marginalized groups. Unfortunately, my experiences are not novel. Such behavior is more commonplace in academia than most would acknowledge. Power dynamics often perpetuate sexism and gender inequalities, allowing some mentors to mistreat mentees due to mentees' subordinate roles.

Black Female Faculty Mentoring

Lorde (2007) reminds us that "In the interest of separation, Black women have been taught to view each other as always suspect, heartless competitors . . . " (p. 38). Many Black women perceive "that there is only a limited and particular amount of freedom that must be divided up between us, with the largest and juiciest piece of liberty going as spoils to the victor or stronger" (p. 39). Indeed, Black women have been cultured to compare and not connect with one another. For me, although many Black women faculty members have been my greatest supporters, many have also been my greatest adversaries. Instead of guiding and advising, some who share my same race and gender chose to ridicule, bully, and demean. I understand now that these verbal and emotional assaults from my sisters were a product of the oppressor's conditioning of Black women. Some Black women internalize a false narrative that there can only be one. While this belief does not justify their actions; it does offer insight. In reconciling my own experiences with Black women in higher education, it is my ardent belief that the advancement of Black women will not occur unless we truly unify and construct a mentor/sponsor/co-conspirator network to ensure the collective uplift of the Black sisterhood. Collins (2000) affirms, "This process of trusting one another can seem dangerous because only Black women know what it means to be Black women. But if we will not listen to [and support] one another, then who will?"

(p. 114). Black women must actively participate and collaborate in this mentoring process for self and group preservation.

White Female and White Male Faculty Mentoring

There is an overwhelming presence of whiteness (Sleeter, 2001) among the demographic makeup of higher education faculty. Matias et al. (2019) also contended, "Women of color in the academy are too often chastised, ostracized, punished, or patronized when sharing their stories about the academy" (p. 54). Considering these truths, my mentoring experiences with white male and female faculty members span from allyship to ambivalence. Although academia is a predominately white space, few white faculty members have intentionally invested in my personal and professional growth and progress. During my graduate training my white allies provided varying support; however, many did not provide the type of mentoring I, a Black woman navigating white spaces, needed in order to not merely survive but to thrive. Many white allies that I reference offered publication opportunities. Though I am appreciative of these projects, too often I sought them out. I approached many white allies and offered my labor and skillset in hopes that they would be willing to collaborate with me—that they would accept me. While these collaborations were beneficial, many were often surface-level interactions, void of reciprocal love mentoring.

White faculty members who displayed ambivalence toward me did so by engaging in what I believe to be unethical practices pertaining to authorship and intellectual property. For instance, as a paid graduate assistant, I helped compose manuscripts and received no authorship credential or written acknowledgment for my work because of my student status. This common practice in academia of having graduate assistants compose literature reviews and using their writings in published papers is not a form of mentoring; it is plagiarism, a blatant violation of intellectual property. In another example of ambivalence, I taught an undergraduate course for free just so I could get higher education teaching experience. When I told a Black male mentor about how my labor was exploited in the College of Education, he responded by stating, "Slavery is over" and encouraged me to quit. Again, abuse of power, in this case by white faculty and administrators, colored my gendered racial experiences in higher education.

BETTIE RAY'S STORY

The path to graduation for many Black students in college can be varied and complex (Dorimé-Williams & Choi, 2021). For Black women attending

PWIs, degree attainment is commonly accompanied by negative encounters and traumatic memories. Too often, the embarrassment and perception of failure—perpetuated by the removal or withdrawal from a program or institution of higher education, and constant messages of inadequacy communicated directly and indirectly by faculty—breeds silence and isolation. I know this to be true, because of my own experiences.

In graduate school I felt like an imposter intruding upon a space that was never intended for me. Despite having graduated from my undergraduate degree program with a 4.0 GPA, I started to doubt my abilities and question whether I belonged in a PhD program. My colleagues where white, the faculty were white; for the first time in my educational tenure no one looked like me. I was the first, the only, Black woman in my program at the time. This hypervisibility, where I was seen but invisible, was evident every day I stepped foot on campus or entered the classroom. I retreated into silos as a coping strategy. I became private, guarded, and largely antisocial. Keep your head down, work hard, get good grades, avoid politics, and you will survive and eventually succeed—or so I thought. Call me naïve, perhaps; but I was conditioned to think this way since grade school. Until graduate school, unbeknownst to me, this type of thinking—which I can now admit was marred in white supremacist ideology—would ultimately contribute to my premature departure from my initial doctoral program.

My story is a small portion of a much larger narrative. Busia (1989, as cited in Dillard, 2011, p. 230) states that it is the "fragments that make up the whole, not as isolated individual and even redundant fragments, but as part of a creative and sustaining whole." Through, or in spite of, my experiences in graduate school I am the unapologetically Black woman, motherscholar, and mentor that I am today.

Over the years, I have found the courage to transform my silence into language and action acknowledging, as Lorde (1996) says, that the very "visibility that makes [me] most vulnerable is that which is the source of [my] greatest strength" (p.42). Writing, as a spiritual practice, helped me to process and metabolize my struggles and challenges while in pursuit of my doctoral degree; and this narrative is no different. In the sections to follow, I recall many of my experiences by memory. Doing so allows me to "[awaken] an opening to the spirit of something that has, until [this] moment, been asleep within [me]" (Dillard, 2011, p. 230). I recall the messy, dark, and (for some) unconscionable encounters that I had with white faculty. I intentionally and deliberately engage in the process of (re)membering as a way to heal from the deep wounds of my past, as well as, to transform my future (Dillard, 2011). It is my hope that, in sharing, I can model for others how they too can embrace their truths and history/herstory unashamedly. I hope that through the power of counter storytelling others might be able to see the *beauty in the ashes*; recognizing that (re)membering is a decolonizing process which enables us to identify the unsung heroes whose mentoring contributions may have been overlooked as a result of our desire to forget the pieces, or fragments, of our lives riddled with pain (and perhaps even shame). I hope to encourage the survivors of reckless mentoring to rise from *the shadows of death* by spirit murdering, and to revive their souls, reclaim their voices, and renew their strength.

This is my story.

(RE)MEMBERING THE ENCOUNTER
I WISH I COULD FORGET

"You are so f***ing inconsiderate!" said Professor Fellows. I sat there in total disbelief. I was in complete shock. Never in a million years would I have expected that one of my own professors would speak to me this way. I grew up in a Christian family, and we never used this type of language—without question, it was forbidden. Nonetheless, there I was in the deep south, more than a thousand miles away from home, and this white man—whom I honestly respected up until this point—hurled one insult after another directly at me. Professor Fellows's frequent and casual use of profanity was not just offensive; it was destructive. What probably lasted for a few short minutes, felt like an eternity. To compound matters, the door was wide open during his outburst. His voice vibrated off the walls and filled the narrowly shaped hallway causing several students to walk by staring curiously into his office. I was noticeably embarrassed, yet he completely disregarded my humanity. He continued with the verbal abuse. I do not remember exactly what he said beyond this point, but I certainly can recall how he made me feel. I was nervous. My heart raced. My hands shook uncontrollably. My eyes were filled with a cloudy mist, but I held in my tears (initially). I had to maintain my composure. I had to be strong. Right? Though I was emotionally injured, I made a conscious decision to remain poised. Professor Fellows's face turned a deep reddish color. It seemed as though my response further angered him. His voice got louder. His eyes were like knives, piercing and deflating my self-worth. In many ways he succeeded in murdering my spirit (Love, 2016; Williams, 1987). A piece of me died that day.

At that moment, I could not hold back my pain any longer, tears rolled down my face uncontrollably as my head dropped down and rested between my knees with my arms clenching the outer side of both my legs. My body was postured in an upright fetal position, and that is when I began to cry silently. This can't be happening—I thought. Seconds passed and I heard some shuffling. What was he doing? As I glanced up, he reached for a box of tissue and placed it in front of me. The nerve of this guy. I sat up quickly, head raised and shoulders back; then I proceeded to wipe my tears away with the bare palms of my hands. I wanted to demonstrate to Professor Fellows that my tears were not a sign of weakness, but instead anger—blood-boiling rage, actually. Of course, he made no attempt to cover up the smirk on his face. Oh, the arrogance of whiteness. I would bet that he may have enjoyed watching me break, presuming that I would not say a word given his favorable status in the department. His colleagues were well aware of his narcissistic behaviors, yet they said nothing—did nothing. If only he could hear my thoughts. In some ways I was ashamed. I allowed Professor Fellows to get the best of me. I wanted to call my husband [who was my boyfriend at the time] and tell him to "straighten him out." Then he would know what it felt like to be humiliated. Seemingly unaware, perhaps, of how he made me feel, in a very sarcastic tone he had the audacity to say to me—something to the effect of—"I'm glad we could have this talk" and "Come back and see me anytime." Why would I want to do that? Could he not recognize his misjudgment in that moment? I suppose not. I could not subject myself to his verbal abuse and condescending behaviors one second longer. I gathered my belongings, got up out of my seat, and hurried out the door. I left Professor Fellows's office exhausted and fatigued as if I had run a marathon. Apart from this encounter, everything about that day remains a bit sketchy. No matter how hard I have tried, the one thing that I will never forget is that this was the day that Professor Fellows took something from me that I have struggled for years to get back.

What led up to this moment? Why was I "f***ing inconsiderate"? Even now, nearly two decades later, I am still unsure. All I know is this. One morning after class, I requested a meeting with Professor Fellows. He obliged. It was supposed to be a quick meeting. Class had relatively gone well. I was one of the highest performing students in his seminar—so the discussion was not related to my grades. Once at his office, as a manner of respect, I waited to speak until he was seated comfortably at his desk. Then he asked about the nature of our meeting. I explained, with excitement in my voice, that one of my research papers had just been accepted for presentation at one of the field's most popular and well-attended conferences. This accomplishment was a huge deal given my status as a newly minted graduate student. Somewhat apprehensively, I informed him of how this opportunity presented a slight scheduling dilemma. I sincerely believed that the problem could be easily fixed. I suppose I hoped (rather naively, it would turn out) that he would agree. Was it too much to think that he would be as excited about this opportunity as I was? He was my professor, I thought he would be proud. I began with a long sigh, and said, "Well . . . you see . . . " I shared with him the nature of the schedule conflict between my outbound flight and our upcoming midterm exam. I had already booked the flight (with guidance from other doctoral students) early in the semester so that I could get the best rate, given I had to pay for my ticket out of pocket. Doctoral students often traveled together and all who were attending the conference had aligned their flight schedules. I had simply done as I was advised.

I felt, given the circumstances, it might be good if I was transparent, honest, and vulnerable; hoping that he would be empathetic, compassionate even. I went out on a limb (something that I do not do often) and expressed to Professor Fellows that I had great anxiety about traveling alone. I did not travel often. Up until this point, I may have flown by myself on three or four occasions prior—at best. Many of the flights were direct; but this one was not. As a Black woman, in my early twenties, I was petrified to travel to an unfamiliar city—let alone, a city with one of the highest crime rates in the country. It was reasonable to be concerned, you would have to be crazy not to. Growing up in a low-income community I was taught to always be aware of your surroundings. Because of the context of my neighborhood, I was no stranger to the threat of crime or violence. My familiarity with the "streets" taught me that the easiest target was always a tourist or someone who was not from the "block." With this at the forefront of my thoughts, I explained to Professor Fellows that I feared having to walk several blocks from the subway to my hotel. Because there were limited outbound flights to the conference location, I had two options; either travel with my colleagues and leave one hour before the exam or take the later flight alone and arrive at nightfall. If these were my two choices, the answer seemed pretty apparent to me; so, I went with the former.

Although my professor was white and I was Black, I thought that he might—if but for a moment—imagine if I were his daughter. Certainly, he would not want his child to travel under these same conditions. So, I mustered up the courage to ask Professor Fellows if it was possible, under the present circumstances, for me to take my exam early. I did not ask to be excused from the exam, nor did I desire to take the exam late. Yet, the look of utter disgust on his face remains etched in my memory. I immediately regretted my decision to meet with him. That is when Professor Fellows began his tirade about how I was "f***ing inconsiderate." I did not understand why he reacted this way, and moreso why he did not see anything wrong with his own behavior. To this day, I am not sure if it was the request itself or the blank look (attributable to my apparent shock) on my face after he frowned at my appeal, that had him so enraged. Nevertheless, his mask came off that day; and from that point forward everything changed.

I am not sure what surprised me more, his reaction or the fact that everyone—both faculty and graduate students—excused it. Once I returned to my office, one of my white classmates stopped by to inquire about what had just happened. I confided in her. After baring my soul, she responded that reporting this exchange would make things "harder for me." Dismayed by the entire encounter, both at my professor's behavior and my colleague's response, I convinced myself that, just maybe, this was an isolated incident. I decided not to file a formal grievance. I returned to Professor Fellows's class the following week, I acted as though nothing had happened. After the semester was over, I learned very quickly that my experience was anything but anomalous.

Isolated, Pushed Out, and Left Behind

The exchange that I had with Professor Fellows was the first of a series of questionable events that transpired throughout the remainder of my graduate school tenure. After a few years, more Black female students were admitted into the doctoral program. I affectionately, now, refer to each of them as my "sistascholars." Collectively, and individually, we endured verbal and emotional abuse from white faculty while enrolled in the program. Such encounters were normalized. A demoralizing culture seemed to permeate the department, and we were the targets. One white faculty was overheard saying, "We have to break them [Black students] down." This is reminiscent of the *keep them in their place* philosophy. A mindset historically rooted in a culture of systemic racism and discrimination (Mills, 2020).

Our collective struggle is captured by a memory that I have of standing in the doorway of my office suite. My sistascholars and I were immersed in deep conversation about the egregious charges in the *Jena Six* case. Six Black youth in Jena, Louisiana, were indicted for attempted second-degree murder and conspiracy to commit murder following a fight that left one white high school student with a slight concussion. Abhorred by the blatant racial injustice surrounding the case, along with the increasingly divisive racial climate on our campus, we stood in solidarity with protesters by dressing in all black clothing. Gathering outside my door our conversation was critical, but peaceful and civil. As the department chair walked by, she gazed at us and then commented, "This looks like trouble." There was no smile on her face, no inclination that she was being facetious; she was serious. It was obvious that she knew the power of her words and what it suggested. Despite the fact that we had done nothing wrong, gathering in the hallways was a common practice for graduate students in our department; at that moment, she chose not to see us as scholars but troublemakers. In her mind, we were all the same.

As long as we were separated, our presence was tolerable; but at the first sign of unity, we became a threat. Following the chair's microaggressive comment (Solórzano et al., 2002), there was a concerted effort to eliminate the perceived "threat." I suppose in some sense we had surpassed the acceptable threshold for Black female admits. There were a total of six of us, and three were pushed out of the program—first ostracized, then humiliated, and ultimately isolated. It almost felt experimental even. We were pitted against one another. Some were treated favorably, while others (including myself) received nothing—almost as if we were the ones randomly selected into the control group. For us, funding and professional development opportunities started to disappear. Mentoring relationships, with white and nonwhite faculty, were nonexistent. The only Black faculty member in the department was untenured. Apart from class, he had very limited interaction with us. I assume this was strategic on his part so as to not complicate his tenure review. We were alone. Segregated from our peers, we were publicly shamed in our classes, our reputations were tainted, and our intellect was called into question, despite our academic success and relatively high GPAs.

The abuse had to stop. Several weeks before I decided to contact the University's diversity officer, he had made a presentation to the College laying out his plan for diversity and his mission to ensure equity and fairness. He seemed to be more progressive in his thinking. He gave the appearance of being an advocate for students of color. After listening to his speech, I gained the courage to call him to share my concerns. Because it was not just me suffering this time, I felt a moral obligation to do something as the most senior in the group. Maybe in some sense, I also felt guilty. Had I filed a formal report during my first exchange, perhaps things might have been different for all of us. With every ring, I could feel my heart beating faster. After a few seconds his administrative assistant answered. She informed me that the diversity officer was unavailable and then jotted down my basic contact information so that he could return my call. The very next day one of my white classmates came by my office inquiring about why I was filing a report. I had not formally spoken with the diversity officer nor had I told anyone, not even my sistascholars, what I was planning to do. Speechless, I listened to my classmate as he discouraged me from making a complaint. He told me that after my call, the diversity officer had contacted the department chair, who then informed members of the faculty that I was attempting to file a formal grievance. It was like a scene from the TV series *Scandal*. I was being intimidated into silence again. I had enough. After suffering years of physical and mental trauma, the stress became overwhelming. With no support at the department or institutional level, eventually I, along with two of my sistascholars, chose to withdraw from the program.

Driven Crazy or Purpose-Driven?

Upon leaving, I went through bouts of depression. I self-medicated to sleep. I became a recluse. Sunday was the only day I felt alive. The church was my sanctuary—literally. It was the only place I felt free. Messages of hope, triumph, and better days were the fuel that kept my flame ablaze. In quiet moments, I could hear an inner voice telling me that it was not over. I believed that something great would rise from the ashes. Daily, I meditated on biblical scriptures. One verse in particular resonated with me the most. Philippians 1:6 said, *He who has begun a good work in you will complete it.* Was God speaking to me? What was He instructing me to do? I prayed earnestly for a sign. I desperately needed direction.

Months passed and then one day I received a phone call from Dr. Blue, my former McNair Scholars Director and undergraduate professor. Dr. Blue was Black, male, and possibly in his early 30's at the time. He had a rare gift for connecting with college students. Dr. Blue was relatable, compassionate, and at times even a bit humorous (in a quirky kind of way). He reached out to me directly after he learned of my decision to withdraw from my doctoral program. This was not uncommon, he regularly checked on several of his students after they had graduated. However, this call was different. The timing seemed divinely orchestrated. Our conversation was reflective, and in many ways, it was the confirmation that I needed. He encouraged me to continue to pursue my doctorate degree. Dr. Blue never pacified my emotions; instead, he reminded me of who I was. He spoke to the scholar, the activist, the straight A student; the young woman who never backed down from challenges—the determined, relentless Bettie Ray that he knew. Aware of my spirituality, he used his familiarity with scriptures to remind me that my doctorate was not just a piece of paper or three letters behind my last name, but a promise from God. My countenance suddenly started to shift. I had not been affirmed in this way since leaving my alma mater—an HBCU. He went on to share, with great depth and transparency, his own challenges in graduate school and his subsequent success thereafter despite his difficult journey both personally and academically. In just a few hours, his intentional and deliberate act of reciprocal love changed the trajectory of my entire life and I made the decision to try again.

I was driven to complete what God had begun in me. After speaking with Dr. Blue, I reapplied to multiple PhD programs and chose to enroll in the one that best aligned with my research interests. I took the lessons that I learned from my previous program, and I approached this new degree with a completely different mindset. I was more calculated and less naïve in my interactions, than I was before. I found my self-worth and gradually regained my confidence. In three years, I completed my doctoral degree with honors and awards, several publications, and a tenure-track position. One phone conversation showed me the transformative power of mentorship. A simple gesture, such as this one, could very well be the difference between emotional health and emotional illness; and in the most crucial cases, quite possibly, the difference between life and death.

The trauma that I faced was very real. Even now, certain things connected to my former program (not excluding writing this narrative) still trigger a form of debilitating anxiety. Nearly twenty years have passed and I am still not sure if I could muster up enough strength to walk through the halls where my initial doctoral program was housed. The very thought makes me seize up. I recognize that other students—some I know personally, and many I do not—never completely bounce back from this type of socioemotional and mental collapse spurred by the reckless actions of faculty. I suppose I should consider myself blessed to have survived; and I do. Yet the truth remains, reckless mentoring is a form of *academic* spirit murdering—whether intentional or not. Murder is a choice and therefore preventable.

MELISSA'S STORY

My experiences as a mentee in the academy have been, almost without exception, extremely positive. My whiteness has provided acceptance and belonging—especially in my chosen field of study, in which nearly all the professors and practitioners áre white. In fact, I have rarely had to ask for mentorship; nearly all of my experiences as a mentee in the academy have been a result of a white mentor signaling to me their interest in me and my academic career. Unlike my co-authors, "reckless" is not a word I would use to describe any mentoring experience I have had in the university; I have never suffered harm nor even encountered ill will as a mentee.

However, if by "reckless" we mean the academy's unabashed, racist pursuit of the white protégé as the ideal (the ideal mentee, the ideal teacher candidate, the ideal future professor), then certainly, given the contrast between my experiences as a mentee and that of my Black colleagues, "reckless" is an apt description of my experiences. In this narrative I will describe particular experiences as the white protégé who was recklessly pursued, and explained how I have leveraged each of those experiences to benefit Black mentees as a cross-racial mentor.

Reckless Signaling: Belonging and Affirmation

As a student in a Master's program at a public university, I watched nervously as our quiet, unassuming, and intellectually intimidating white cis female professor returned our first papers. As she handed me mine, she said in her whisper of a voice, "Melissa, I'd like to talk with you in the hallway about this during the break." I leafed through the paper, scanning the loopy handwriting that covered the margins, trying to discern where I might have gone wrong and why my mistake would warrant a private and immediate conference. Moments later, I walked nervously to the hallway and stood as confidently as I could manage in front of Dr. Cohen. "Melissa," she murmured, "I have never met a student at this university with your intellectual promise. I would like, with your permission, to be your mentor during your time here and to be a part of your life for as long as you'll have me."

Dr. Cohen was one of many professors who offered to mentor me throughout my academic career; this anecdote is one of at least a dozen I could have written here. And the frequency of these interactions illustrates the finding that intellect and ability are more easily recognized in white students than in Black students (Guiffrida, 2005). White faculty often inflate their expectations of white students while saddling their Black students with lower expectations and homogenization (Green et al., 2017). Thus, even as a first-generation, low-income white student, I received many signals—and still do, as an untenured faculty member who has had a number of white senior faculty offer mentorship—that I "deserved" to be at the university, that I belonged, and that my abilities were not in question.

As a white faculty member, I see this frequent signaling of belonging as a privilege of my whiteness, and given my experience of it, hope to re-imagine that signaling to the benefit of my Black students. While there are white low-income and first-generation students who benefit from these frequent messages of affirmation and offers of mentorship, Black students receive them far less frequently, especially when their race intersects with other minoritized identities in the academy (Reddick & Young, 2012). As a way to dismantle my white privilege within the academy, I make intentional efforts to reach out to Black students and to signal to them that I see their Blackness, that I care about them as individuals, and that they belong.

I send these signals in multiple ways in and out of my classes. The door to my campus office is covered in quotes about white supremacy from Black thinkers and writers, I incorporate antiracist and culturally sustaining education into every one of my courses, my syllabus reflects my pro-Black activism, and I talk openly with my classes about my research in critical whiteness studies in teacher education. I share this here not as a way to claim or prove wokeness, but for a white mentor and reader of this chapter who may not understand what is meant by "signaling." Indeed, among my white colleagues, many of them express surprise when I explain to them that their own pride in their neutrality keeps their Black students from approaching, relating to, and even trusting them. Further, I want my white students to understand my positionality and know that their interactions with me will be informed by my commitment to growth as an antiracist educator. And for my Black students, I hope to send a clear signal: I'm learning. I'm with you. Race matters. You matter.

Two years ago, in my second semester at my current university, a student I did not know, named Emily, emailed me. Her friend was in my *Introduction to Secondary Education* course, she explained, and had told her about me. Emily was not a secondary education major, and would therefore never be a student in any of my courses nor an advisee of mine, but she wanted to know if she could meet with me. We scheduled a time for her to come to my office, and Emily cut to the chase. At our predominantly white university, she was having trouble finding any professors who cared about her Blackness and about Black issues, but her friend had told her that I might. "Would you mentor me?" Emily asked. We talked about her definition of mentoring, her expectations for our relationship, and I agreed.

White faculty take signaling for granted in several ways. First, having ourselves been invited to and included in white academic culture, we assume our invitation to be meritorious, even when we believe ourselves to be racially conscious. This thinking can be especially true when, as in my case, we claim other minoritized identities—for me, low socioeconomic status and a first-generation university student. Our relief to have been invited to mentorship eases our experiences of imposter syndrome while distancing us from the white supremacy of the reckless pursuit of mentees in the university. And this is precisely the role of whiteness—to maintain its insidious violence through the appearance of meritocracy.

In addition, white faculty like me underestimate the sway of our racial biases. As Dr. King wrote, "the greatest threat to antiracism is the white liberal" (King, 2010). Given the overwhelming number of white liberals that are faculty on university campuses, King's words are especially sobering: "The white liberal must rid himself [and herself] of the notion that there can be a tensionless transition from the old order of injustice to the new order of justice . . . " (p. 90). What is needed is disruption, and if we are to disrupt our own biases with regards to our Black students, we are going to need to methodically and intentionally make choices about our mentorship that create a transition of disruption in our service commitments, our colleges, and our departments.

Finally, white faculty underestimate the reach of signaling for the Black student. As my experience with Emily demonstrates, faculty who make concerted efforts to signal their support of Black excellence will find that their signals will travel beyond their classroom and their own students. White faculty must be prepared for, and welcome, those signal boosts, and be ready to share with their colleagues of color the mentorship of Black students and students of color. Signal boosting means Black students will ask more of us—they will ask us to attend their performances, to participate with them in protests, and to meet their loved ones. We must be ready to say yes to all of it, and to disrupt our preconceived notions of the students for whom we are responsible, especially when signal boosting costs us our comfort, our time, and our energies.

Reckless Relationality: The Möbius Strip

Given my family's low socioeconomic status and inability to financially contribute to my college education, I competed for and won a substantial academic scholarship that made it possible for me to attend a private, religious, four-year undergraduate liberal arts college. The scholarship was not just monetary; the small group of us who were award-winners had obligations to fulfill and were given additional benefits. One of them was an assigned faculty or staff mentor throughout our four years of study. Again, being seen as the ideal white protégé, I was not surprised to find that I was assigned to a white director in the admissions office who had taken a liking to me during the scholarship competition process; she had told me multiple times during my senior year of high school that she would very much like to mentor me and that I showed tremendous intellectual and leadership promise.

As a first-generation, low-income white woman entering higher education, I often questioned my abilities and whether I belonged in such an institution. My gender and low-income status engendered numerous insecurities. Despite possessing intersections of marginalized identities, my mentor affirmed my capabilities as a student. I met with my mentor a couple times per month on campus; she knew the details of my academic progress, my career goals, and also, my personal life. I was in her life, too; I visited her home a few times, met her children and her spouse, and attended off-campus events with her. I still recall a dinner at her beautiful house near the ocean at which three of her mentees and I were invited. She treated us to a New England lobster bisque, the pot of which I can still envision simmering on the back of her stove (and the likes of which, given my more humble upbringing, I had never before eaten). We talked around the fire in her fireplace about our goals, each of us sharing our plans for graduate school, our work for social justice, our career plans, and books we were reading. My mentor was, as always, absolutely engaged with what we had to say, asking incisive questions that sometimes made us uncomfortable but always led to deeper connections between our learning and our lives.

During my undergraduate years, this experience of reciprocal love—inclusive of both my personal and intellectual lives—was common and an encouraged part of our religious campus culture. My faculty mentors regularly invited students to their homes for dinner discussions, met us at off-campus events, partnered with us in community service ventures, and helped us through our questions and conflicts, whether they were personal, religious, or academic. Parker Palmer, a Quaker educator, writes about this seamlessness that can be fostered between our inner and outer lives as a Möbius strip (Palmer, 2009). A Möbius strip is a single shape with just one side—what appears to be the inside of the loop is also its outside. Given the debate in the literature between the binaries of mentoring—formal versus informal, academic versus affective, career versus psychosocial, instructional versus developmental—Palmer's work has important implications for mentoring theory and practice. Applied to mentoring, Palmer (2009) would suggest that each of these aspects of mentoring can co-create the other. As I experienced as an undergraduate, these various facets of mentoring are inseparable—we mentor not just students, but complex human beings in need of love.

I have found what I am now calling Möbius strip mentoring to be particularly important in cross-racial mentoring with Black students. Since my early days of teaching as an urban high school teacher in a majority-minority high school and now in my current professorship at a predominantly white institution, I have been learning to move more and more seamlessly among the supposed binaries of mentoring with my Black students. For me, this means an integration of my personal and professional lives as both a model and invitation to my students to similarly express all facets of their lived experiences. More recently, I asked three Black students who had previously taken one of my undergraduate secondary education courses to co-author with me the concluding chapter of this book. In keeping with my own undergraduate experiences of Möbius strip mentoring, I extended the invitation to my students to visit my home for a dinner conversation that would form the basis of our chapter. They quickly agreed, but I could tell as the date approached that they were nervous. I received a few emails from them asking if they should bring any food with them and if they needed to wear anything in particular. *No, no,* I assured them again and again, *you are welcome in my home however you arrive! Just come!*

As life would have it, the day of the scheduled dinner tested every bit of my attempts with my students to seem easygoing. My husband, the cook of our family, spent the day in the hospital with his suddenly sick father. I was suddenly thrust into all the roles—solo parenting our daughter with multiple disabilities, pulling dinner together, hosting, and having a coherent academic conversation to boot. Momentarily, I considered rescheduling with my students, and then I remembered my words to them—*come as you are!*—and realized that I could extend the same sentiment to myself. I ordered dinner from a local pizza shop, dressed my daughter in her PJs before my students arrived, and met my students at the front door with full disclosure: *This is us today,* I told them. *Come on in.* And of course, we had a wonderful—if imperfect—evening. Later my students told me that mine was the first invitation they had received to the home of a faculty member and how meaningful the experience was for them. This, for me, is how white mentors can show up for Black students—by inviting our students into our lived experiences and modeling the kind of honest, whole personhood we invite from them.

Given the centuries of harm inflicted by white practices of hierarchy, domination, and subjugation, the Möbius strip as a model of mentoring provides three ways forward for cross-racial mentorships. First, mentoring that integrates our inner and outer lives disrupts the traditional hierarchy of mentorship by positioning the mentor and the mentee as humans sharing and seeking to understand one another's lived experiences. As I reveal my inner life—for example, by responding with emotion to a mentee's disclosure, by apologizing when I do wrong, or by asking questions when I do not understand my mentee—I practice a humility that is necessary for the cross-racial relationship to thrive. Living into my imperfections and my full humanity necessarily means that I recognize my incompleteness, especially with regards to my racial experience, and this cultural humility creates space for my learning and my students' experiences as people of color. Second, Möbius strip mentoring fills that space with care and in so doing, generates possibilities for justice. The relationship extends beyond "protective hesitation" common in the hierarchy of cross-racial relationships (Thomas, 2001). Much is known about the incompleteness of kindness; on the other hand, an ethos of critical care—that is, care oriented in equity and criticality—moves the individuals involved in the mentorship towards an actualization of the goals of activism and transformation.

Finally, as I bring my whole self to my mentoring, my personhood is amplified, and my sense of the individual student is amplified as a result. In other words, Möbius strip mentoring causes me to see the uniqueness of each protégé's experience; my Black student is not a representative of his/her Black community but a unique individual at intersections of identities and experiences I have yet to discover. The Black mentee is, in the description one of my students explained to me, "always Black and also, not only Black" (Bowman et al., 2000). Thus, mentoring within and among and through the binaries of traditional mentorship resists and disrupts the homogenization Black students too often experience in the academy, especially in predominantly white institutions.

DISCUSSION

In acknowledgment of our shared and divergent mentoring experiences and the different and difficult higher education experiences faced by countless Black students, we bring attention to the larger theme of systemic and structural issues that negatively influence cross-racial mentoring throughout academia. Racial bias impedes the educational progress of Black students (D'Augelli & Hershberger, 1993). Allen (1992) stressed that "when African Americans are made to feel unwelcome, incompetent, ostracized, demeaned, and assaulted, their academic confidence and performance understandably suffers" (p. 41). Moreover, it is difficult to refute that in higher education academic progression and success cannot be adequately achieved when a student must constantly combat racism and covert acts of discrimination (Robertson et al., 2005). Indeed, racial bias is pervasive, infecting the minds, hearts, and souls of many higher education faculty. Whether consciously or not, the toxic culture of higher education (as told in Abiola's story), the dehumanizing encounters with faculty (as told in Bettie Ray's story), and the racist pursuit of a white protégé as the ideal graduate prototype (as told in Melissa's story), is reckless and detrimental to the lives, bodies, and spirits of Black college students.

When examining the intersections of our respective mentoring stories through a racialized, gendered, and classed lens, it is evident that we each experienced some form of harm. As Black female graduate students, Abiola and Bettie Ray were affected by systemic and structural barriers while in pursuit of their doctorate. Existing institutional policies and practices reinforced their marginalization—leaving them unprotected, exploited, criminalized, silenced, and pushed out. Although they persisted, securing their doctorate degrees in atmospheres that revered and protected whiteness (Matias et al., 2019) and binary ways of mentoring, the challenges they endured could have derailed their paths and were indicative of the ever-present toxic and dehumanizing culture of academia (Winkle-Wagner, 2015).

Melissa, a first-generation, low-income white cis woman personally experienced white faculty members' reckless pursuit of an ideal white protégé. Her narrative describes how she was oftentimes the recipient of signaling by white faculty. Notwithstanding the intersection of her gendered identity and working-class background, Melissa openly acknowledged that her own white privilege afforded her frequent, unsolicited opportunities for mentorship as both a graduate student and untenured faculty member. Yet, she boldly calls out the myth of meritocracy in higher education for what it is—the blatant racist institutionalized practice of valorizing whiteness at the expense of Blackness/otherness. Aware of the systemic and structural barriers connected to mentoring support, Melissa leverages her power through reverse signaling to nurture cross-racial mentoring relationships with her Black students.

Albeit our stories reinforce instances of reckless mentoring, each narrative is balanced by an equally reflective memory of mentorship as responsive and culturally sensitive. Within Abiola, Bettie Ray, and Melissa's descriptions of their mentoring experiences emerge three collective themes: mentoring as intentionality, mentoring as reciprocal love, and mentoring as transformative practice.

The first theme, *mentoring as intentionality* is illustrated through each narrative as a conscious and deliberate investment of time. Our stories tell how our mentors were not only able to see our academic potential but how they chose to invest in our professional and personal growth using time apart from class to do so. Our mentors invited us into their personal spaces. Abiola and Melissa's mentors opened their homes to socially engage with them and their families in authentic ways; whereas Bettie's mentor candidly shared intimate aspects of his life connected to his own personal and academic challenges while pursuing his doctorate. These acts by their mentors were done with intentionality.

The second theme, *mentoring as reciprocal love* is demonstrated through an ethos of care. Through the reflections of our lived experiences we describe how our mentors fostered our social, emotional, and academic well-being. Beyond strengthening our intellectual capacity, each mentor affirmed our humanity and for Bettie, in particular, her spirit. Our mentors recognized that we were more than mere students—that we existed outside institutional walls. They came to know us and used this knowledge as a tool to build deeper, more meaningful connections.

The third and final theme, *mentoring as transformative practice*, is revealed through the positive tangible impact that our mentors had on our success as students. Because of our mentors' supportive nature, their guidance enhanced our professional development and buttressed our confidence to persist in the face of difficulty. Their contributions extended past verbal encouragement into actionable results. Whether it was through securing funding, regular phone calls, or dinner invitations; when tracing back our most transformative educational moments we each identified something that our mentors "did" (not only what they said). Their commitment to act in our best interest left a sustaining impact on our lives and helped to shape our very own mentoring practices.

Considering, at times, our dichotomous experiences in higher education, what is clear is reckless mentoring interactions are textured, layered, and intimately tethered to our spirits. What is also clear from our collective narratives is that counteracting reckless mentoring, especially among Black and marginalized students, requires intentionality, reciprocal love, and transformative practice. These three themes undergird what we regard as *culturally responsive mentoring*.

CULTURALLY RESPONSIVE MENTORING

Juxtapose to reckless mentoring is the notion of culturally responsive mentoring. While reckless mentoring often captures what faculty "should not do," culturally responsive mentoring demonstrates what faculty "could do." The use of "could" here emphasizes possibility. It encourages faculty to shift their thinking and (re)imagine mentoring not as it *is*, but as it *could be* (Greene, 1995). Just as with other asset-based approaches, culturally responsive mentoring is not a checklist of strategies but a mindset. How one thinks about mentoring shapes how they mentor. Thus, effectively mentoring Black college students requires a radical (re)imagining of student-faculty relationships. Faculty must, in principle, put away old practices and embrace new possibilities.

We acknowledge that the concept of culturally responsive mentoring is not new. In fact, Merriweather (2012) was one of the first to introduce the term, roughly a decade ago, in her review of literature on mentoring practices for adult learners. Her in-depth synthesis revealed that a dearth of research, at the time, viewed mentoring through a cultural lens and rarely drew a connection between cultural responsivity and general models of mentoring. Merriweather (2012), referencing the work of Lechuga (2011), pointed out that attention to power dynamics, acknowledging positionality, and consciously creating spaces for mentee's voice are each considered effective practices in which faculty can participate to foster success for all students. Yet, she stressed that being culturally responsive in the practice of mentoring requires action, on the part of the faculty mentor, to assess, educate, protect, guide, encourage and socialize mentees of color. In giving critical attention to the role and responsibilities of mentoring for diverse student populations, Merriweather (2012) started a worthwhile and much-needed discussion on culturally responsive mentoring, which she defines as "a holistic, equity-based approach based on cultural competence and critical consciousness of the individual, social context, and political playing field" (p. 106). Although this definition frames culture from a broad perspective, Merriweather is quick to suggest that more research should be open to the possibility of examining mentoring through a racialized lens to help "move mentoring from a normative state of cultural neutrality to a state of cultural specificity that both demonstrates honor and respect for the process as a whole" (p. 107).

This book builds upon the earlier work of Merriweather (2012) and follows her recommendation to consider mentoring from an "Afrocentric perspective" (p. 107). Each chapter, included within this text, explicitly centers the mentoring experiences of Black college students. In conjunction with Merriweather's recommendation, our specific attention to Black students is especially significant given that research has suggested that Black students in comparison to white students are less likely to have faculty mentors, and this lack of mentorship negatively impacts their educational progress (Nettles & Millet, 2006). By clearly addressing what Black students need and expect from all faculty—white faculty in particular—at least three goals might be reached through this book: 1) to illuminate and recast focus on culturally responsive mentoring, 2) to add to the growing knowledge in this specialized area, and, most importantly, 3) to improve the higher education schooling experiences of Black students.

THE BOOK: *MENTORING WHILE WHITE*

The combined chapters bring together a group of well-respected, leading, and emerging scholars who have tackled the complexities of student-faculty mentoring relationships through either cutting-edge research and/or innovative practices. Modeled in each chapter are the ongoing themes of intentionality, reciprocal love, and transformative practice—first introduced here through our own collective narratives. We contend that these themes align well with Merriweather's (2012) conceptualization of culturally responsive mentoring and thus, we use them to guide our discussion on how faculty could become more culturally responsive in the practice of mentoring Black students.

Mentoring While White offers practical recommendations for white faculty—and by extension, predominantly white colleges and universities—on how to provide greater support to Black college students and to affirm their importance and value in academic spaces. We argue that white faculty mentors (and possibly others) should be prepared to engage with racial differences, but also see their Black mentee as an individual and not a representative of Blackness. This book grapples with race, not as the sum total of Black identity, but rather as an intersecting axis that spans across multiple identity markers, which unveil experiences that are both varied and unique.

Mentoring While White is divided into five sections, each covering a different perspective on mentoring based on overlapping identities that speak to the lived experiences of Black college students. Part I of this book is entitled "Mentoring and Lived Experiences." It includes one chapter (the current chapter) which intersects each of the editors' experiences of mentoring—from the position of an African immigrant, African American, and white woman—that frame the central themes (i.e., mentoring as intentionality, mentoring as reciprocal love, and mentoring as transformative practice) that undergird each subsequent chapter. Part II, "Mentoring and Black College Students," includes two chapters (chapters 2 and 3). This section explores the varied dimensions of mentoring from a holistic perspective, giving attention to what it means to be a Black student in higher education. Part III, entitled "Mentoring and Intersectionality," includes five chapters (chapters 4–8). These chapters discuss the role of intersecting identities: Black and male (chapters 4 and 7); Black and women (chapter 5); Black, queer, and women (chapter 6), and Black and possessing diverse abilities (chapter 8). The authors suggest that the recognition of these overlapping identities is vitally important in shaping authentic student-faculty mentoring relationships. Part IV, entitled "Antiracist" includes chapters 9 and 10. Both chapters address the need to "call out" (i.e., to bring attention to, or heighten awareness of, an issue) and challenge anti-Black structures in academia as a means of supporting and effectively engaging in race-conscious mentoring practices. Part V, "Mentoring and Social Media," contains one chapter (chapter 11). This sole chapter demonstrates how one major online mentoring community (R.A.C.E. Mentoring), with a race specific focus, helps to bridge communication gaps between faculty and Black students while also providing guidance on how to successfully navigate academic culture. Part VI, "Mentoring in Practice," the final section of the book integrates the voices of Black undergraduate college students enrolled at a PWI (chapter 12). These students reflect and narrate their own experiences with the hope of stimulating dialogue about what students need and expect from faculty in order to cultivate productive and sustaining mentoring relationships.

Mentoring While White is intended to open up conversations with faculty about uncovering possibilities of mentoring Black students differently. James Baldwin (1962), at the height of the Civil Rights Movement, was quoted as having said, "Not everything that is faced can be changed; but nothing can be changed until it is faced" (p. 38). To this we add, *anything is possible when we can face change together*. This book, in a sense, symbolically represents the extension of our hands as an invitation to you, the reader, to take the first step together in this journey to (re)imagine mentoring through a culturally responsive lens.

REFERENCES

Allen, W. R. (1992). The color of success: African-American college student outcomes at predominantly White and historically Black public colleges and universities. *Harvard Education Review, 62*(1), 26–44.

Allen, A., & Butler, B. R. (2014). African American women faculty: Towards a model of coethnic mentorship in the academe. *Journal of Progressive Policy & Practice, 2*(1), 111–122.

Baldwin, J. (1962, January 14). As much truth as one can bear. *New York Times,* BR11, 38.

Blackwell, J. E. (1989). Faculty mentoring minority. In M. C. Adem & E. Wadsworth (Eds.), *Report of the Stoney Brook Conference* (pp. 25–44). Dix Hills, NY: General Hall.

Bowman, S. R., Kite, M. E., Branscombe, N. R., & Williams, S. (2000). Developmental relationships of Black Americans in the academy. In *Mentoring dilemmas* (pp. 39–62). Psychology Press.

Brittain, A. S., Sy, S. R., & Stokes, J. E. (2009). Mentoring: Implications for African-American college students. *Western Journal of Black Studies, 33,* 87–97.

Brunsma, D. L., Embrick, D. G., & Shin, J. H. (2017). Graduate students of color: Race, racism, and mentoring in the white waters of academia. *Sociology of Race and Ethnicity, 3*(1), 1–13.

Busia, A. (1989). What is your nation? Reconnecting Africa and her diaspora through Paule Marshall's *Praisesong for the widow.* In C. Wall (Ed.), *Changing our own words: Essays on criticism, theory, and writing by black women* (pp. 116–129). Rutgers University Press.

Campbell, T. A., & Campbell, D. E. (2007). Outcomes of mentoring at-risk college students: Gender and ethnic matching effects. *Mentoring & Tutoring, 15*(2), 135–148.

Carbado, D. W., Crenshaw, K. W., Mays, V. M., & Tomlinson, B. (2013). Intersectionality: Mapping the movements of a theory. *Du Bois Review: Social Science Research on Race, 10*(2), 303–312.

Collins, P. H. (2000). *Black feminist thought: Knowledge, consciousness and the politics of empowerment.* 2nd ed. New York. Routledge.

Collins, P. H. & Bilge, S. (2016). *Intersectionality.* Cambridge: Polity.

Crenshaw, K. (1989). Demarginalizing the intersection of race and sex: A Black feminist critique of antidiscrimination doctrine, feminist theory, and antiracist politics. *University of Chicago Legal Forum, 14,* 538–554.

Crenshaw, K. (1991) Mapping the margins: Intersectionality, identity politics, and violence against women of color. *Stanford Law Review, 43*(6), 1241–1299.

Dahlvig, J. (2010). Mentoring of African American Students at a Predominantly White Institution (PWI). *Christian Higher Education, 9*(5), 369–395.

Davis, D. (2007). Access to academe: The importance of mentoring to Black students. *Negro Educational Review, 58*(3/4), 217–231.

Defreitas, S.C., & Bravo, A. (2012). The influence of involvement with faculty and mentoring on the self-efficacy and academic achievement of African-American and Latino college students. *Journal of the Scholarship of Teaching and Learning, 12*(4), 1–11.

Dillard, C. B. (2011). Learning to remember the things we've learned to forget: Endarkened feminisms and the scared nature of research. In N. K. Denzin & M.

D. Giardina (Eds), *Qualitative inquiry and global crisis* (pp. 226–243). Taylor & Francis Group.

Dorimé-Williams, M. L., & Choi, S. (2021). Class, sex, and the role of involvement on Black collegians degree attainment. *Journal of Diversity in Higher Education.* https://doi.org/10.1037/dhe0000325.

Ellis, C. (2004). *The ethnographic I: A methodological novel about autoethnography.* Walnut Creek, CA: AltaMira Press.

Ellis, C. (2009). *Revision: Autoethnographic reflections on life and work.* Walnut Creek, CA: Left Coast Press.

Ellis, C., Adams, T. E., & Bochner, A. P. (2011). Autoethnography: an overview. *Historical Social Research, 36*(4), 273–290.

Gay, G. (2018). *Culturally responsive teaching: Theory, research, and practice* (3rd ed.). Teachers College Press.

Grant, C., & Ghee, S. (2015). Mentoring 101: Advancing African-American Women Faculty and Doctoral Student Success in Predominantly White Institutions. *International Journal of Qualitative Studies in Education (QSE), 28*(7), 759–785.

Grant-Thompson, S. K., & Atkinson, D. R. (1997). Cross-cultural mentor effectiveness and African American male students. *Journal of Black Psychology, 23*, 120–134.

Green, T. D., Ammah, B. B., Butler-Byrd, N., Brandon, R., & McIntosh, A. (2017). African-American mentoring program (AAMP): Addressing the cracks in the graduate education pipeline. *Mentoring & Tutoring: Partnership in Learning, 25*(5), 528–547. https://doi.org/10.1080/13611267.2017.1415807.

Greene, M. (1995). *Releasing the imagination: Essays on education, the arts, and social change.* Jossey-Bass.

Guiffrida, D. A. (2005). Othermothering as a framework for understanding African-American students' definitions of student-centered faculty. *The Journal of Higher Education, 76*(6), 701–723.

Harris, T., & Lee, C. (2019). Advocate-mentoring: A communicative response to diversity in higher education.

Harris, V. T. (2012, May). The effectiveness of African American and Hispanic mentoring programs at predominantly White institutions (Working Paper CHEWP.3.2012). Retrieved from https://pdfs.semanticscholar.org/5372/e686c58dfd73892e179e9d69d521b35c018b.pdf.

Holman Jones, S. (2005). Autoethnography: Making the personal political. In N. K. Denzin & Y. S. Lincoln (Eds.), *Handbook of qualitative research* (pp. 763–791). Sage.

Ishiyama, J. (2007). Expectations and perceptions of undergraduate research mentoring: Comparing first-generation, low-income white/Caucasian and African-American students. *College Student Journal, 41*(3), 540–549.

Jackson, C. H., Kite, M. E., & Branscombe, N. R. (1996). African-American women's mentoring experiences. Paper presented at the 104th Annual Meeting of the American Psychological Association. Toronto, Ontario, Canada.

Jackson, I., Sealey-Ruiz, Y., & Watson, W. (2013). Reciprocal love: Mentoring Black and Latino males through an ethos of care. *Urban Education, 49*, 394–417.

Johnson-Bailey, J. and Cervero, R. M. (2002). Cross-cultural mentoring as a context for learning. *New Directions for Adult and Continuing Education, 96*, 15–21.

Johnson-Bailey, J., & Cervero, R. M. (2004). Mentoring in Black and White: The intricacies of cross-cultural mentoring. *Mentoring & Tutoring, 12*, 7–21.

Kincheloe, J. L., & Tobin, K. (2015). The much exaggerated death of positivism. In *Doing Educational Research* (pp. 15–32). Brill Sense.

King Jr, M. L. (2010). *Where do we go from here: Chaos or community?* (Vol. 2). Beacon Press.

Kohl, E. & McCutcheon, P. (2015). Kitchen table reflexivity: negotiating positionality through everyday talk. *Gender, Place & Culture, 22*(6), 747–763.

Lechuga, V. M. (2011). Faculty-graduate student mentoring relationships: Mentors' perceived roles and responsibilities. *Higher Education, 62*(6), 757–771. https://doi.org/10.1007/s10734-011-9416-0.

Lige, Q. M., Peteet, B. J., & Brown, C. M. (2017). Racial identity, self-esteem, and the impostor phenomenon among African American college students. *Journal of Black Psychology, 43*(4), 345–357. https://doi.org/10.1177/0095798416648787.

Lorde, A. (2007). *Sister outsider: Essays and speeches*. Freedom, CA: Crossing Press.

Love, B. L. (2016). Anti-Black state violence, classroom edition: The spirit murdering of Black children. *Journal of Curriculum and Pedagogy, 13*(1), 22–25.

Love, B. (2019). *We Want to Do More than Survive: Abolitionist Teaching and the Pursuit of Educational Freedom*. Boston: Beacon Press.

Lundberg, C. A., & Schreiner, L. A. (2004). Quality and frequency of faculty–student interaction as predictors of learning: An analysis by student race/ethnicity. *Journal of College Student Development, 45*(5), 549–565. doi:10.1353/csd.2004.0061.

Matias, C., Walker, D. & del Hierro, M. (2019). Tales from the ivory tower: Women of color's resistance to whiteness in academia. *Taboo: The Journal of Culture & Education, 18*(1), 35–58.

McCormick, T. (1997). An analysis of five pitfalls of traditional mentoring for people on the margins in higher education.

Merriweather, L. (2012). A need for culturally responsive mentoring in graduate education. *All About Mentoring, 42*, 103–108.

Mills, K. J. (2020). "It's systemic": Environmental racial microaggressions experienced by Black undergraduates at a predominantly White institution. *Journal of Diversity in Higher Education, 13*(1), 44–55.

Milner, H. R., Husband, T., & Jackson, M. P. (2002). Voices of persistence and self-efficacy: African American graduate students and professors who affirm them. *Journal of Critical Inquiry into Curriculum and Instruction, 4*(1), 33–39.

Milner, H. R. (2007). Race, culture, and researcher positionality: Working through dangers seen, unseen, and unforeseen. *Educational Researcher, 36*(7), 388–400.

National Center for Education Statistics. (2017). *The condition of education 2017: Characteristics of postsecondary faculty*. Retrieved from https://nces.ed.gov/fastfacts/display.asp?id=61.

Palmer, P. J. (2009). *A hidden wholeness: The journey toward an undivided life*. John Wiley & Sons.

Reddick, R. J., & Pritchett, K. O. (2015). "I don't want to work in a world of white-ness": White faculty and their mentoring relationships with Black students. *Journal of Professoriate, 8*(1), 54–84. Retrieved from https://caarpweb.org/wp-content/uploads/2015/06/8-1_Reddick_p54.pdf.

Reddick, R. J., & Young, M. D. (2012). Mentoring graduate students of color. In S. Fletcher & C. Mullen (Eds.), *The SAGE handbook of mentoring and coaching for education* (pp. 412–429). Thousand Oaks, CA: SAGE.

Sleeter, C. E. (2001). Preparing teachers for culturally diverse schools: Research and the overwhelming presence of Whiteness. *Journal of Teacher Education, 52*(2), 94–106.

Strayhorn, T. L., & Terrell, M. C. (2007). Mentoring and satisfaction with college for Black students. *The Negro Educational Review, 58*, 69–83.

Sutton, E .M. (2006). Developmental mentoring of African American college men. In M. J. Cuyjet, (Ed.), *African American men in college* (pp. 95–111). San Francisco, CA: Jossey-Bass.

Thomas, D. A. (2001). The truth about mentoring minorities. Race matters. *Harvard business review, 79*(4), 98–107.

Williams, P. (1987). Spirit-murdering the messenger: The discourse of fingerpointing as the law's response to racism. *University of Miami Law Review, 42*(1), 127–157.

Winchell, M. (2020, July - Sept). Minding the (opportunity) gap: Critical conscious-ness pedagogy in college gateway courses. *Multicultural Perspectives, 22*(3), 133–138.

Winkle-Wagner, R. (2015). Having their lives narrowed down? The state of Black women's college success. *Review of Educational Research, 85*, 171–204.

NOTES

1. While we acknowledge APA guidelines to capitalize all racial identities, we are choosing instead to capitalize Black only as a way of dismantling anti-Blackness in academia.

2. For the purpose of this chapter, *reckless mentoring* is defined as a behavior per-formed by a mentor to a mentee in which the mentor interacts with a mentee without thinking or caring about the implications and consequences of the mentor's actions.

3. Spirit-murdering, a term first coined and conceptualized by Patricia Williams (1987), is a crime of racism, a death of the spirit, "an offense so deeply painful and assaultive" (p. 129) against the humanity and spirits of people of color "through sys-temic, institutionalized, anti-Black, state-sanctioned violence" (Love, 2016, p. 22).

PART II

Mentoring and Black College Students

Chapter Two

Faculty Mentoring Promotes Sense of Belonging for Black Students at White Colleges

Key Insights from Those Who Really Know

Terrell L. Strayhorn

WHAT WE KNOW FROM PRIOR RESEARCH

Studies have consistently shown that strong, supportive relationships can help individuals successfully negotiate adulthood transitions (Bernier et al., 2005). For example, informal contact with nonfamilial (or nonkin) adults who endorse prosocial values may help reduce substance abuse, delinquency, and gang involvement (Baetz & Widom, 2019; Rhodes, 2002; Tolan et al., 2014). Frequent interaction with adults who stress the importance of education seems to facilitate development of academic skills, learning curiosity, and positive attitudes toward schooling (Gipson & Mitchell, 2017; Kelley & Lee, 2018). College students may enjoy similar benefits when interacting with campus personnel in such meaningful ways (Hirt et al., 2008; Strayhorn & Terrell, 2007).

MENTORING STUDIES

A long line of scholarship shows that the impact of interpersonal support depends, in part, on the quality and nature of students' relationships with other members of the campus community, especially faculty members who act as "agents of the institution," reflecting its values and mission. Contact (both formal and informal) between faculty mentors and students has a positive influence on students' academic performance, retention, and satisfaction with college, to name a few outcomes (Gershenfeld, 2014; Mangold et al., 2003; Strayhorn & Saddler, 2009). Formal mentoring refers to students' engagement with faculty through educationally purposeful activities like undergraduate research, advising, service-learning, and internships. Such arrangements often operate according to structured agreements, marked by intentional matching and guidelines specifying the frequency of meetings, role expectations, and desired outcomes (Parise & Forret, 2008). Talking about nonacademic matters, attending cultural events, and hanging out in campus lounges are examples of informal contact (Rose et al., 2005). Formal faculty mentoring experiences generally have a greater impact than informal contact on college students' learning and development (Wanberg et al., 2006), especially for racial/ethnic minoritized students such as Latinx (Bordes & Arredondo, 2005; Zalaquett & Lopez, 2006) and African Americans (e.g., Strayhorn & Terrell, 2007).

MENTORING PROGRAMS

Based on these findings, colleges and universities have established mentoring programs that match faculty with [minoritized] students for one-on-one coaching, out-of-classroom social activities, and individualized support for coping with academic and life stressors. The underlying assumption driving most mentoring programs is that those who participate in such programs are more likely than nonparticipating peers to thrive academically and professionally. For instance, the Search for Education, Elevation, and Knowledge (SEEK) mentoring program at CUNY College of Staten Island was designed to "help disadvantaged college students via holistic approaches, to fulfill their academic potential" using a mix of goal-setting strategies (Sorrentino, 2007, p. 243). Mentoring programs of this kind improve students' study skills, ease their social adjustment (to college), reduce anxiety, and promote psychological well-being (Jacobi, 1991; Redmond, 1990). The underlying causal mechanism points to several facilitating factors including growth-minded feedback, generativity (i.e., feeling cared about), and affirmation of students' *sense of self* at times when it may be threatened (Rhodes et al., 2000).

In response to such evidence, professional societies and colleges have invested in the development of formal mentoring programs that connect students with faculty in specific fields. For instance, Patitu and Terrell (1997) conducted a study to evaluate components of the NASPA Minority Undergraduate Fellows Program (MUFP). Analyzing survey data from seventy-seven mentors and seventy-six protégés at seventy predominantly White institutions (PWIs), they found that MUFP was effective in socializing students, mostly people of color, to their professional field. Similar conclusions about the efficacy of formal mentoring programs were drawn based on a survey student of 1,135 undergraduate science majors engaged in research with faculty members (Lopatto, 2003).

MENTORING ROLES & DEFINITIONS

Researchers have examined the various roles and functions that mentors serve for protégés, dating back to early work (Kram & Isabella, 1985). Mentors can act as sponsors for protégés, offering career-related support and advice. Healy (1997) pointed out that mentoring is "a dynamic, reciprocal relationship in a work environment between an advanced career incumbent (mentor) and a beginner (protégé) aimed at promoting the career development of both" (p. 10). Mentors can also afford protégés (or "mentees") privileged opportunities for visibility, networking, or career advancement that they might not get otherwise. Beyond career support, mentors can also serve as role models or confidantes by providing academic advice, counseling, and friendship when needed. In short, mentors serve in a variety of roles ranging from advisor, guide, and teacher to coach and partner, as explained by Mertz (2004) and affirmed later by Dawson (2014). And though tallies vary significantly, Jacobi (1991) identified over fifteen definitions of mentoring in the literature, while Nora and Crisp (2007–2008) reported thirty, each varying in scope, nature, and impact.

Of course, not all mentoring experiences produce positive results for students—scholars have directed attention to negative mentoring, even as it relates to minoritized students (Wilson, 1997). Negative mentoring experiences "can take a variety of forms, from mismatches between mentor and protégé to sabotage or deceit on the part of the mentor" (Simon & Eby, 2000, p. 1085). Generally speaking, negative mentoring refers to specific behaviors of the mentor that can lead to negative perceptions or experiences for protégés. Negative mentoring behaviors include manipulation, neglect, lack of experience, incompatibility, and general dysfunction or personal problems.

A published typology of negative mentoring experiences outlined multiple dimensions including outcome severity, specificity, and mentor function (Simon & Eby, 2003). Other studies linked negative mentoring to protégé stress and dissatisfaction (Eby & Allen, 2002; Eby et al., 2000).

With so much written about mentoring, one might wonder: What else is there to say? Although a preponderance of research has reported that strong, positive relationships with faculty mentors ease students' adjustment to college, facilitate learning, and increase academic performance, even for first-year and minoritized students (Strayhorn, 2008); not much has been said about the importance of sense of belonging, which is also a major determinant of college students' success (Strayhorn, 2019). Far less is known about whether and how students' engagement with faculty mentors enhances their sense of belonging in college. This is the gap addressed by the study that informed the present chapter.

PURPOSE

The purpose of this chapter is to provide new insights about the important role that faculty mentoring plays in the academic success of Black college students, using sense of belonging as a theoretical framework or lens for examining this topic. Drawing upon insights from an institutional study comprising in-depth interviews, the chapter offers vivid examples of faculty support, mentoring roles, and specific behaviors that enable sense of belonging and academic success of Black students at PWIs. Before summarizing the study, the next section describes sense of belonging as a psychological concept.

SENSE OF BELONGING: A THEORETICAL LENS

Definitions of sense of belonging vary across studies. Generally, it reflects the extent to which individuals feel accepted, valued, and able to assume a role in a group. It is also about feeling respected, valued for who you are, and/or a level of supportive energy and commitment from others. Indeed, sense of belonging helps individuals find value in life and cope with intense, painful emotions (Guo & Cheng, 2016; Hill, 2006; Treichler & Lucksted, 2018).

A steady and growing body of research shows that sense of belonging is correlated with a number of factors like grades (Anderman & Freeman, 2004), retention (Hoffman, Richmond, Morrow, & Salomone), happiness (De Souza & Halafoff, 2018), and life satisfaction (Guo & Cheng, 2016). For instance, difficult life experiences or stereotypes about minoritized groups can negatively influence students' efficacy (i.e., confidence), self-esteem, and sense of belonging. Reduced sense of belonging can hijack students' academic abilities and compromise performance and persistence, especially in high-pressure environments like standardized testing, college transition, or hostile, unwelcoming campuses. Consequently, researchers have shown that anxiety, depression, and loneliness increase during college students' adjustment period (Asher & Weeks, 2014; Drake et al., 2016). When students feel anxious about "fitting in" or making new friends their sense of belonging—or feeling accepted and respected by others—takes on heightened importance (Strayhorn, 2019).

Sense of belonging is a basic need essential for optimizing human functions. For this reason, students may search for ways to satisfy this specific need. They will generally look for physical and social cues that signal that they matter (to another or a group) and have a "place in the space," so to speak, through curriculum, programming, and personnel who look like them. Cues range anywhere from proximity, eye contact, attention, and vocal pitch to more obvious things like feeling respected, having friends in class, or seeing themselves (or core aspects of self) reflected in the learning environment. Two other concepts deserve mention, including ego-extension and pluralistic ignorance. Ego-extension refers to the sense of experiencing self *through others*, namely that others take pride in one's accomplishments or hardship in one's failures (Erikson, 1956). Pluralistic ignorance, on the other hand, refers to a psychological state of shared delusion, wherein people wrongly assume that they feel differently than their peers (Westphal & Bednar, 2005). Applied to college contexts, it is when first-year students pretend to be "fine" because they wrongly assume that they're the only one(s) feeling homesick or doubting their readiness for the demands of college life.

Given the importance of strong, positive relationships to sense of belonging and the fact that *true mentoring* requires a level of personal commitment and generativity that characterizes meaningful relationships, sense of belonging served as a useful theoretical framework for this chapter. If nothing else, it provided language for talking about these issues and how they relate to one another. Figure 2.1 presents a graphical representation of the theory.

THE STUDY

This chapter draws upon data from an ongoing study of Black students attending historically Black colleges and universities (HBCUs) and PWIs. Although the larger study consists of student responses to web-based surveys and in-depth interviews at multiple institutions, this chapter is based on qualitative information from a single institution for which complete data were

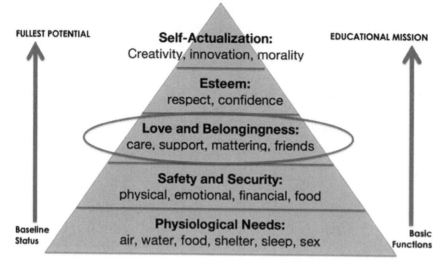

FULLEST POTENTIAL   **Self-Actualization:**   EDUCATIONAL MISSION
                          Creativity, innovation, morality

                                   Esteem:
                               respect, confidence

                          Love and Belongingness:
                          care, support, mattering, friends

                            Safety and Security:
                          physical, emotional, financial, food

Baseline   **Physiological Needs:**   Basic
Status   air, water, food, shelter, sleep, sex   Functions

Figure 2.1 Strayhorn's (2019) Sense of Belonging Theory

readily available. The campus is best described as a large, public research university in the Midwestern region of the country, with a comprehensive suite of student activities for involvement, ranging from student government to fraternities, intramural sports to a campus gospel choir. At the time of the study, the university enrolled approximately 30,000 students, 56 percent of whom were women. Just under 10 percent of all students were African American/Black according to the University's institutional research unit.

Data were collected through one-on-one and focus group interviews using a semistructured protocol. Interview questions explored students' experiences in college, especially the nature of their interactions with peers, staff, and faculty. For instance, participants were asked: "What has college been like for you?" and "Who's been most helpful to you in college?" Follow-up probes like "describe a time when . . . " or "tell me more about . . . " provided respondents an opportunity to expound upon their comments, clarify the meaning of their words, and offer examples to illustrate their point. Interviews generally lasted ninety to 120 minutes on average.

Wherever possible, extensive verbatim quotes and rich, thick descriptions are included in the next section. Showing the data in this way and demonstrating how findings emerged from the *actual words* of students establishes an audit trail which helps strengthen credibility and ensure transferability. In keeping with previous work (Strayhorn, 2010; Strayhorn et al., 2010), data were analyzed using a systematic process that moved from identifying a set of preliminary codes using a form of open coding, to sorting resultant codes and categories into major themes.

KEY INSIGHTS

Three major themes emanated from the present analysis. In keeping with the argument that opened this chapter, we found that even when Black college students enroll at PWIs, many of them experience difficulty adjusting to the campus environment; report hostile, unwelcoming climates characterized by overt and subtle forms of discrimination/racism; and feel insignificant or invisible to campus personnel, which prevents Black students from feeling a sense of belonging. According to interview participants, faculty mentors play critical roles in 1) affirming Black students' experiences, 2) enhancing their belonging, and 3) enabling their success in college. Participants also pointed out ways that White[1] faculty helped them as well.

The quotes presented in this section are representative of the major themes that emanated from this analysis, remaining entirely faithful to the overall sentiments shared by other students in the larger study. Illustrative examples from student interviews are excerpted below, followed by a discussion of recommendations for diverse faculty in higher education.

AFFIRMING STUDENTS' EXPERIENCES

Participants spoke at length about the various ways that faculty mentors eased their adjustment to the college environment or helped them to persist by affirming their experiences, both on-and off-campus. For instance, Elijah (a pseudonym, as are all names in this study) offered the following comment when reflecting on his interactions with a faculty mentor:

> It all just depends, in my opinion, on who you get and what you kinda [sic] need from them. I remember that my first year was very hard for me. It wasn't just the academics—yeah, they were hard as hell but it was like my life decided to fall apart the moment I got to college. That was the year my dad got really sick; I got super depressed; and I had to miss a sh*t load of days for a couple of weeks until I could get some help. It was Dr. Huggins [pseudonym] who really helped me. She put me in touch with the counselor, but really . . . most of all, she just told me that it was life and it would be "OK."

Here is another example that demonstrates how faculty at PWIs affirm Black students' racialized experiences:

> A lot of times it's harder for us [Black students] here [at this PWI] because people really don't get it. They really don't think it's like it is, feel me? Like I told this one professor that I wanted to apply for this scholarship that would give me an internship in New York for the summer. He was like "well, you know you've

got to have pretty good grades to get that . . . and blah blah blah." I had started to tune him out by then 'cuz I've got like a 3.8. Yeah, I got dreds [dreadlocks] and I don't talk like I write, but I'm not stupid. I told my mentor, Dr. Wilson, and she was like "he soooo [emphasis added] racist." Then she helped me find somebody to nominate me for the internship, which I got anyway! (Maurice)

Elijah and Maurice's comments reflect the spirit and tenor of Kim, Krystal, and so many others in the study. Their quotes are illustrative, providing explicit examples of the point that faculty mentors of any race can help Black students by affirming their experiences in college. Some Black faculty at PWIs have a unique vantage point or perspective, given their shared racial history, to help Black students make meaning of racial microaggressions, process racist events or develop healthy coping mechanisms for responding productively in such contexts. The strength of conviction reflected in faculty members' words and the ethic of care displayed matters most to students and positively influences their belonging beliefs.

HELPING STUDENTS ADJUST

Black college students in this study report undergoing an overwhelming process of college transition, identity negotiation, and reconciliation of previously existing social ties to friends, intimate partners, and family (broadly conceived). Working simultaneously through such core issues as "who am I" or "what's my purpose in life," while managing or redirecting existing social relations with people who may or may not understand one's goals left some students feeling "overwhelmed," stressed out, or "on the verge," as one put it. Left unattended, heavy emotions developed into other psychological struggles like anxiety, depression, and loneliness. Consider the following quote from Marshall, a first-year student who met his faculty mentor, Dr. Dee, through a five-week summer bridge program on campus:

For me it was like from the very beginning, like day one, my world got crazy. . . . Well, crazier the moment I got in college. No cap [colloquial phrase meaning "no lie" or "for real"]. It was like my girlfriend was trippin' like she didn't know we'd be apart. My old job was trippin' acting like I had to come back to work or be fired, and I was trippin' too . . . like sometimes I wanted to be bothered and other times I didn't want nobody. Dr. Dee was legit like the only person who I felt like cared about me . . . he would listen, help me, tell me it was normal [to feel that way], and actually check up on me from time to time, especially during campus break periods.

Students spoke at length about how faculty mentors made them feel like they had what it takes to excel in college, despite issues of self-doubt. Feeling "out of place," lonely, or socially and physically dislocated, as if they don't belong, raised doubts about their capability and threatened their sense of self-confidence, according to Black students in the study. Lack of confidence manifested through "crazy checks," in the words of students, where they pondered rhetorical questions like: "Did that *really* just happen?" "Am I losing it?" or "Is it just me?" In such instances, productive faculty mentors played a vital role of not just affirming Black students' experiences, but also reducing such doubts, boosting their confidence, reframing negative experiences into "teachable moments," and helping them design a plan for confronting offenders or moving forward, which enhanced their sense of belonging.

ENABLING STUDENTS' ACADEMIC SUCCESS

Beyond affirming their experiences and enhancing a sense of belonging, Black college students described how faculty mentors—including White faculty members—helped to enable their academic success. Participants identified a number of specific things that faculty did to support their academic success, including offering tutoring or out-of-class assistance, sharing scholarship information, providing feedback on papers/assignments, and writing letters of recommendation, to name a few. Interestingly, a number of participants talked at length about faculty members who read, reviewed, and/or provided feedback to students even though they were not the course instructor.

Participants identified many things that faculty mentors did to help them overcome setbacks, deal with other faculty, or even score higher on a future test after past failure. However, it was not the mere act or incident of faculty mentors "doing something" to help a student succeed that seemed to matter most to Black students in the study; rather, it was the meaning that Black students attached to such actions and the extent to which those actions showed how faculty mentors "went above and beyond the call of duty," as one student described, that stood out as impacting students' belonging beliefs. Consider the following quotes from Logan and Brianna, both STEM majors, that echo the sentiments of so many others:

> I call Dr. Robinson my mentor because he does a lot more than he *has* (emphasis added) to [do] really. I mean, I guess all teachers [professors] have to like teach classes, grade papers, and tell us what we gotta [sic] do to get a good grade (laughing). But, Dr. Robinson don't [sic] just teach me . . . he tells me about stuff like scholarships, grad schools, and even like kept it real with me about

fraternities and stuff. He don't [sic] have to do that, but he does and I know it's because he really care [sic]. (Logan)

For as long as like forever, I've dreamed of going to graduate school at [said institution]. I tried to keep my grades up so that I could apply one day. But, I had no idea that Dr. Harris [a White woman] would have my back like that . . . I mean, she spent her own money to take me to [said institution] to meet the Dean and some other people. She paid for my food, lab jacket, and basically *made them* (emphasis added) accept me for a summer program. She ain't [sic] have to do all that . . . facts. (Brianna)

Both Dr. Robinson and Dr. Harris did things to demonstrate their care and concern for Logan and Brianna, respectively. The depth of their conversations, the length of their visits, and the level of their public support for proteges stood out as significant—as acts of care and concern—to and for these students.

Another point deserves mention here. Black college students identified a menu of school-related things that faculty mentors did to support their academic success. But several students (like Brianna) talked about how faculty helped them by providing more basic needs like food, money, and clothing or school supplies (e.g., lab jacket). A few students mentioned how their mentor helped them find a place to stay during winter break when the campus (residence hall) was closed or invited them over to eat with their family during holidays, if they had no place to go. Providing these basic, physiological needs like apparel, food, and shelter signaled to students that mentors care, that proteges matter, and they belong.

DISCUSSION

The purpose of this chapter was to provide new insights about the important role that faculty mentoring plays in the academic success of Black college students at PWIs. Drawing upon insights from an institutional study comprising one-on-one and group interviews, three major themes were identified including how faculty mentors helped Black students at PWIs by affirming their experiences, helping them through difficult transitions, enabling their academic success, and thus, fostering their sense of belonging in college. Insights presented in this chapter connect with prior research in a number of ways.

A long line of research confirms that a sense of belonging matters and powerfully influences student success in both K-12 (Goodenow, 1993) and collegiate (Strayhorn, 2019) settings. The same is true for Black students at

PWIs, and faculty mentors can play a vital role in providing the academic and social support needed for students to feel like they matter and someone else cares about their success, which is known as ego-extension (Erikson, 1956; Schlossberg, 1985). Information presented in this chapter helps to make clear that social support alone—that is, mere presence of a faculty mentor—is insufficient for changing or raising Black students' thoughts and behaviors. Rather, when faculty mentoring helps Black students process their experiences, work through difficult transitions, and feel like they *matter and belong* then real magic happens. That kind of support can ease students' adjustment to college, reduce feelings of anxiety, and push students to stay when dropping out seems so much easier.

Sense of belonging has been identified as important to the health, especially mental health, of Black college students. Anxiety and isolation can be detrimental to overall well-being (Choenarom et al., 2005), especially during college transition for Black students at PWIs. Faculty mentors make a difference by providing the social support that helps Black students feel like they belong. Feelings of belonging were potent buffers against self-doubt, depression, and "crazy checks" or what scholars refer to as pluralistic ignorance (Westphal & Bednar, 2005). Faculty mentors told Black students that they were okay and that things would work out, provided hope for the future, and helped them set a plan of action for working through issues.

RECOMMENDATIONS FOR CULTURALLY RESPONSIVE MENTORING

Findings from the study that informed this chapter have a number of practical implications, especially for faculty mentors generally and White faculty working with Black college students specifically. For instance, it is important for mentors to get to know their protégés well. Faculty should know students' names, their future aspirations, and academic interests. Acquiring this knowledge takes time and so faculty would be well-served to set aside time—through office hours and other means—to talk with students out of class about these topics.

Institutions can play a critical role by encouraging or incentivizing faculty to get to know their students. Creating "high touch" environments where students feel cared about and connected to faculty is not just good for promoting belonging, but is also a proven strategy for student success. Mentoring program coordinators should include such expectations in program guidelines and mentor training exercises. Provosts and Deans can revisit existing reward structures to give weight to factors, such as, how much time faculty spend with students out of class. Identifying campus leaders in charge of faculty development may be a way to streamline student-focused training or to pick a point of contact for mentors who want to help.

Recall that several students shared how some faculty mentors gave them money, paid for school supplies, or helped them find a place to stay during school breaks. These actions are vital to students' academic success and personal well-being, but clearly go beyond the scope of duty for faculty and *may* even present a liability for colleges and universities. Institutions can alleviate this concern and help students by forming institutionally funded food pantries, clothing closets, and scholarships (or book funds) that help underwrite hidden costs of the curriculum. Partnering with groups like the College and Food Bank Alliance can provide important resources.

It is true that many more Black students enroll in college today than was even possible in past decades. Yet even when they do enroll, many Black students drop out or abandon their degree plans due to lack of support. Faculty mentors can play a pivotal role and enhance Black student's sense of belonging at PWIs, as described herein. Of course, doing so takes time, patience, *authentic* care and concern, as well as trust—and, unlike iPhones and tablets—trust cannot be manufactured, it is built or earned over time. The forging of this type of trust can be very hard work. However, hard work is no excuse for retreat. Faculty mentors—not just *members*—go above and beyond the call of duty to affirm Black students' experiences, boost their sense of belonging, and, thus, enable their academic success. To do anything less would be . . . well, not mentoring.

REFERENCES

Anderman, L. H., & Freeman, T. M. (2004). Students' sense of belonging in school. In M. L. Maehr & P. R. Pintrich (Eds.), *Advances in motivation and achievement: Vol. 13 Motivating students, improving schools: The legacy of Carol Midgley* (pp. 27–63). Greenwich, CT: Elsevier.

Asher, S. R., & Weeks, M. S. (2014). Loneliness and belongingness in the college years. In R. J. Coplan & J. C. Bowker (Eds.), *The handbook of solitude: Psychological perspectives on social isolation, social withdrawal, and being alone* (pp. 283–301). Hoboken, NJ: Wiley.

Baetz, C. L., & Widom, C. S. (2019). Does a close relationship with an adult reduce the risk of juvenile offending for youth with a history of maltreatment? *Child Maltreatment.* doi:https://doi.org/10.1177%2F1077559519883010.

Bernier, A., Larose, S., & Soucy, N. (2005). Academic mentoring in college: The interactive role of student's and mentor's interpersonal dispositions. *Research in Higher Education, 46*(1), 29–51.

Bordes, V., & Arredondo, P. (2005). Mentoring and 1st-year Latina/o college students. *Journal of Hispanic Higher Education, 4*(2), 114–133.

Choenarom, C., Williams, R. A., & Hagerty, B. M. (2005). The role of sense of belonging and social support on stress and depression in depressed individuals. *Archives of Psychiatric Nursing, 19*, 18–29.

Choy, S. P., Horn, L. J., Nunez, A. M., & Chen, X. (2000). Transition to college: What helps at-risk students and student whose parents did not attend college. *New Directions for Institutional Research, 107*, 45–63.

Dawson, P. (2014). Beyond a definition: Toward a framework for designing and specifying mentoring models. *Educational Researcher, 43*(3), 137–145.

De Souza, M., & Halafoff, A. (2018). *Re-enchanting education and spiritual wellbeing: fostering belonging and meaning-making for global citizens*. London; New York, NY: Routledge.

Drake, E. C., Sladek, M. R., & Doane, L. D. (2016). Daily cortisol activity, loneliness, and coping efficacy in late adolescence: A longitudinal study of the transition to college. *International Journal of Behavioral Development, 40*(4), 334–345.

Eby, L. T., & Allen, T. D. (2002). Further investigation of proteges negative mentoring experiences: Patterns and outcomes. *Group and Organizational Management, 27*, 456–479.

Eby, L. T., McManus, S. E., Simon, S. A., & Russell, J. E. A. (2000). The protege's perspective regarding negative mentoring experiences: The development of a taxonomy. *Journal of Vocational Behavior, 57*, 1–21.

Erikson, E. (1956). The problem of ego identity. *Journal of the American Psychoanalytic Association, 4*, 56–121.

Gershenfeld, S. (2014). A review of undergraduate mentoring programs. *Review of Educational Research*.

Gipson, J., & Mitchell, D. M., Jr.,. (2017). How high-impact practices influence academic achievement for African American college students. *Journal Committeed to Social Change on Race and Ethnicity, 3*(2), 124–144.

Goodenow, C. (1993). The psychological sense of school membership among adolescents: Scale development and educational correlates. *Psychology in the Schools, 30*, 79–90.

Guo, T.-C., & Cheng, Z.-C. (2016). Sense of belonging based on novel posting. *Online Information Review, 40*(2), 204–217.

Healy, C. C. (1997). An operational definition of mentoring. In H. T. Frierson, Jr. (Ed.), *Diversity in higher education* (pp. 9–22). Greenwich, CT: JAI Press, Inc.

Hill, D. L. (2006). Sense of belonging as connectedness, American Indian worldview, and mental health. *Arch Psychiatr Nurs, 20*(5), 210–216. doi:10.1016/j.apnu.2006.04.003.

Hirt, J. B., Amelink, C. T., Bennett, B. R., & Strayhorn, T. L. (2008). A system of othermothering: Relationships between student affairs administrators and students at historically Black colleges and universities. *The NASPA Journal, 45*(2), 210–236.

Hoffman, M., Richmond, J., Morrow, J., & Salomone, K. (2002–2003). Investigating sense of belonging in first-year college students. *Journal of College Student Retention: Research, Theory & Practice, 4*(3), 227–256.

Hurtado, S., Han, J., Sáenz, V., Espinosa, L., Cabrera, N., & Cerna, O. (2007). Predicting transition and adjustment to college: Biomedical and behavioral sciences aspirants' and minority students' first-year of college. *Research in Higher Education, 48*(7), 841–887.

Jacobi, M. (1991). Mentoring and undergraduate student success: A literature review. *Review of Educational Research, 61,* 505–532.

Kallison, J. M. (2017). The effects of an intensive postsecondary transition program on college readiness for adult learners. *Adult Education Quarterly, 67*(4), 302–321.

Kelley, M. S., & Lee, M. J. (2018). When natural mentors matter: Unraveling the relationship with delinquency. *Child and Youth Services Review, 91,* 319–328. doi:https://doi.org/10.1016/j.childyouth.2018.06.002.

Kram, K. E., & Isabella, L. A. (1985). Mentoring alternatives: The role of peer relationships in career development. *Academy of Management Journal, 28*(1), 110–132.

Lopatto, D. (2003). The essential features of undergraduate research. *Council of Undergraduate Research Quarterly, 24,* 139–142.

Mangold, W. D., Bean, L. G., Adams, D. J., Schwab, W. A., & Lynch, S. M. (2003). Who goes, who stays: An assessment of the effect of a freshman mentoring and unit registration program on college persistence. *Journal of College Student Retention: Research, Theory & Practice, 4*(2), 95–122.

Mertz, N. T. (2004). What's a mentor, anyway? *Educational Administration Quarterly, 40*(4), 541–560.

Nora, A., & Crisp, G. (2007–2008). Mentoring students: Conceptualizing and validating the multi-dimensions of a support system. *Journal of College Student Retention: Research, Theory & Practice, 9*(3), 337–356.

Parise, M. R., & Forret, M. L. (2008). Formal mentoring programs: The relationship of program design and support to mentors' perceptions of benefits and costs. *Journal of Vocational Behavior, 72*(2), 225–240.

Patitu, C. L., & Terrell, M. C. (1997). Participant perceptions of the NASPA Minority Undergraduate Fellows Program. *NASPA Journal, 17*(1), 69–80.

Paul, E. L., & Brier, S. (2001). Friendsickness in the transition to college: Precollege predictors and college adjustment correlates. *Journal of Counseling and Development, 79,* 77–89.

Redmond, S. (1990). Mentoring and cultural diversity in academic settings. *American Behavioral Scientist, 34*(2), 188–200.

Rhodes, J. E. (2002). *Stand by me: The risks and rewards of mentoring today's youth.* Cambridge, MA: Harvard University Press.

Rhodes, J. E., Grossman, J. B., & Resche, N. L. (2000). Agents of change: Pathways through which mentoring relationships influence adolescents' academic adjustment. *Child Development, 71,* 1662–1671.

Rose, G. L., Rukstalis, M. R., & Schuckit, M. A. (2005). Informal mentoring between faculty and medical students. *Academic Medicine, 80*(4), 344–348.

Schlossberg, N. K. (1985). *Marginality and mattering: A life span approach.* Paper presented at the annual meeting of the American Psychological Association, Los Angeles, CA.

Simon, S. A., & Eby, L. T. (2003). A typology of negative mentoring experiences: A multidimensional scaling study. *Human Relations, 56*(9), 1083–1106.

Sorrentino, D. M. (2007). The SEEK mentoring program: An application of the goal-setting theory. *Journal of College Student Retention: Research, Theory & Practice, 8*(2), 241–250.

Strayhorn, T. L. (2008). The role of supportive relationships in facilitating African American males' success in college. *NASPA Journal, 45*(1), 26–48.

Strayhorn, T. L. (2009). Bridging the gap from high school to college for "at risk" first-year students. *E-Source for College Transitions, 6*(3), 9–11.

Strayhorn, T. L. (2010). Racial and sexual identity politics in college: New directions in campus equity. In T. E. Dancy, II (Ed.), *Managing diversity: (Re)Visioning equity on college campuses* (pp. 141–158). New York: Peter Lang.

Strayhorn, T. L. (2019). *College students' sense of belonging: A key to educational success for all students* (2nd ed.). New York: Routledge.

Strayhorn, T. L., Blakewood, A. M., & DeVita, J. M. (2010). Triple threat: Challenges and supports of Black gay men at predominantly White campuses. In T. L. Strayhorn & M. C. Terrell (Eds.), *The evolving challenges of Black college students: New insights for policy, practice and research* (pp. 85–104). Sterling, VA: Stylus.

Strayhorn, T. L., & Saddler, T. N. (2009). Gender differences in the influence of faculty-student mentoring relationships on satisfaction with college among African Americans. *Journal of African American Studies, 13*(4), 476–493.

Strayhorn, T. L., & Terrell, M. C. (2007). Mentoring and satisfaction with college for Black students. *The Negro Educational Review, 58*(1–2), 69–83.

Tognoli, J. (2003). Leaving home: Homesickness, place attachment, and transition among residential college students. *Journal of College Student Psychotherapy, 18*, 35–48.

Tolan, P. H., Henry, D. B., Schoeny, M. S., Lovegrove, P., & Nichols, E. (2014). Mentoring programs to affect delinquency and associated outcomes of youth at risk: A comprehensive meta-analytic review. *Journal of Experimental Criminology, 10*(2), 179–206.

Treichler, E. B. H., & Lucksted, A. A. (2018). The role of sense of belonging in self-stigma among people with serious mental illnesses. *Psychiatr Rehabil J, 41*(2), 149–152. doi:10.1037/prj0000281.

U.S. Department of Education. (2019). *The condition of education*. Washington, DC: U.S. Government Printing Office.

Wanberg, C. R., Kammeyer-Mueller, J., & Marchese, M. (2006). Mentor and protege predictors and outcomes of mentoring in a formal mentoring program. *Journal of Vocational Behavior, 69*(3), 410–423.

Westphal, J. D., & Bednar, M. K. (2005). Pluralistic ignorance in corporate boards and firms' strategic persistence in response to low firm performance. *Administrative Science Quarterly, 50*, 262–298.

Wilson, R. (1997). Negative mentoring: An examination of the phenomenon as it affects minority students. In J. Frierson, H. T. (Ed.), *Diversity in Higher Education* (Vol. 1, pp. 177–185). Greenwich, CT: JAI Press, Inc.

Zalaquett, C. P., & Lopez, A. D. (2006). Learning from the stories of successful undergraduate Latina/Latino students: The importance of mentoring. *Mentoring & Tutoring, 14*(3), 337–353.

NOTES

1. Racial and ethnic groups are designated by proper nouns and are capitalized. Therefore, we use "Black" and "White" instead of black and white (colors) when referring to human racial and ethnic groups.

Chapter Three

Let's Work

Identifying the Challenges and Opportunities for Mentoring across Difference

Richard J. Reddick, Delando L. Crooks,
M. Yvonne Taylor, Tiffany N. Hughes,
and Daniel E. Becton

Faculty mentorship and socialization of graduate students has a direct impact on student retention (Gardner & Barnes, 2007; Gardner, 2008; Weidman et al., 2001). As the academy attempts to diversify to meet the needs of an increasingly diverse student body and global society, it is imperative that White[1] faculty members endeavor to successfully mentor students who do not look like them (Austin & McDaniels, 2006; Hall & Burns, 2009; Reddick & Young, 2012; Weidman et al., 2001). This work cannot be performed by Black, Indigenous, and People of Color (BIPOC) faculty members alone. Specifically, in graduate education, White faculty members' socialization process is different from Black graduate students' experience, potentially presenting challenges in effective mentorship and socialization processes for Black graduate students. Because of these challenges, this chapter provides considerations for White faculty members who are engaged in mentoring and socializing Black graduate students.

To begin, this chapter presents the multiple and intersectional identities of Black graduate students. Next, the psychological impacts of mentorship and multiple ways of mentoring are discussed. We conclude by urging White faculty to unveil, critique, and dismantle the hidden curriculum to unburden the experiences of students of color (Jackson, 1968; Margolis & Romero, 1998).

With these four considerations, we keep honesty and authenticity central in the mentee-mentor relationship.

BLACKNESS AND BEYOND: AFFIRMING BLACK GRADUATE STUDENTS' OTHER IDENTITIES

As we consider White faculty members' mentorship of Black graduate students, it is important to stress that Black graduate students are not mono-lithic, neither are their experiences with oppression. As with any individual or group of people, Black graduate students have varied and intersectional identities, and White faculty should be aware of that. Some of these identities may be international or they may intersect with White faculty members' own characteristics and identities: common intersecting identities can help mentors develop a bonding connection with students, furthering the mentorship relationship (Reddick & Young, 2012). In this section, we will present the intersectionality of identities, differences between race and ethnicity, socio-economic factors, religious identity, considerations of gender, sexuality, and gender identity, and finally, ability status.

INTERSECTIONALITY

Intersectionality has become an important concept to explain the complexity of oppression within the academy and in popular culture. Legal scholar Kimberlé Crenshaw (1989) coined the term to describe people with multiple identities—specifically race and gender—and the disparate outcomes they may experience due to the ways in which systems of oppression—such as the law—act upon those those intersectional identities. For example, although a Black woman's gender may be the same as a White woman's, the intersection of race and gender present different Black women with a different experience of oppression and different outcomes caused by how White supremacist and patriarchal systems interface with their raced and gendered identities. A White woman who must address a group of faculty members who identify and present as men, for example, is seen differently than a Black woman in the same situation. Sexism may play a role for both, but anti-Blackness coupled with misogyny (termed "misogynoir" [Bailey, 2010]) causes a different reading of the Black woman and a different, potentially oppressive, experience or outcome for her (Collins, 1990; Crenshaw, 1989; hooks, 1981). An example is evident in the pay gap between White and Black women. While finding points of connection are important for bonding between White faculty and Black students, it is equally important to remember to avoid presuming that those commonalities ensure that their students will all have the same experiences and outcomes. Assuming a monolithic Black experience is dangerous and does not account for differences between race and ethnicity, gender, sexuality, and so on.

RACE DOES NOT EQUAL ETHNICITY

"I had to explain to the [faculty member and administrator] that not all Black people were African Americans. He thought saying 'Black' was a slur," said a Black graduate student in a recent study (personal communication, 2019). The faculty member, having come of age during the 1970s and 1980s, when Black people in America had begun to increasingly use "African American" as their ethnic descriptor, thought using it for all Black people was the appropriate thing to do. However, as the graduate student explained to him, the university enrolls Black students from across the African diaspora. Students may hail from countries in Africa, the Caribbean, United Kingdom, South America, or any part of the world—or from families who have recently immigrated from abroad. Not every student who identifies as Black is African American, and not every African American prefers to be referred to as such. Understanding that there is a Black diaspora—and avoiding assumptions—is an important early step for a White faculty member engaging in mentorship with a Black student.

Additionally, like K-12 teachers, White faculty within postsecondary institutions are not immune to framing Black students through a deficit-rather than asset-based lens (Brown, 2016). Black American students often bring with them deep, rich cultural ties and sense of responsibility, which can help drive them to academic achievement, as they are less likely to see their pursuit as an individual goal, but a collective accomplishment for their community (Carson, 2009; McCallum, 2017). Immigrant students from the African diaspora may have backgrounds quite distinct from those of their African American peers (George Mwangi et al., 2019). Black students may have strong religious ties that influence their academic motivation and success (Jett, 2010). These points of difference and variances among Black identities are worth noting as they do not fit the general narratives about Black students. They may also provide a point of connection for the White faculty mentor.

SOCIOECONOMIC STATUS

Another aspect of difference has to do with socioeconomics. Dominant narratives in media and society portray Black people in ways that lead to preconceived notions of lack and hardship (Collins, 1991; Hartman, 2019; hooks, 1981). Additionally, a great deal of earlier education research focused on deficit thinking regarding the resources that Black students bring to educational environments (Brown, 2016). These deficit-framed narratives and research can influence unconscious biases and cause people who have little day-to-day interaction with Black people to make assumptions about their socioeconomic conditions or the previous educational attainment of Black graduate students.

RELIGIOUS IDENTITY

The importance and influence of the Black Church as a source of community, sustenance and liberation for Black Americans is well known (Lincoln & Mamiya, 1990; Pinn, 2002). However, not all Black students are Black Americans, and not all Black Americans have the same shared experience of Baptist church-going. Many, such as those in South Louisiana, are Catholic. The Black Muslim tradition is also strong in Black American culture (Lincoln, 1994). More recently, younger Black Americans, have begun foregoing religious identification or reclaiming African spiritual traditions as a form of liberation from White supremacy (Finley & Gray, 2016). Prevailing narratives about Black people still tend to adhere to a singular story about religious affiliation and commitment within Black communities, but again, these narratives are too simplistic.

GENDER, SEXUALITY, AND SEXUAL IDENTITY

Gender, sexuality, and sexual identity are also identities that intersect with Blackness that White faculty members who want to successfully mentor Black graduate students should consider. Black men, women, and nonbinary students may each have different challenges on predominately White campuses. Black women, for example, must often contend with invisibility and hypervisibility simultaneously (Collins, 1990; hooks, 1981). Their gender coupled with their Blackness mean that their experience of misogyny in academia is compounded by their simultaneous navigation of anti-Blackness (Collins, 1990; hooks, 1981). Black men are often assumed to be athletes on campus, resulting in being perceived as less intelligent (Fuller, 2017; Vachuska & Brudvig, 2018).

The study of queer and transgender identities within the academy is a fast-growing field of research; however, these studies often continue to center the experiences of White queer and transgender students and faculty

(Renn, 2010; Stewart et al., 2015; Vacarro, 2012). Black students may also hold queer and transgender identities. Queer Black male students have said that they feel invisible on predominantly White campuses (Gonzales, 2019). As LGBTQ acceptance within some Black communities is still a challenge, queer and trans Black graduate students may be more apt to "cover" or mitigate their queerness to be more acceptable to group norms (Yoshino, 2006). This form of passing may render their LGBTQ identity invisible, yet this identity may be shared with a White faculty member with the potential to foster a sense of kinship. Kinship communities, or chosen families, as elucidated in Nicolazzo's work (2016), are highly important for trans students' sense of safety and acceptance on college campuses and could be crucial in the retention and success of trans Black graduate students.

ABILITY STATUS

Students, faculty, and staff experience varying types of ability, but hidden disabilities often go unnoticed. These include attention deficit disorder, autism spectrum disorder, hearing disabilities, and other forms of disability not readily apparent to the naked eye. Still, disability is an identity characteristic, and recognition among universities that accommodations must be made for students has been growing in recent years (Taylor, 2019). Ability status can impact anyone, including Black graduate students. The little research on the topic has shown that navigating hidden disabilities in college causes students considerable emotional and psychological stress and negative feelings (Olney & Brockelman, 2003). It can be speculated that coming forward with a disability and need for accommodations may be especially challenging for a Black graduate student who already contends with stereotype threat, which is fear that their something about their behavior or disability may be "proving" a common stereotype correct about Black people, or imposter phenomenon, which are feelings of inadequacy that contribute to a sense of not belonging (Cokley et al., 2013). They may fear that disclosing a disability might cause their mentor to view them as less than capable of graduate study. As with LGBTQ status, if students do not witness faculty discussing their own status, they are implicitly being told that their status is invisible or problematic.

Recognizing that Black graduate students may hold any number or combination of these identities is important for any faculty member who wishes to successfully mentor them. It is especially true for White faculty members, who may be more prone to seeing the student primarily through race or consider race the only identity that matters. Seeing the student's race and culture is undoubtedly important. Recognizing the strengths and assets race and cultural identity give their students and the assets students bring to the academy are valuable to the mentoring relationship. Understanding their students as multifaceted, whole beings with varied interests, identities and experiences are important building blocks of mentoring relationships. Additionally, being able to recognize, affirm, and help graduate students find community and acceptance of their other identities on campus and in the academy will also bode well for psychological considerations in successful mentoring. Faculty can learn more about every student in their classrooms by employing surveys prior to class to learn about their students. In doing so, they can gain information not only about student identities, but their interests and hopes for their education. Such surveys can aid in building rapport and connection with students and build a sense of community and belonging that creates a healthier social-emotional environment for learning, not only for Black students but all students.

APPROACHING MENTORSHIP WITH PSYCHOSOCIAL CONSIDERATIONS

Effective mentoring not only addresses career development, it also includes a psychosocial component (Kram, 1988; Reddick & Young, 2012). The psychosocial aspect of mentoring is concerned with the basic needs of a mentee (Reddick, 2009) and with "caring about students as *people* as well as learners" (Reddick & Young, 2012, p. 421). Reddick (2009) argues psychosocial considerations should precede instrumental (career-focused) approaches in higher education mentoring. Reddick (2009) adds that for graduate students of color, psychosocial mentoring is needed to address "challenges such as perceived racism, or racial microaggressions" (p. 71). This echoes the work of several researchers who assert that graduate students of color require faculty members who provide support beyond traditional academic advice (Griffin & Reddick, 2011; Guiffrida, 2005; Stanley & Lincoln, 2005; Young & Brooks, 2008).

Effective mentoring, then, requires reflection and developmental "work." As Young and Brooks (2008) argue, an effective mentoring relationship is "empathetic rather than sympathetic" and requires "responsibility and commitment" from both mentor and mentee (p. 399). In order to facilitate a generative space, mentors must affirm both themselves and their mentees as complex individuals whose concerns exceed the academic or professional realms. Rather than dispensing knowledge, as one might view instrumental techniques, effective mentors recognize that they are also implicated as a subject. That is, the mentor has to suspend their own values and commitments in order to be present to the mentee. In the psychosocial domain, one's identities are rendered vulnerable and acknowledged as in flux.

By demanding that faculty and staff fracture from themselves as knowers, higher education mentoring presents a developmental challenge. As articulated in Robert Kegan's (1980) constructive-developmental theory, this refers to "a transformational change, a qualitative shift in how people understand themselves, their worlds, and the relationship between the two" (Helsing, 2010, p. 679). Researchers argue that education leaders today regularly face "adaptive" challenges, which evade scripted solutions and fundamentally challenge leaders' "values, beliefs, habits, ways of working, or ways of life" (Helsing et al., 2008). Developmental possibilities occur when someone faces a "disorienting dilemma" that exposes the limits of their current meaning-making structure (Mezirow, 1991). If this challenge is also met with support, a person can uncover hidden assumptions and beliefs, thereby developing new conceptual capacities (Helsing, 2010, p. 679).

Mentors in higher education are therefore called to be humble, vulnerable, and willing to grow. Literature in adult developmental psychology (e.g., Kegan, 1994) suggests that development is inhibited when individuals become overidentified with a subject position. Disorienting dilemmas may render conscious what was previously an irreducible identification, such as how a professor understands themselves as a *teacher* or as a *thinker*, or how an administrator identifies as a *leader* or as an *organizer*. Development involves the disintegration and reintegration of the conception of "self" such that one's identity is reformulated in a more complex manner. As Helsing (2010) writes, this "includes the capacities of the prior stage but adds new capacities as well" (p. 679). For instance, a midcareer faculty member who assumes an administrative role may lean on experiences from a career of researching and supporting students, yet at the same time find themselves learning and developing new skills—much like their students may experience.

This developmental demand is also reflected in mentoring research. As Reddick and Young (2012, p. 419) note, mentors may have "too strong of an attachment to a certain style of 'being' a professor, which can encourage 'cloning' or constrict innovation." Such an attachment represents the psychological challenge described above. In order to facilitate a mentee's creative flourishing, the mentor must also relinquish certainty in who they are. When Reddick and Young (2012, p. 423) write that "what makes a good mentor may be more an issue of what they do, rather than who they are," this is because the latter is at least partially constituted by the former.

Kegan's (1994) constructive-developmental theory urges us to consider the structure of meaning-making as well as noncognitive dimensions to development. Addressing the structure, not simply the content, of a person's meaning-making process means focusing on "the principles that organize an individual's thinking, feeling, and social relating (or *how* the individual thinks and feels) as separate from *what* the individual thinks and feels"

(Helsing, 2010, p. 679). Kegan incorporates affective, interpersonal, and intrapersonal domains as well as the cognitive dimension, considering the self an "integrating, unifying system" (Helsing, 2010, p. 680). Thus, for effective psychosocial mentoring to take place, a mentor must be: a) present to a mentee's holistic experience, b) vulnerable to potential changes in their own meaning-making principles, and c) attuned to the interrelation of ideas, feelings, and relationships.

These actions illustrate that the essential resource of all mentoring is trust. Without it, there is no possibility of meaningful connection; trust is "the cornerstone of effective mentoring" (Reddick & Young, 2012, p. 421). Yet the pathway to psychosocial connection can be obfuscated by sociological terrain: mentors tend to "choose to mentor others who look like them" which disadvantages people from underrepresented racial backgrounds (Caver & Livers, 2002, p. 7). At predominantly White institutions (PWIs), students of color often have multiple sources for instrumental (professional) support, but few people in whom they can trust and confide (Reddick & Young, 2012, p. 420). When staff and faculty demonstrate trustworthiness to one student, however, their reputation often reaches generations of successive students (Reddick & Young, 2012, p. 422), and they may become a "magnet" for budding scholars (Reddick, 2015, p. 47).

Mentors for students of color can build trust by demonstrating a commitment to a race-conscious, antiracist worldview (Brown et al., 1999; Scheurich & Laible, 1995; Young & Brooks, 2008). This commitment is both personal and individualized (navigating one's social, political, and professional relationships in an antiracist manner), as well as using one's positionality and power to advocate for, and advance systemic and structural changes in institutions. By using one's positionality to advocate and insist on the importance of assessments about the racial climate and campus culture at an institution, for example, provides a service to students of color and helps on the individual level, as a mentor can better establish trust with a mentee, with an honest presentation of the realities of existing on campus (Reddick & Young, 2012). Furthermore, research indicates that mentors can build cross-racial rapport through sharing experiences in which they themselves faced isolation and/or discrimination (Reddick, 2009). In addition to demonstrating solidarity in the struggle against oppression, this shows that challenges are part of the learning process (Reddick & Young, 2012).

The mentoring space is thus a liminal one that requires honesty and ambivalence. As Reddick and Young (2012, p. 415) write, "Indeed, the level of honesty required may place mentors at cross-purposes with institutional goals." Staff and faculty are caught in a web in which institutions advocate a desire for integration, but leave fundamental Whiteness unaddressed as an organizing institutional factor (Bonilla-Silva, 2015). White employees are complicit in systems of privilege even if they are unaware or ideologically opposed. For example, they may not be aware of the impact of racist architecture on their campus, or they may unwittingly support neoliberal rhetoric about student success that disproportionately penalizes students of color.

Cross-racial mentoring is thus necessary for White mentors who must step back from their own racialized experience to recognize it as nonuniversal. Ultimately, mentoring is "complex, dynamic, and riddled with contradictions" (Reddick, 2009). It therefore demands a meaning-making structure complex enough to "hold both sides of an ambivalent feeling simultaneously" (Helsing, 2010, p. 681). Effective mentors exhibit the empathy, courage, and self-awareness to embrace structural shifts in their own meaning-making systems. Once this is realized by White faculty and staff, they will understand their shortfalls and introduce other forms of mentoring. Ultimately, the effective mentor will not only embrace approaches to supporting their mentees that are familiar and comfortable, but also consider new methods as opportunities for growth and development that support their junior colleagues.

MULTIPLE WAYS OF MENTORING

When we consider what a mentoring relationship consists of, researchers have provided many definitions of the role. All, however, can agree that mentorship is a supportive, developmental relationship, assumed to benefit both the mentor and the mentee (Kram, 1988; Mertz, 2004; Reddick & Young, 2012). Mentoring relationships are also flexible. They can form spontaneously or in a more arranged fashion (Mertz, 2004), that is, in a naturally developing relationship between two parties, as well as in a designed programmatic format. While it is often assumed that these relationships work best when mentees share an ethnic background and similar research interests with their mentors, these factors do not preclude White mentors from maintaining successful mentoring relationships with students of color (Brown & Grothaus, 2019; Brown II et al., 1999). Considering there are more White faculty that can serve as mentors to Black graduate students, we present examples of different types of mentorship and mentorship in different spaces.

TYPES OF MENTORSHIP

Kram (1988) puts forth the idea that mentorship is multifunctional; it facilitates both the psychosocial and career development of the mentee. Building on this foundational idea, Mertz (2004) posits that professional development and career advancement can be looked at as separate functions that align to prepare mentees for postgraduate success. While it is not necessary for each function of mentorship to be fulfilled by the same individual, it is advisable that graduate students of color, particularly those at PWIs, have access to this full range of support as they progress in their studies and prepare for life in academia (Brown II et al., 1999; Davis, 2007; Reddick & Young, 2012).

Psychosocial well-being

Black faculty only account for 6 percent of full-time postsecondary faculty (National Center for Education Statistics, 2020). As such, it is imperative that White faculty confidently step in the role of mentors for developing Black scholars (Brown II et al., 1999; Reddick & Young, 2012). Holding a marginalized identity can lead to challenges as graduate students of color learn to navigate the landscape of the academe. As mentioned earlier, psychosocial support is important in helping these students work through perceived racism on their journey to the professoriate (Reddick & Young, 2012). To successfully facilitate these difficult conversations, mentors from nonmarginalized identities must have a genuine commitment to antiracism (Brown II et al., 1999; Reddick & Young, 2012). Mentors who cannot directly relate to experiences of racism can draw on *proximal experiences of being othered*—their own experiences of isolation or discrimination, to empathize with their advisees (Reddick, 2009). Ultimately, being willing to listen to students without being dismissive of their concerns is an important element of the cross-racial mentoring relationship (Reddick & Young, 2012).

Career development

The effect of mentorship on a graduate student's career is profound (Brown II et al., 1999; Davis, 2007; Holmes et al., 2007; Mertz, 2004; Reddick & Young, 2012). Though they may enter their programs with an interest in the professoriate, the relationship they have with their mentor and what they observe may turn their interests outside of academia. Research shows that the opposite is true as well (Davis, 2007). Students who enter graduate studies with no plans to pursue tenure-track positions may alter their career goals based on a good mentoring relationship. This illustrates just how pronounced the impact of mentorship is on a graduate student and underscores the importance of establishing good mentoring practices with underrepresented populations in order to encourage future participation in the academe (Brown II et al., 1999; Mertz, 2004; Reddick & Young, 2012).

MENTORSHIP CAN COME FROM ANYWHERE

Traditionally, when one thinks of graduate student mentors, one may picture a faculty member offering guidance and support to a pupil. While faculty-student mentorship remains the most common structure of mentoring relationships for graduate students, it is complemented by similarly supportive relationships formed with staff and their fellow graduate student peers. This supportive network is also called "constellation mentorship" (Johnson & Ridley, 2008; Reddick, 2011). Staff members and administrators should welcome the opportunity to mentor graduate students. These individuals hold a host of knowledge that is valuable to students, and particularly graduate students of color. University staff members have knowledge of the institution and its values, procedures, and power structures. They can also offer guidance to graduate students in the arena of professional development by ensuring that graduate students of color are made aware of useful workshops and funding opportunities that students sometimes miss. These mentors often prove to be integral to students in navigating the graduate student process successfully.

One of the initial impacts that mentors have on Black graduate students is in offering them realistic expectations for their institution, department, and faculty advisors (Reddick & Young, 2012). This is a prime opportunity for more advanced students within the graduate program to form informal mentorship to new grads. It is also important for Black graduate students to develop relationships with peers and near-peers, as these individuals will be their collaborator colleagues in the future. These relationships can be facilitated by departments in setting up formal programs with mentor pairings for first-year students. They can be nudged by faculty advisors who encourage their advising families—other students mentored by the same advisor—to share what they have learned from their experience with newer advisees. Or, they can occur naturally based on shared interests and goals (Mertz, 2004). Constellation mentorship, including staff and peers, will provide Black graduate students with the implicit rules necessary for their success, also known as the hidden curriculum. For instance, discussing the intricacies of applying to graduate school and in-person visits with multiple mentors—a mentor who has expertise in the proposed field of study, a mentor who shares aspects of identity with the mentee, and a near-peer mentor who may have recently experienced graduate school, are examples of how a constellation can inform and elucidate what lies ahead for a student.

UNVEILING THE HIDDEN CURRICULUM

Effectively mentoring Black graduate students includes helping them learn what they do not know. Many scholars have called this the "hidden curriculum" (Apple, 2004; Gair & Mullins, 2001; Margolis et al., 2001; Margolis & Romero, 2001; Reddick & Young, 2012). More specifically, Margolis et al. (2001b) cite the hidden curriculum "as values, dispositions, and social and behavioral expectations that brought rewards for students in school" (Jackson, 1968). Additionally, Gair and Mullins (2001) and Reddick and Young (2012) add that the hidden curriculum is a representation of privilege and dominant social ideologies in the academic context. Furthermore, the replication of inequalities in academics allows the hidden curriculum to be both visible and invisible to underrepresented students, in this case Black graduate students. Therefore, effectively mentoring Black graduate students includes unveiling the hidden curriculum and helping them navigate it. We present the hidden curriculum based on the institution, field of study, and effectively empowering Black graduate students to be successful in their graduate experiences.

TYPES OF INSTITUTIONS

Higher education institutions are categorized by their research or professional agenda. In graduate education, the hidden curriculum depends on its reproduction and advancement of its institutional priorities and its educational disciplines (Gair & Muillins, 2001). According to the Carnegie Classifications of Institutions (2018), institutional categories are based on the amount of research and scholarship doctorates offered, research expenditures amount, and its level of research production. Institutions are designated into three groups:

1. pursuing very high research activity (R1)
2. high research activity (R2)
3. doctoral and professional university (Carnegie Classification of Institutions, 2018).

R1 or R2 institutions will emphasize research in its curriculum while institutions in the doctoral and professional university category prioritizes professional education and career training in its curriculum.

Based on the institutions' classification, their priorities may be viewed as common knowledge, however, incoming students may be unaware of the institutional emphasis or its effect on their graduate school experience.

Additionally, because classifications are fluid, institutions trying to advance its category can cause additional pressure on researchers, including graduate students. These institutions' faculty and staff are aware of these dynamics and may assume that students are as well. Conversely, some faculty are aware, yet do not disclose this information because of enrollment, rankings, or other forms of prestige equated to academic capitalism. Yet faculty and staff should unveil their institutional emphasis to promote informed student decisions and implement the navigational tools for their success. This act is the first step of unveiling the hidden curriculum to students; however, there will be other implicit rules that need to be uncovered in their specific education concentration.

FIELD OF STUDY

The graduate education curriculum typically presents required courses and milestones needed to matriculate in respective programs and concentrations. However, the curriculum does not incorporate the best practices to excel in coursework while completing unstated program expectations. Some examples of unstated expectations at institutions are hierarchy and power differentials, publishing, conference presentations—and several more. These unstated expectations are present in both research and professional schools, but vary by concentration and graduate program, whether a sciences or humanities concentration. For example, disciplines like sciences and clinical settings employ efficiency, integrity, and teamwork within their hidden curriculum (Bandini et al., 2017). These disciplines also have the negative implicit exceptions, such as, like hierarchy control, long work hours, unwavering availability, and teamwork dynamics (Austin, 2002).

At the most basic level, the hidden curriculum in graduate education can begin with simple expectations like reading and writing. Both are necessary for progressing in graduate education but are almost always assumed as common knowledge, regardless of students' prior educational experience. The hierarchy of publishing is also worth highlighting. Publishing is necessary when pursuing an academic career and creates a hierarchy in the job market. Types of publishing are books, academic journals, book chapters, op-eds, white papers, etc., and also varies based on disciplines. The hierarchy is set with this implicit consideration of competitive journals, type of research (quantitative, qualitative, or mixed), journal references, and others. Black faculty and even Black graduate students entering academia have mentioned the burden of proving their intellectual abilities by the demand to publish higher quality and more of it to be considered competitive with their non-Black counterparts (Matthew, 2016).

There is a further dimension to the hidden curriculum: understanding that journals that focus expressly on underrepresented and communities of color are not always viewed as favorably by senior scholars, regardless of the level of rigor required in these journals. This unfortunate reality was exposed in the case of Dr. Paul Harris, who was originally denied tenure at the University of Virginia in 2020 (Flaherty, 2020). Taylor Harris, his wife, disclosed a document that voiced this form of bias: "One comment from the committee of White faculty, was that a journal that had published his work appeared to be self-published. It was the *Journal of African American Males in Education.* The acceptance rate for articles? About 20 percent. Some of the biggest names in his field publish in that journal" (Harris, 2020). While Dr. Harris' negative tenure decision was eventually reversed, and Dr. Harris took a tenured position at Penn State, one must consider what might have happened had Dr. Harris instead been a graduate student, or if the issue was not covered in the media (Hudson, 2021).

Along with publishing, conference attendances and presentations are also another implicit expectation for students. The quality and focus of conferences are important and are necessary for networking or tailoring their research to fit different disciplines and increase career opportunities. Conferences can also be leveraged for advancing papers and publication into students' disciplines. These implicit expectations can be overwhelming for Black graduate students, especially when incorporating their intersectional identities or their psychological state. Adding insult to injury, these implicit expectations are not only from institutions and faculty members, but can be reinforced by their peers (Bandin et al., 2017).

Graduate students' identities are not accounted for in the curriculum like they are for traditional undergraduate students. Colleges and universities receive incentives when accounting for undergraduates' identities; however, at the graduate level, marginalized and alienated identities are less pronounced. These identities and experiences are social and cultural capital not supported by the institution nor its curriculum but can be for their White or affluent peers, who often have their assumptions challenged and gain perspective from their classmates' lived experiences. Graduate students who are socialized and aware of the hidden curriculum often cause Black graduate students to experience the earlier mentioned imposter syndrome, including self-doubt and inadequacy. The hidden curriculum is constantly changed and reproduced by the institution, faculty members, and peers, particularly when the deficit narratives about the value of research in marginalized communities are perpetuated, rather than challenged. Indeed, it could be considered an incomplete education, or even educational malpractice to only create awareness of the hidden curriculum, but do nothing to resist or critique it. Mentors can do this by co-authoring and co-presenting with Black students, and submitting their scholarship to Black journals—so they can experience the rigor of those peer review processes.

UNVEILING AND EMPOWERING

White faculty and staff can and should serve as mentors to not only relieve their Black counterparts' workload, but also to effectively unveil the hidden curriculum and empower Black graduate students to persist. It is imperative to understand mentorship has many interpretations (Gofton & Regehr, 2006). Effective mentorship serves as a coping mechanism with the hidden curriculum and allows students to gain positive effects from the implicit curriculum (Bandini et al., 2017). Exposing Black graduate students to the hidden curriculum would allow them access to informal networks often intended for White middle-class males (Gofton & Regehr, 2006).

Giving students this knowledge of the hidden curriculum would positively improve their confidence, academic performance, professional development, and their agency (Gofton & Regehr, 2006; Romero, 2017). According to Romero (2017), knowledge of the hidden curriculum will allow students to alter the curriculum with their identities, and promote equity in their graduate departments. Yet this is only the first step; strong mentors will help their students understand ways to resist and challenge the hidden curriculum. Their strong advocacy and support for scholarship on marginalized communities, in venues for marginalized communities, is one way that senior White scholars can work to both illuminate the hidden curriculum as well as work to dismantle it. Efforts such as this will unveil the hidden curriculum for future generations of Black graduate students, and their transitions out of their graduate education.

TRANSITIONING FROM GRADUATE EDUCATION

Students' abilities to learn and maneuver their concentration's hidden curriculum will affect their transition out of their graduate education. At the end of students' graduate journey, the hidden curriculum will continue with unstated expectations in the job market like the institutional fit (academic or administrative), negotiations (benefits or workload), and managing racial microaggressions and cultural taxation (such as navigating assumptions of disbelief that they are members of the faculty or having excessive advising, teaching, or service responsibilities). The importance of deconstructing the hidden curriculum with Black graduate students will allow them to observe hidden networks and identify when the hidden curriculum changes for themselves in their future careers, whether for career advancement or self-development.

RECOMMENDATIONS FOR CULTURALLY RESPONSIVE MENTORING

It is necessary and important for White faculty and staff members to serve as Black graduate student mentors. It will not always be easy, but in this chapter we have highlighted four considerations when doing this work; identify and appreciate their other identities, psychologically appreciate them as humans, consider the multiple ways they can be mentored, and unveil the hidden curriculum and their graduate programs' socialization process. When mentoring Black graduate students, we recommend White mentors first consider that the mentorship relationship will require work from both mentor and mentee (Reddick & Young, 2012). The mentor has to be honest and attribute compassion, humanism, and vulnerability with their Black graduate student mentors.

In order to do this, we recommend simply getting to know your students, appreciating them for who and where they are. This process can be initiated by beginning with a questionnaire or survey that gathers information about your students: their identities, interests, and goals. The COVID-19 pandemic has also shown us that community building can indeed occur online, which means there are more ways to provide students access and personal time than traditional in-person office hours. We recommend devoting time with regular scheduled check-ins. We also recommend resisting the more paternalistic top-down version of mentoring by being vulnerable, authentic, and personable, and understanding students' needs within and outside of their academic responsibilities. Understanding mentorship as a developmental relationship, and assisting mentees to thrive through transitions—entering the academic environment, achieving milestones in their academic program, and assisting them as they transition beyond their academic degrees—is an essential aspect of how effective mentors can support mentees not only for a brief period, but well beyond the formal connection one may have as members of the same institutional community.

Our research collective may serve as an example of this. The senior author serves as the doctoral advisor to the graduate students on the team, and we regularly engage in research and writing together. Graduate student members of the team are at varying levels in their doctoral journeys and career experiences. The age range among them spans twenty-five years, and identities include Black, White, Jewish, Christian, and agnostic, as well as those who identify as men and women and who are queer and straight. We leverage our collective wisdom and experiences—not essentializing all of our worth in our academic status, but valuing experiences as activists, professionals in the field of education and media, and community leaders. Our whole lives— partners and families, physical and mental health, and sense of belonging— matter as we work and learn together. Indeed, we regularly come together with all in the advising family (including our graduates, whom we celebrate) to share knowledge and collectively resist White supremacy through our work in academia. As the senior author, Rich regularly shares how he was lovingly mentored by both BIPOC and White faculty and administrators, and he shares those networks with the advising family.

White mentors cannot provide all the answers nor are they expected to. Instead, White mentors should offer their extended networks and connect students with people possessing the necessary answers. These connections are not to be confused with a relinquishment of mentorship responsibilities, but as constellation mentoring.

Constellation mentorship gives students the agency to seek and exchange knowledge among gained networks. Additionally, it will further expose their graduate programs' socialization process whether during their graduate application process, graduate school career, or their postgraduate school transition. This unveils the ever-changing hidden curriculum and will increase Black graduate students' persistence in their graduate education and future careers. Promoting the persistence and overall success of Black graduate students is necessary, and White faculty and staff mentorship is essential to do so.

REFERENCES

Apple, M. (2004). The hidden curriculum and the nature of conflict. In M. Apple (Ed.), *Ideology and Curriculum* (pp. 77–98). Routledge.

Austin, A. E. (2002). Preparing the next generation of faculty: Graduate school as socialization to the academic career. *Journal of Higher Education, 73*(1). https://doi.org/10.1080/00221546.2002.11777132.

Bandini, J., Mitchell, C., Epstein-Peterson, Z. D., Amobi, A., Cahill, J., Peteet, J., Balboni, T., & Balboni, M. J. (2017). Student and faculty reflections of the hidden curriculum: How does the hidden curriculum shape students' medical training and professionalization? *American Journal of Hospice and Palliative Medicine, 34*(1), 57–63. https://doi.org/10.1177/1049909115616359.

Bonilla-Silva, E. (2012). The invisible weight of Whiteness: The racial grammar of everyday life in contemporary America. *Ethnic and Racial Studies, 35*(2), 173–194. http://doi.org/10.1080/01419870.2011.613997.

Brown, E. M. & Grothaus, T. (2019). Experiences of cross-racial trust in mentoring relationships between Black doctoral counseling students and White counselor educators and supervisors. *Professional Counselor, 9*(3), 211–225. https://doi.org/10.15241/emb.9.3.211.

Brown, K. D. (2016). *After the "at-risk" label: Reorienting educational policy and practice.* New York: Teachers College Press.

Brown II, M. C., Davis, G. L., & Shederick A. McClendon. (1999). Mentoring graduate students of color: Myths, models, and modes. *Peabody Journal of Education, 74*(2), 105–118. https://doi.org/10.1207/s15327930pje7402_9.

Carson, L. (2009). "I am because we are": collectivism as a foundational characteristic of African American college student identity and academic achievement. *Social Psychology of Education, 12*, 327–344. http://doi.org/10.1007/s11218-009-9090-6.

Caver, K. & Livers, A. (2002). "Dear White boss . . . " *Harvard Business Review, 80*(11), 76–83.

Cokley, K., McClain, S., Enciso, A., & Martinez, M. (2013). An examination of the impact of minority status stress and impostor feelings on the mental health of diverse ethnic minority college students. *Journal of Multicultural Counseling and Development, 41*, 82–95. https://doi.org/10.1002/jmcd.12040.

Collins, P. H. (2002). *Black feminist thought: Knowledge, consciousness, and the politics of empowerment* (2nd ed). New York: Routledge.

Crenshaw, K. (1989). Demarginalizing the intersection of race and sex: A Black Feminist critique of antidiscrimination doctrine, Feminist theory and antiracist politics. *University of Chicago Legal Forum,* 139–167. https://chicagounbound. uchicago.edu /uclf/vol1989/iss1/8.

de Royston, M. M., Vakil, S., Nasir, N. S., Miraya Ross, K., Givens, J., & Holman, A. (2017). "He's more like a 'brother' than a teacher": Politicized caring in a program for African American males. *Teachers College Record, 119*(4), 1–40.

Davis, D. J. (2007). Access to academe: The importance of mentoring to Black students. *Negro Educational Review, 58*(3/4), 217–231.

Finley, S., & Gray, B. (2015). God is a White racist: Immanent atheism as a religious response to Black Lives Matter and state-sanctioned anti-Black violence. *Journal of Africana Religions, 3*(4), 443–453. doi:10.5325/jafrireli.3.4.0443.

Flaherty, C. (2020, June 22). "Botched": Two black scholars say UVA denied them tenure after belittling their work and their contributions to their fields, erring in procedure along the way. *Inside Higher Education.* https://www.insidehighered.com/news/2020/06/22/two-black-scholars-say-uva-denied-them-tenure-after-belittling-their-work.

Fuller, R. D. (2017). Perception or reality: The relationship between stereotypes, discrimination, and the academic outcomes of African American male college athletes. *Journal of Sport and Social Issues, 41*(5), 402–424. https://doi. org/10.1177/0193723517719664.

Gair, M., & Muillins, G. (2001). Hiding in plain sight. In E. Margolis (Ed.), *The hidden curriculum in higher education* (pp. 21–43). New York: Routledge.

George Mwangi, C. A., Changamire, N., & Mosselson, J. (2019). An intersectional understanding of African international graduate students' experiences in U.S. higher education. *Journal of Diversity in Higher Education, 12*(1), 52–64. https:// doi.org/10.1037/dhe0000076.

Gofton, W., & Regehr, G. (2006). What we don't know we are teaching: Unveiling the hidden curriculum. *Clinical Orthopaedics and Related Research, 449,* 20–27. https://doi.org/10.1097/01.blo.0000224024.96034.b2.

Gonzalez, A. (2019). Experiences of LGBTQ male students of color in a predominantly White environment. *Ursidae: The Undergraduate Research Journal at the University of Northern Colorado, 6*(8). https://digscholarship.unco.edu/urj/vol6/iss2/8.

Griffin, K. A., & Reddick, R. J. (2011). Surveillance and sacrifice: Gender differences in the mentoring patterns of Black professors at predominantly White research universities.. *American Educational Research Journal, 48*(5), 1032–1057. https://doi.org/10.3102/0002831211405025.

Guiffrida, D. (2005). Othermothering as a framework for understanding African American students' definitions of student-centered faculty. *Journal of Higher Education, 76*(6), 701. https://doi.org/10.1080/00221546.2005.11772305.

Harris, T. (2020, June 10). Whiteness can't save us: Whiteness cannot give us what we need, and this is not a disappointment. This is a testimony. *Catapult.* https://catapult.co/stories/taylor-harris-on-police-violence-racism-church-parenting-black-kids.

Helsing, D., Howell, A., Kegan, R., & Lahey, L. (2008). Putting the "development" in professional development: Understanding and overturning educational leaders' immunities to change. *Harvard Education Review, 78*(3), 437–465.

Helsing, D. (2010). Human development. In R. A. Couto (Ed.), *Political and civil leadership: A reference handbook* (pp. 678–687). Thousand Oaks, CA: SAGE.

Holmes, S. L., Land, L. D., & Hinton-Hudson, V. D. (2007). Race still matters: Considerations for mentoring Black women in academe. *Negro Educational Review, 58*(1–2), 105–129.

Hudson, W. (2021, May 11). After fighting to gain tenure, Dr. Paul Harris leaves UVA on his own terms. *Diverse Issues in Higher Education.* https://diverseeducation.com/article/214500/.

Jett, C. C. (2010). "Many are called, but few are chosen": The role of spirituality and religion in the educational outcome of "Chosen" African American male mathematics majors. *Journal of Negro Education, 79*(3), 324–334.

Johnson, W. B., & Ridley, C. R. (2008). *The elements of mentoring.* New York: Palgrave Macmillan.

Kegan, R. (1980). Making meaning: The constructive-developmental approach to persons and practice. *The Personnel and Guidance Journal, 58*(5), 373–380. https://doi.org/10.1002/j.2164-4918.1980.tb00416.x.

Kegan, R. (1994). *In over our heads: The mental demands of modern life.* Cambridge, MA: Harvard University Press.

Kram, K. E. (1988). *Mentoring at work: Developmental relationships in organizational life.* Lanham, MD: University Press of America.

Lincoln, C. E. & Mamiya, L. H. (1990). *The Black church in the African-American experience.* Durham, NC: Duke University Press.

Lincoln, C. E. (1994). *The black Muslims in America* (Third ed.). Grand Rapids, MI: Eerdmans.

Margolis, E., & Romero, M. (2001). "In the image and likeness . . . ": How mentoring functions in the hidden curriculum. In E. Margolis (Ed.), *The hidden curriculum in higher education* (pp. 79–96). New York: Routledge.

Margolis, E., Soldatenko, M., Acker, S., & Gair, M. (2001). Peekaboo: Hiding and outing the curriculum. In E. Margolis (Ed.), *The hidden curriculum in higher education* (pp. 1–20). New York: Routledge.

Matthew, P. A. (2016). *Written/unwritten: Diversity and the hidden truths of tenure.* Chapel Hill: University of North Carolina Press.

McCallum, C. (2017). Giving back to the community: How African Americans envision utilizing their PhD. *Journal of Negro Education, 86*(2), 138–153.

Mertz, N. T. (2004). What's a mentor, anyway? *Educational Administration Quarterly, 40*(4), 541–560. https://doi.org/10.1177/0013161X04267110.

Mezirow, J. (1991). Transformative dimensions of adult learning. San Francisco: Jossey-Bass. National Center for Education Statistics. (2020). *The condition of education—Characteristics of postsecondary faculty.* Retrieved from https://nces.ed.gov/programs/coe/indicator_csc.asp#f2.

Nicolazzo, Z. (2016). *Trans* in college: Transgender students' strategies for navigating campus life and the institutional politics of inclusion.* Sterling, VA: Stylus.

Olney, M., & Brockelman, K. (2003). Out of the disability closet: Strategic use of perception management by select university students with disabilities. *Disability & Society, 18*(1), 35–50. https://doi.org/10.1080/0968759032000044193.

Pinn, A. B. (2002). *The Black church in the post-civil rights era.* Maryknoll, N.Y: Orbis Books.

Reddick, R. J. (2009). Fostering cross-racial mentoring: White faculty and African American students at Harvard College. In S. Sánchez-Casal & A. A. Macdonald (Eds.), *Identity in education* (pp. 65–102). New York: Palgrave Macmillan.

Reddick, R. J. (2011). Intersecting identities: Mentoring contributions and challenges for black faculty mentoring black undergraduates. *Mentoring & Tutoring: Partnership in Learning, 19,* 319–346. https://doi.org/10.1080/13611267.2011.597121.

Reddick, R. J., & Young, M. D. (2012). Mentoring graduate students of color. In S. Fletcher & C. Mullen (Eds.), *The SAGE handbook of mentoring and coaching for education* (pp. 412–429). Thousand Oaks, CA: SAGE.

Reddick, R. J. (2015). Of feral faculty and magisterial Mowglis: The domestication of junior faculty. *New Directions for Higher Education, 171*, 43–51. https://doi.org/10.1002/he.20141.

Renn, K. A. (2010). LGBT and queer research in higher education: The state and status of the field. *Educational Researcher, 39*(2), 132–141. https://doi.org/10.3102/0013189X10362579.

Romero, M. (2017). Reflections on "The Department is Very Male, Very White, Very Old, and Very Conservative": The functioning of the hidden curriculum in graduate sociology departments. *Social Problems, 64*(2), 212–218. https://doi.org/10.1093/socpro/spx004.

Scheurich, J. J., & Laible, J. (1995). The buck stops here—in our preparation programs: Educational leadership for all children (no exceptions allowed).

Educational Administration Quarterly, 31(2), 313–322. https://doi.org/10.1177/00 13161X95031002009.

Stanley, C. A., & Lincoln, Y. S. (2005). Cross-race faculty mentoring. *Change, 37*(2), 44–50. https://doi.org/10.3200/CHNG.37.2.44-50.

Stewart, D. L., Renn, K. A., & Brazelton, G. B. (Eds.). (2015). Gender and sexual diversity in US higher education: Contexts and opportunities for LGBTQ college students. *New Directions for Student Services, 152.*

Taylor, Z. W. (2019). Web (in)accessible: Supporting access to Texas higher education for students with disabilities. *Texas Education Review, 7*(2), 60–75.

The Carnegie Classification of Institutions of Higher Education (n.d.). About Carnegie Classification. http://carnegieclassifications.iu.edu/.

Twale, D., Weidman, J., & Bethea, K. (2016). Conceptualizing socialization of graduate students of color: Revisiting the Weidman-Twale-Stein framework. *The Western Journal of Black Studies, 40,* 80–94.

Vaccaro, A. (2012). Campus microclimates for LGBT faculty, staff, and students: An exploration of the intersections of social identity and campus roles. *Journal of Student Affairs Research and Practice, 49*(4), 429–446. https://doi.org/10.1515/jsarp-2012-6473.

Vachuska, K. & Brudvig, J. (2018). Discourse from #TheRealUW: What tweets say about racial concerns at a predominately White institution. *Social Sciences, 7*(21), 1–13. https://doi.org/10.3390/socsci7020021.

Weidman, J. C., Twale, D. J., & Stein, E. L. (2001). *Socialization of graduate and professional students in higher education: A perilous passage?* San Francisco: ERIC Clearinghouse on Higher Education.

Young, M. D., & Brooks, J. S. (2008). Supporting graduate students of color in educational administration preparation programs: Faculty perspectives on best practices, possibilities, and problems. *Educational Administration Quarterly, 44*(3), 391–423. https://doi.org/10.1177/0013161X08315270.

Yoshino, K. (2006). *Covering: The hidden assault on our civil rights.* New York: Random House.

NOTES

1. Racial and ethnic groups are designated by proper nouns and are capitalized. Therefore, we use "Black" and "White" instead of black and white (colors) when referring to human racial and ethnic groups.

PART III

Mentoring and Intersectionality

Chapter Four

Critical Race Mentoring

Theory into Practice for Supporting Black Males at Predominantly White Institutions

Horace R. Hall and Troy Harden

In order to grasp the postsecondary struggles of Black[1] men, it is vital that we first acknowledge the academic and social experiences that precede their foray into college. Research has long informed us that Black youth are a demographic that perpetually remains neglected by schools and society (Hall, 2019; Hilliard, 2003; Noguera, 2012; Willie & Willie, 2005). Prior to college, many Black males face a range of institutional obstacles—teacher bias and low expectations, disparities in school discipline, and limited access to college readiness courses—that excessively position them into low-achieving academic tracks (Ferguson, 2001; Howard, Flennaugh, & Terry, 2012; Noguera, 2003; Oaks, 2005). Outside of school, they also endure a litany of harsh conditions—underemployment, low economic status, neglected neighborhood infrastructure, extreme community violence, and ultrapolicing—particularly if they are living in hypersegregated communities (Kunjufu, 2010; Mandara & Murray, 2000; Shabazz, 2015).

In and outside of schools, anti-Black perceptions, policies, rules, and procedures abound and cut across years of Black male development and growth. The racial inequities that this group faces are reproduced in two overlapping ways: one, through biased institutional practices and two, through cultural representations of racial difference (Lewis & Diamond, 2015; Forman, 2017). With respect to the latter, Black boys and men are often socially stigmatized as less than or abnormal through such descriptors as "stupid," "aggressive," "libidinous," and "predatory" (Hall, 2006; Kunjufu, 2010). Regarding institutional practices, disproportionate sanctions—arrests, suspensions, and expulsions—against Black males give rise to racism and generate feelings of despair and failure. It is this unreceptive and discriminatory treatment of their Black bodies and minds that reduces their affinity for education and thus chances at success, pushing them, as studies have shown, out of their schools and into high risk factors of poverty, poor health, or incarceration (Fergus & Noguera, 2014; Forman, 2017; Morris, 2015).

Despite the odds stacked against Black males in America, many still show a level of resilience and resistance that propel them over longstanding social and economic hurdles and towards the threshold of higher education. Upon entering the hallowed gates of academies, however, they are soon reminded of the arduous road left in their wake. For those attending predominantly White institutions (PWIs), a multiplicity of factors gradually become apparent— unwelcome campus climates, overt and covert racism, stereotype threats, and limited representation in curriculum—that tarnish their college experience and dispirit some from completing a bachelor's degree (Harper, 2009; Perna et al., 2007; Salami & Walker, 2014; Steele, 2003). As college campuses are places where students live, work, learn, and gather for an extended period of time, PWIs become foundational spaces that Black men must learn to traverse in order to graduate. As such, the academies themselves must be truly committed to proving that they value diversity and cultivating an environment respectful and accepting of Black history, heritage, and culture.

For almost two decades, the frequently used phrase *"There are more Black men in prison than in college"* (Schiraldi & Ziedenberg, 2002) has served to magnify the status of young Black males in America. Though now firmly debunked[2] as a specious argument, the underrepresentation of Black men in college and university settings still lingers as a significant issue (Toldson, 2019). Data from the National Center for Education Statistics, as well as the American Council on Education, indicate that Black men only account for 4.3 percent of total enrollment at four-year postsecondary institutions in the United States—a virtually unchanged percentage since 1976 (ACE, 2019; NCES, 2019). Accordingly, those Black men pursuing bachelor's degrees at PWIs starting in 2011 had higher dropout rates and lower six-year completion rates than any other ethnic group. Furthermore, the gender gap between college Black males and females persists, as nearly two-thirds of Black undergraduates and more than two-thirds of master's and doctorate students are Black women (NCES, 2019).

Concerning the attrition of Black males in U.S. academies, scholars over the past twenty years have supplied educators, policymakers, and stakeholders with best practices for supporting Black student achievement (Brittain et al., 2009; Lee, 1999; Sands et al., 2007; Strayhorn & Terrell, 2007). One uniform recommendation has been *mentoring*. In its broadest terms, mentoring is a helping process whereby a supportive and experienced person nurtures the development and advancement of another person with lesser experience (Roberts, 2000). There are four general types of mentoring: 1) *formal*—assigning mentors and mentees to scheduled face-to-face sessions over a period of time; 2) *informal*—traditionally a voluntary relationship that evolves naturally; 3) *one-on-one*—individual mentees and mentors agree on expectations or planned goals of their partnership; and 4) *group mentoring*— mentor(s) facilitate guidance and discussion with a preidentified group of mentees on topics based on mentees' expressed issues and concerns (Chaoe & Walz, 1992; Hall, 2006; Johnson, 2002).

Making use of research literature, PWIs have initiated mentoring programs as a means of increasing retention and degree completion rates of their Black male undergraduates (Brooms 2016; Dahlvig, 2002; DeAngelo et al., 2015). Studies reveal that many of these programs employ a formal mentoring approach that emphasizes work-based learning (e.g., class performance, major selection, degree persistence) and/or relational needs (e.g., being away from home, diverse campus climate, network building) to help students transition out of high school and home life to the college environment and beyond (Cuyjet, 2006; Johnson-Ahorlu, 2013; Pope, 2002). While Black males have reported positive mentoring influences at PWIs (Brooms, 2016; Harper, 2012; Pope, 2002), scholars denote that one significant gap in the process is the absence of a validating space where they can voice and confront psychological stressors related to racism they encounter on campus (Ancis et al., 2000; Cuyjet, 2006).

As previously noted, Black males have substantively different psychosocial experiences to that of their ethnic counterparts. For Black men attending PWIs, college is but an extension of the larger society where anti-Black treatment—subtle and overt, verbal and nonverbal—decreases their likelihood of academic success. Thus, we argue that mentoring programs must additionally build into their agendas opportunities for dialogue and action that helps Black students identify, challenge, self-determine, and transform the often tacit nature of racism ever-present in their college experience. We suggest the use of CRT as a combined theoretical and methodological framework for enriching mentoring practices intended to support Black men in navigating and building resilience against higher education influences in campus curriculum and policies that systematically operate as a silencer of racial identities, subordinate narratives, and diverse cultural ways of existence. In the following chapter, we offer a cursory review of literature describing CRT; how this theory intersects with mentoring practices; its various tenets and how each apply to student mentoring; and then finally recommendations for readers planning or already engaged in such endeavors.

CRITICAL RACE THEORY: A LENS FOR DECONSTRUCTING RACISM AT PWIS

Critical race theory derives out of the critical legal studies (CLS) movement of the mid-1970s, which largely focused on inequities within US jurisprudence (Tate, 1997). It later developed into a more expansive social scientific approach to the study of race and racism in society through the work of civil rights leader and well-regarded Black legal scholar Derrick Bell Jr. In his seminal book, *Faces at the Bottom of the Well* (1992), Bell's principal argument was that racism is much more than a single determining factor of a given inequality. More accurately, it is a systemically fixed and enduring facet of hierarchical social structures (Bell, 1992). Put another way, because racism is so deeply embedded in the social and moral fabric of society, it is often confused as a natural process rather than a by-product of systemic racial domination (Bonilla-Silva, 2017). In today's perceived "postracial" society, CRT is ever more essential as it reminds us that race and racism are socially endemic, and diagnosis of these phenomena demands meticulous analyses of systems of inequality beyond random incidences of bigotry (Crenshaw, 1988; Delgado, 1995).

Since the emergence of critical race theory, scholars in the field have built into its application several key interlacing tenets for translating the lived experiences of People of Color within multiple sites of oppression—e.g., education, housing, employment and healthcare (DeCuir & Dixson, 2004; Ladson-Billings & Tate, 1995; Yosso, 2002). Given the specific context of this chapter, we have chosen to draw on the five CRT tenets used in Hiraldo's (2010) analysis of diversity and inclusivity within higher education to explore how different forms of racial inequities endured by Black males can be confounded through mentoring. Below is a summary of each tenet:

1. *Counterstorytelling*—experiential knowledge and counterstories of People of Color that speak to racism in personal relationships, places of work, or in educational and judicial systems (Bonilla-Silva, 2003);
2. *Whiteness as Property*—based on power relations and property interest for those identifying as White, benefiting from social advantages where White racial identity provided the basis for allocating societal benefits both private and public (Harris, 1993);
3. *The Permanence of Racism*—the transformation of racial prejudice through the use of power directed against racial groups. Color-blindness and antiaffirmative policies aid in the permanence of racism, yet are disrupted through equal if not more force against persistent racial inequities (Ladson-Billings, 2005);

4. *Interest Conversion*—the premise that People of Color's need to accomplish racial justice only advances when it coincides with the benefits and interests of the White power structure (Bell, 1992);
5. *Critique of Liberalism*—interrogating meritocracy, objectivity, piecemeal change, and race neutrality which camouflage the self-interest, power, and privilege of dominant groups in society through colorblindness (DeCuir & Dixson, 2004).

An additional component of CRT, not included in Hiraldo's (2010) scrutiny of college life, is *intersectionality*. Originating from the Black feminist work of critical race theorist Kimberlé Crenshaw, this concept provides a basis for recognizing how complex identities overlap and shape specific ways cultural biases are experienced through race, class, gender, sexual orientation, religious affiliation, and other social constructs (Crenshaw, 2011). This relatively newer tenet is connected to CRT's earliest roots with those legal scholars endeavoring to produce coalitions between diverse groups aiming to resist and change the status quo. Despite our focus on Hiraldo's five tenet framework here, the authors fully recognize the import of intersectionality and speak to its usage in our later recommendations for deepening higher education mentoring practices.

With respect to the use of CRT in examining PWIs, much has been critiqued around diversity and the unique needs of Black students (Harper, 2009; Hiraldo, 2010; Ladson-Billings & Tate, 1995; McCabe, 2009). What must first be noted is that we are talking about academies that were *never* designed for People of Color. These structures, since their US origins, have consigned powerless populations to the fringes of academic life. As such, CRT has been employed to study the circumstances of these groups, revealing how historical and contemporary aspects of academia perpetuate White supremacy and maintain subordinate and dominant racial statuses on college and university sites (Harper et al., 2009). It goes without saying, however, that racial prejudice and marginalization have no place on any campus or in any classroom as such abuses leave Students of Color susceptible to feelings of ostracism, shame and detachment. Nonetheless, we still find in present-day that Black students' cultural heritage and histories are mostly absent from or rendered invalid within PWI institutional policies, practices, guidelines, and curriculum (Hiraldo, 2010; Ladson-Billings & Tate, 1995).

CRT scholars have also called into question the ethos of PWIs in relation to broader politicized social movements. For example, since the 1990s, critical race theorists have analyzed hard attacks by right-wing conservatives on affirmative action programs. Opponents of such assert that higher education is being controlled by a liberal agenda that "victimizes" White people and that efforts of inclusion only soften academic rigor and freedoms within higher education (Anderson, 2016; Harris et al., 2015). This backwards assessment further reinforces racial group inequities that have long-existed in our society, which clearly work against those universities attempting to presently construct more inclusive and equitable environments. CRT scholars have challenged these conservative claims by positing that antiaffirmative action efforts fundamentally use race-neutral meritocracy, as well as color-blind language and ideology, to divert attention away from biased programs and practices, such as legacy admissions and residential preferences, which have unfairly benefited White students (Savas, 2014; Yosso & Lopez, 2010).

In addition to the above racist practices that Black students face, critical race theorists have also studied employment experiences of racially diverse staff at PWIs. Ample research has shown that a majority of Black staffers receiving PhDs in education primarily earn them in administrative positions with very little opportunities for upward mobility beyond practitioner roles and into the rank of full-time faculty (Patton et al., 2007). Subsequently, Black staff members are not becoming part of the driving force in higher education. Professors, ordinarily White and situated as "owners" of curriculum, use their autonomy to design courses according to their own cultural knowledge and background. This outcome ultimately works against People of Color as it is proof of the notion of Whiteness as property, cementing within PWIs only those perspectives beheld as official and credible with respect to racial identity and discourse (Patton et al., 2007).

CRITICAL RACE MENTORING (CRM)

While there is a substantial body of literature that focuses on mentoring at PWIs, reports on such programs explicitly operating on tenets of CRT are sparse at best. We argue, however, that CRT ought to be an integral component in mentoring Black males as this framework not only can engage them in examining race within multiple societal contexts, but also support them in navigating unfamiliar academic terrains that they, their families, or their peers may have never faced (Saufley et al., 1983; Von Robertson & Chaney, 2017). By integrating CRT into mentoring practices, mentees and mentors can work together to cultivate shared knowledge and strategies for helping Black students remain in college and finish their degrees. Furthermore, the use of CRT in mentoring can render greater attentiveness for academies genuinely seeking to know and act upon issues that Black students endure and how racial inequities, perpetuated by PWI traditions and standards, adversely affect students' life choices and chances for success.

Given the above discussion, we propose the following mentoring model—what we term here *Critical Race Mentoring (CRM)*. It is largely based on our combined forty-plus years of mentoring Black students from elementary to college levels. The foremost goal of our proposal is to assist Black college males in naming and questioning inequitable societal structures, while becoming viable change agents in driving PWI institutional practices towards racial equity. From our established mentoring endeavors, we find that Black college students, by and large, already possess the cognitive and cultural skillsets needed to persevere at PWIs. They require, however, additional support systems to guide, affirm, and sustain them in their academic pursuits. With this, CRM necessitates three central prerequisites: 1) *institutional commitment*, 2) *effective matching*, and 3) *safe spaces*. Even though CRM serves as a direct "mainline" for empowering Black males, it is the institution itself that must be willing to contribute in authentic equitable ways that directly speak to the intellectual and communal development of this student population.

As Black males are expected to succeed in higher education, PWIs must completely back their mentoring program(s). This entails, on the one hand, the institution at-large providing appropriate financial and social resources for mentoring operations while, on the other, locating staff and faculty willing to serve as directors and mentors of the program, and who are prepared to create a culturally and socially ethical campus environment the very moment Black students step onto its grounds (Frierson, Wyche, & Pearson, 2009; Furr, 2002; Saufley, Cowan, & Herman, 1983). Secondly, matched mentors and mentees must be regularly assessed for efficacy. Although pairing based on race is extensively viewed as key in mentoring literature, what must also be acknowledged is that such relationships may not be feasible where access to Black staff and faculty is limited. In these cases, mentor partnering should be considered beyond race, looking alternatively at peer-mentoring or pairing with staff and faculty who are sensitive to and competent of the ethnocultural experiences of Black males (Brooms, 2016; Sinanan, 2016; Strayhorn & Terrell, 2007).

The last precondition for CRM is the necessity for safe and trustful spaces—on and off campus. Whether in a formal, informal, one-on-one, or group setting, our mentoring proposal requires that mentees feel as consistently safe as possible, particularly given the often racially hostile climate of PWIs. In CRM, where voiced realities (oral or written) counter racism, students need to be ensured that their physical and psychological well-being, as well as their academic standing, will not be threatened. Hence, safety and trust must be co-constructed with university staff, faculty, and students as earnestly as possible. The path to doing so involves mentors truly rejecting traditional mentoring hierarchies and flattening their status over students. More specifically, disruption, if not eradication, of this power dynamic necessitates program mentors honestly being on the side of mentees and not concerned with superficially "checking boxes" of university diversity or protocols.

If Critical Race Mentoring is to organically and authentically take shape as a viable concept and practice, then program mentors have to decenter themselves and allow for the needs, issues and self-determination of mentees to take precedence. CRM is about developing and maintaining an atmosphere of Black student empowerment and solidarity, where mentees can share their ideas without being judged, punished, or have their offerings exploited, commodified and coopted for institutional benefit or professional gain. To make it plain, CRM is about putting mentees first. If student-centeredness is compromised in any way, mentees will soon recognize it and whatever full potential CRM might achieve will certainly be wasted. In the next section, we present a general curriculum outline for CRM framed within each of the five aforementioned CRT tenets.

CRM CURRICULUM: WHERE CRT MEETS MENTORING PRACTICES

In institutional settings such as PWIs, Black males find little cultural validation, which can result in feelings of alienation and disempowerment (Harper, 2009). CRM curriculum ideally nullifies this by engaging mentees and mentors in various undertakings like workshops, conferences, civic forums, guest speaker seminars, school and community-based research projects, and partnerships with faculty to appraise course materials for cultural relevance. It is important to note that these are not meant to be feel-good or pacifying activities. Rather, they are envisioned to be student-directed, and intently focused on addressing the needs, issues and concerns of Black students first. The substantial cultural knowledge and real-life experiences that they bring function to enhance the intellectual and social life of academies and PWIs should recognize this. Introducing CRT into the above activities provides us with the substance, methodologies, and plausible outcomes for our conceptual model.

COUNTERSTORYTELLING

Black people represent a unique history in education, from early legal battles for integration and equity like *Brown v. Board of Education* (1954/55) to more recent ones such as the *NAACP v. State of New Jersey* (2019).[3] At the center of past and present litigations are the voices of those who have been the most excluded by systems of oppression. CRT argues that efforts to create just policies and practices only become actionable when they benefit White groups. In such instances, Black folks' initial complaint becomes relegated to the margins of sociopolitical life. While much has been written about the inclusion of these identities in CRT, we offer here that counterstorytelling can be an essential tool for unpacking Black male student experiences with discrimination in higher education. By positioning their narratives at the fore of educational discourse and policies, it is hoped that their individual and collective grievances will be honored without cooptation or dilution, leading to pathways of true equitable representation and respect.

Mentoring relationships are inherently intimate and allow for up-close and personal tellings of resilience at both institutional and community levels. As many Black males share stories about encounters with racism and stereotyping or being the first to enter or graduate from college, it is usually faculty and staff who are soundboards for their disclosures (Baker, 2013). These personal accounts, however, are often ignored by administrators and in college climate studies (Guiffrida & Douthit, 2010). Hence, strategies to ensure that these voices are recognized are indispensable. One key approach is to have mentors unapologetically lift up these countertellings and engage Black male students in recording their institutional realities. Mentoring sessions—one-on-one or in groups—are moments where mentees can talk about or write down their classroom or campus experiences. If agreed upon by mentees, this documentation—anonymous or not—can be used to inform strategic plans for articulating the future direction, mission, and goals of PWIs.

WHITENESS AS PROPERTY

Being aware of the history of why and how higher education spaces were founded and financed is central. It is perhaps no secret that many American universities prior to the Civil War were built by slaves and indentured servants (Harris et al., 2019; Wilder, 2013). By uncovering the precedent that White professors and even White students used slaves on campus, it is reasonable to ask: "Who are higher education institutions for today?" Judging by the official school curriculum, also called "master scripts"[4] (Swartz, 1992, p. 341), we see that White experiences are still the norm for scholarly aptitude and success. With Whiteness positioned as the curriculum standard and institutional benchmark for advancement, Black cultural ways of being and knowing tend to be distorted through misrepresentations or omitted altogether from master scripts. Hence, classroom content that does not reflect the dominant social class must be brought under control, altered and then "mastered" before becoming a feature of hegemonic school curriculum (Swartz, 1992).

Dissecting and disrupting master scripts calls for various approaches within CRM. First, mentees should be familiarized with and encouraged to examine architectures of the past. This entails having group dialogue that focuses on the interlocking relationship between White supremacy and academies, as well as the methods by which master scripts have repressed Black perspectives over time, legitimizing and maintaining Eurocentric curriculum. Secondly, similar to our proposed activities in counterstorytelling, CRM must provide space and time for Black males to create self-narratives that reveal their encounters with the largely standardized discourse and ways of confronting it. Third, we advise that mentee narratives become part of a larger antiracist discussion with representative faculty, staff and administrators who ideally are faithful to reforming university curriculum, policies, and practices that fail to recognize how academic spaces were never truly intended to be inclusive of the multiple realities and identities of People of Color.

THE PERMANENCE OF RACISM

Although there have been widespread efforts challenging higher education inequities, arguably many have fallen short due to the ever-evolving nature of racism (Delgado, 1995). In recent years, scholars have studied PWI institutional processes and procedures that continue to benefit Whites, while depriving historically oppressed groups (Feagin & O'Brien, 2003; Smith, 2013). This enduring injustice manifests in classrooms where color-blind, liberal ideology abounds, subordinating racialized experiences of Students of Color within the master script (Delgado & Stefancic, 1997). Moreover, the phenomenon of microaggressions—often indirect, unconscious insults (verbal/nonverbal/visual) aimed at People of Color—exist in both academic and social spaces. Although Black students see themselves as equal to their White counterparts and deserving of the same treatment and opportunities, the PWI experience can be an unexpected wake-up call when Students of Color are faced with institutional microaggressions[5]. They then find themselves ill-prepared to handle these sudden affronts in classes and on campuses, which can result in suffocation, if not killing, of their dreams in obtaining a college degree (Harper, 2009).

The question then becomes, how do universities assist Black students in dealing with an injustice they did not create? The short answer, within the context of PWIs, is that combating systemic racism must be a collective institutional effort—the kind of effort that is *not* solely incumbent on faculty, staff or students in righting the wrongs of universities and how they have functioned for generations. Any antiracist campaign must move away from neoliberal modes of production that fault and punish smaller groups for not being efficient enough. Instead, this form of justice work embodies a multilateral approach that holds upper administration responsible for developing institutional changes across campus and in classrooms that are dedicated to affirming (not antiaffirming) the racial identities, realities, and needs of students, especially those from historically underrepresented groups.

INTEREST CONVERGENCE

Diverse student recruitment at PWIs is a prime example of interest convergence, where Whites are the primary beneficiaries of diversity initiatives. As a relatively new endeavor in the long history of PWIs, diversity efforts focus on universities fulfilling their mission statements and policies by creating a more inclusive environment, while also being able to market themselves as academies that can reliably recruit and admit Students of Color (Bugeja, 2013). Although inclusivity has become an emphasis for colleges across the U.S., diversity does not automatically mean equity, especially for Black students. No doubt, their visibility benefits White students desiring to see or interact with others from different backgrounds. Yet, diversity can be nothing more than a buzzword when these same institutions neglect to provide supportive mechanisms and structures for Black enrollees to be successful and persevere (Eakins & Eakins, 2017). Growth in student diversity is designed to engender more cross-race cultural learning, yet we find this CRT tenet questions: "How might the issues and concerns of Black students remain exclusive and singularly addressed without being commandeered by a White, integrationist market agenda?"

Over the years, PWI strategic plans have stressed a need for recruiting and retaining Black males given their scarcity in postsecondary academies (Von Robertson & Chaney, 2017). With the marketplace insisting upon added campus diversity, CRM programs can make the most of this demand by holding school officials' feet to the fire, particularly if university mission statements explicitly convey a need for increasing greater institutional access and persistence for Students of Color. Indeed, White students' desires to attend and live on a college campus where diversity numbers are high should not come at the expense of Black students' physical, mental, emotional, and intellectual well-being. CRM addresses interest convergence arguments by having its organizational body of students, faculty and staff develop campaign initiatives (e.g., forums, petitions, student councils, interactive websites) that call for "race-woke" dialogue and actions with upper administrators about how institutional objectives can, in one vein, reliably attend to the needs of Black students and Students of Color overall while, in a parallel vein, deal with institutional obligations of diversity. Fully unpacking this dichotomy cannot be realized in a single meeting on antiracism or by watching a series of diversity training videos. Instead, all university stakeholders should engage in time-extensive, multipronged sessions that carefully analyze the impacts of race and racism relative to diversity protocols and university budgetary lines, which have up to now unfairly advantaged White students' needs over minorities.

THE CRITIQUE OF LIBERALISM

CRT scholars contend that colorblindness is an integral facet of liberal ideology (Delgado, 1995; Hiraldo, 2010). Many Americans claim not to see color and argue that race, despite all of its complexities, no longer needs to be stressed (Gotanda, 1991), especially given societal gains from the Civil Rights Movement to the presidency of Barack Obama. Even so, colorblindness does nothing more than characterize the racist experiences of Black people as stochastic and disconnected from bygone days of domestic racial oppression (Crenshaw, 2011). With respect to PWIs, colorblindness weakens efforts to build equitable and inclusive campuses because it, unwittingly or not, consumes Black existence through its default academic space of liberal Whiteness (Robertson & Chaney, 2017). Hence, Black students resisting colorblindness, consciously or not, are then labeled as "too Black" or academically unfit for higher education and must be "vomited out" by the institution (Harper, 2012). As long as this liberal ideology negates the real and recent oppression of Black students, amending policies and practices of PWIs cannot and will not ever go far enough in disrupting the extant status quo.

We believe that CRM is one prescription for the consumption and spewing out of Black lives in academia. In order to contradict liberal excuses for colorblindness, it is necessary that college participants—students, staff, faculty, administrators, trustees, and donors—hear and acknowledge the present-day, widespread racist experiences of Black people, from community injustices (e.g., police shootings, underemployment, healthcare disparities, and housing discrimination) to unfair educational policies and practices (e.g., underfunded schooling, Eurocentric curriculum, biased teachers, and uneven school discipline). Here, we are not talking about PWI campuses tolerating student-led rallies, boycotts, teach-ins, or hunger strikes. These forms of protest are often dismissed by authority as youth merely acting out, which can result in their punishment. Instead, we argue that governing bodies must engage in respectful dialogue early with Black students about their needs, issues, and concerns, and learn how to collaboratively build viable pathways for these students to enter, move through, and complete their scholarly aims. Being that a diversified student body is an imperative at PWIs for fiscal and social purposes, these institutions must then assertively work to keep Black males in attendance.

RECOMMENDATIONS FOR CULTURALLY RESPONSIVE MENTORING

Today, education is arguably more important than at any other time in history. With the ever-increasing rate of scientific and technological advancements in the world, the right to a quality education must extend to all. The overwhelming literature on the low academic achievements of Black males, however, has presented a dismal picture of reversing longstanding trends in their academic trajectories. If PWIs are to respond proactively to the issue of enduring campus absence and underachievement by large segments of Black males, then these institutions have to gain greater insight and awareness into the dominant structural forces operating in the lives of Black men, as well as how they respond to such forces. While considerable attention has been paid to the role of educators and curriculum in helping to level the higher education playing field, we contend that university boards and power-brokers must also be held accountable in creating an equitable academic and social space. At the end of the day, while we can ask faculty, staff, and students to be willing to engage in transformative work, it is undoubtedly PWI policies and structures that must be open to change. Given the sordid legacy of PWIs, their formation, and fiscal backing, we do not expect them to change overnight. However, one semester at a time will definitely help to move this work forward.

In closing, we offer a few additional recommendations for creating an effective critical race mentoring program. These suggestions may also coincide with helping improve the overall learning experience for Black males attending predominantly White institutions.

1. *Real support*—Colleges and universities need to show a high level of commitment to Black students beyond enrollment sales pitches. This certainly involves the backing of mentoring programs, but also demands that governing officials hire Black administrators, staff, and faculty who can serve as role models and help cultivate social networks for students. Genuine support also entails rethinking, redressing and revising institutional policies that at face value do not appear to be anti-Black. Yet, if properly examined, PWI rules and guidelines actually speak to the permanence of racism through the color-blind treatment of Black students with respect to procedures, curriculum, and campus programs/resources. Acknowledging this ought to compel higher administrative bodies to see that racial inequity is not "race-neutral" (e.g., antiaffirmative action arguments), but rather a collection of policies that perpetuate chronic Black stumbling blocks in and outside of the academia.

2. *"Woke" mentoring*—the recruitment of Black faculty and staff who are conscientious of relevant issues surrounding Black males is integral to Critical Race Mentoring. As mentioned previously, it is not enough to simply enlist mentors who are of the same race or ethnicity. A critical race mentoring space, whether in a one-on-one or group format, has greater potential to advance when mentors can culturally and socially can connect with, relate to, and learn with/from mentees. Specifically, woke mentoring, through collaborations with mentors and mentees, involves providing insights, tactics, and practices that universities, and the social organizations outside of them, can use to measurably transform organizational culture, operationalize equity, and move from a dominant organizational hierarchy to one of solidarity.

3. *Mentor training*—for university employees interested in taking part in CRM, they need to be required to attend training sessions focused on institutional and social hurdles encountered by Black males. Led by an experienced/knowledgeable program director(s), these orientations should instruct potential mentors on not only best practices, but also how to engage them in antiracist conversations and work that addresses the historical, personal and political impacts of systemic racism and inequities faced by Black peoples. As previously mentioned, this kind of training is not a quick one-day experience. Rather, it assumes a methodical timeline of multiple sessions necessitating participants explore personal reflections on their biases and prejudices with an earnest commitment to learning about cultural differences, developing cross-cultural skills, and confessing their mistakes all along the way.

4. *Intra-/interpartnership financial support*—internal and external funding for CRM resources and supplies (e.g., stipends, educational materials, field-based research, conferences, food, etc.), without question, helps with program operations, as well as generating consistent student membership. As such, stipends and course releases should be made available for mentors as an added incentive for dedicating their time to students. Internal funding across university offices and departments— student affairs, career access and attainment, admissions, advising, and financial aid—can also assist in proliferating much needed resources where individual campus budgets are insufficient or may not exist for grant programs, scholarships, research activities and new hires. External university partnership (e.g., alumni organizations or private entities) funding can also be used via direct program donations or financial backing for CRM activities. It must be kept in mind that funders within the private sector may very well be looking for opportunities to contribute

and stretch their outreach dollars to particular Black student programs and racial justice initiatives.

5. *Intersectionality*—although the Black male mentoring framework proposed here is based on Hiraldo's (2010) five CRT tenet analysis of racial inequities within higher education, the authors believe that the CRT tenet of intersectionality should be also be used in CRM as way to further nuance the multifaceted cultural issues facing Students of Color. Incorporating intersectionality is key to the work of higher education mentoring as it one, emphasizes how complex facets of identity (e.g., race, class, gender, etc.) further stress the point that PWI institutions were not created for all students despite campuses becoming more "diverse"; and two, with an emphasis on individual and group interlocking systems of oppression (e.g., racism, sexism, homophobia, classism, etc.), CRM programs can improve their efforts to identify and dismantle PWI policies and practices that perpetuate discrimination across a broad spectrum of cultural identities.

Despite the odds stacked against Black males in America, many possess a level of resilience and fortitude that propels them over longstanding educational and socioeconomic and hurdles and towards the doorstep of higher education institutions. Their access into the academy, however, is far from being absent of many of the same societal adversities that they have previously faced. As colleges are sites where young adults experience years of ongoing social development, these institutions must consider how their policies and procedures, as well as the overall environment, either support or ignore ethnic student demographics. Indeed, research on Black male enrollment and attrition rates speak directly to the ways in which this group still struggles with entering and thriving in U.S. academies, especially at PWIs. If these institutional spaces are truly committed to problem-solving this enduring phenomenon, then appropriate interventions must be implemented in order to reach the goal of racial equity. In this chapter, we have suggested college student mentoring, infused by five CRT tenets, as one action-step towards meeting the above objective.

Our proposed programmatic endeavor of Critical Race Mentoring is intended to provide Black male students with academic, social and cultural support systems needed for college persistence and degree attainment through its encouragement of naming and questioning inequitable societal structures in and outside of the university. It is our hope and intent that program participants become viable change agents for others and themselves in moving PWI practices towards racial justice. That said, CRM is by no means meant to be a "Band-Aid" for somehow slowing the bleeding of decades of past and present racial afflictions. Rather, the authors see this design of mentoring as a counternarrative exchange and pathway to compel PWI university boards, administrators, staff and faculty to rethink and revise institutional decisions that have been a long established source of racial prejudice and injustice. Collective input from CRM mentors and mentees serve as entreatments for how academies move past "diversity" platitudes and towards intently living up to their commitment of affirming multiple cultural identities and needs, the redistribution of material resources for historically underrepresented groups, and the involvement of these groups in decision-making impacts from local departments up to the Board of Trustees.

Obviously, racism is a social disease larger than any university or college can alone remedy. Nevertheless, the work of defending against this sickness, within the confines of academia, should not solely be incumbent upon faculty or staff. Nor should students alone feel charged with eradicating a force they did not create. In the context of higher education, the fight against racial institutional injustice is a multilateral process, where upper administration becomes largely accountable for developing and establishing changes based on equal input from students, staff, and faculty councils. Black males navigating higher education deserve more than voguish pledges of good intentions from their institutions, which do little to diminish the reproduction of racist structures and social systems. If what a university does around diversity even partly defines what it stands for, then these academies should feel obligated to fulfill their promises of equity to prospective Black students, and ethnic students overall. We believe that CRM is one approach to changing an institution's story from past-present White supremacy to one of present-future racial justice and promise.

REFERENCES

American Council on Education. (2019). *Race and ethnicity in higher education: A status report*. American Council on Education.

Ancis, J. R., Sedlacek, W. E., & Mohr, J. J. (2000). Students' perceptions of campus climate by race. *Journal of Counseling and Development, 78*(2), 180–186. https://doi.org/10.1002/ j.1556–6676.2000.tb02576.x.

Anderson, C. (2016). *White Rage: The Unspoken Truth of Our Racial Divide*. New York: Bloomsbury.

Baker, C. N. (2013). Social support and success in higher education: The influence of on-campus support on African American and Latino college students. *The Urban Review, 45*(5), 632–650. https://doi.org/10.1007/s11256-013-0234-9.

Bell, D. (1992). *Faces at the bottom of the well: The permanence of racism*. Basic Books.

Bonner, F. A., II. (2010). Focusing on achievement African American student persistence in the academy. In T. Strayhorn and M. Terrell (Eds.), *The evolving challenges of black college students new insights for policy, practice, and research.* (1st ed., pp. 66–84). Stylus Publishing, LLC.

Bonilla-Silva, E. (2017). *Racism without racists: Color-blind racism and the persistence of racial inequality in America.* Rowman & Littlefield.

Brittain, A. S., Sy, S. R., & Stokes, J. E. (2009). Mentoring: Implications for African-American college students. *Western Journal of Black Studies, 33*(2), 87–97.

Brooms, D. R. (2016). Building us up: Supporting Black male college students in a Black male initiative program. *Critical Sociology, 44*(1), 141–155 https://doi.org/10.1177/0896 920516658940.

Bugeja, M. (2013). The new R&R: Recruitment and retention of students. *The Education Digest, 78*(7), 25–28.

Chaoe, G. T. & Walz, P. M. (1992). Formal and informal mentorships: A comparison of mentoring functions and contrast with nonmentored counterparts. *Personnel Psychology, 45*(3), 619–636. https://doi.org/10.1111/j.1744-6570.1992.tb00863.x.

Crenshaw, K. W. (1988). Race, reform, retrenchment: Transformation and legitimation in anti-discriminatory law. *Harvard Law Review, 101*(7), 1331–1387.

Crenshaw, K. W. (2011). Twenty years of CRT: Looking back to move forward. *Connecticut Law Review, 43*(5), 1253–1352.

Cuyjet, M. J. (2006). *African American men in college.* Wiley.

Dahlvig, J. (2010). Mentoring of African American students at a predominantly white institutions (PWI). *Christian Higher Education, 9*(5), 369–395. https://doi.org/10.1080/15363750903404266.

D'Abate, C. P. & Eddy, E. R. (2008). Mentoring as a learning tool: enhancing the effectiveness of an undergraduate business mentoring program, *Mentoring & Tutoring: Partnership in Learning, 16*(4), 363–378. https://doi.org/10.1080/13611260802433692.

DeAngelo, L., Mason, J., & Winters, D. (2015). Faculty engagement in mentoring undergraduate students: how institutional environments regulate and promote extra-role behavior. *Innovative Higher Education, 41*, 317–332.https://doi.org/10.1007/s10755-015-9350-7.

DeCuir, J. T., & Dixson, A. D. (2004). "So when it comes out, they aren't that surprised that it is there": Using critical race theory as a tool of analysis of race and racism in education. *Educational Researcher, 33*(5), 26–31. https://doi.org/10.3102/0013189X033005026.

Delgado, R. (Ed.) (1995). *Critical race theory: The cutting edge.* Temple University Press.

Delgado, R., & Stefancic, J. (Eds). (1997). *Critical White studies: Looking behind the mirror.* Temple University Press.

Eakins, A., & Eakins, S. L. (Fall, 2017). African American students at predominantly White institutions: A collaborative style cohort recruitment & retention model. *Journal of Learning in Higher Education, 13*(2), 51–57.

Feagin, J. R., & O'Brien, E. (2003). *White men on race: Power, privilege, and the shaping of cultural consciousness.* Beacon Press.

Fergus, E. & Noguera, P. (2014). *Schooling for resilience: Improving life trajectories for Black and Latino boys*. Harvard Education Press.

Ferguson, A. A. (2001). *Bad boys: Public schools in the making of black masculinity*. University of Michigan Press.

Forman, J. (2017). *Locking up our own: Crime and punishment in black America*. Farrar, Straus and Giroux Publishers.

Freeman, K. (1999). No services needed? The case for mentoring high-achieving African American students. *Peabody Journal of Education, 74*(2), 15–26. https://doi.org /10.1207/s15327930pje7402_3.

Freire, P. (2000). *Pedagogy of the oppressed*. Continuum.

Frierson, H. T., Wyche, J. H., & Pearson, W. (2009). *Black American males in higher education: Research, programs and academe*. Emerald.

Furr, S. R. (2002). African-American students in a predominantly-White university: Factors associated with retention. *College Student Journal, 36*(2), 188–202.

Gotanda, N. (1991). A critique of 'our constitution is color-blind.' *Stanford Law Review, 44*(1), 1–68.

Guiffrida, D. A., & Douthit, K. Z. (2010). The Black student experience at predominantly white colleges: Implications for school and college counselors. *Journal of Counseling and Development, 88*(3), 311–318. https://doi.org/10.1002/j.1556-6678.2010.tb00027.x.

Hall, H. R. (2006). *Mentoring young men of color: Meeting the needs of African American and Latino students*. Rowman & Littlefield.

Hall, H. R. (2019). What do Black adolescents need from their schools?: Knowing students' obstacles for building on their academic success. *Association for Supervision and Curriculum Development (ASCD), 76*(8), 52–57.

Harris, L. M., Campbell, J. T., & Brophy, A. L. (2019). *Slavery and the university: Histories and legacies*. Georgia University of Georgia Press.

Harris, J. C., Barone, R. P., & Davis, L. P. (Winter 2015). Who benefits?: A critical race analysis of the (d) evolving language of inclusion in higher education. *Thought & Action, 31*(2), 21–38.

Harris, C. I. (June, 1993) Whiteness as property. *Harvard Law Review, 106*(8), 1707–1791.

Harper, S. R. (2009). Niggers no more: A critical race counternarrative on Black male achievement at predominantly White colleges and universities. *International Journal of Qualitative Studies in Education, 22*(6), 697–712. https://doi.org/10.1080/09518390 903333889.

Harper, S. R., Patton, L. D., & Wooden, O. S. (2009). Access and equity for African American students in higher education: A critical race historical analysis of policy efforts. *The Journal of Higher Education, 80*(4), 389–414. https://doi.org/10.1080/00221546.2009.11 779022.

Harper, S. R. (2012). *Black male student success in higher education: A report from the national Black male college achievement study*. University of Pennsylvania, Center for the Study of Race and Equity in Education.

Hilliard, A. (2003). *No mystery: Closing the achievement gap between Africans and excellence*. In T. Perry, C. Steele & A. Hilliard (Eds.), Young, gifted and Black:

Promoting high achievement among African American students (pp. 131–166). Beacon Press.

Hiraldo, P. (2010). The role of critical race theory in education. *The Vermont Connection, 31*(7), 53–59.

Howard, T. C., Flennaugh, T. K., & Terry, C. L. (2012). Black males, social imagery, and the disruption of pathological identities: Implications for research and teaching. *Education Foundations, 26*(1), 85–102.

Johnson-Ahorlu, R. (2013). "Our biggest challenge is stereotypes": Understanding stereotype threat and the academic experiences of African American undergraduates. *Journal of Negro Education, 82*(4), 382–392.

Johnson, W. B. (2002). The intentional mentor: Strategies and guidelines for the practice of mentoring. *Professional Psychology: Research and Practice, 33*(1), 88–96. https://doi.org/10.1037/0735-7028.33.1.88.

Kunjufu, J. (2010). *Reducing the Black male dropout rate*. African American Images.

Ladson-Billings, G., & Tate IV, W. F. (1995). Toward a critical race theory of education. *Teachers College Record, 97*(1), 47–68.

Ladson-Billings, G. (2005). The evolving role of critical race theory in educational scholarship. *Race Ethnicity and Education, 8*(1), 115–119.

Lee, W. Y. (1999). Striving toward effective retention: the effect of race on mentoring African American students. *Peabody Journal of Education, 74*(2), 27–43. https://doi.org/10.1207/s15327930pje7402_4.

Lewis, A. E., & Diamond, J. B. (2015). *Despite the best intentions: How racial inequality thrives in good schools*. Oxford University Press.

Mandara, J. & Murray, C. B. (2000). Effects of parental marital status, income, and family functioning on African American adolescent self-esteem. *Journal of Family Psychology, 14*(3), 475–490. https://doi.org/10.1037/0893-3200.14.3.475.

McCabe, J. (2009). Racial and gender microaggressions on a predominantly White campus: Experiences of Black, Latina/o and White undergraduates. *Race, Gender, & Class, 16*(12), 133–151.

Morris, M. W. (2015). *Pushout: The criminalization of Black girls in schools*. The New Press.

National Center for Education Statistics. (2013). *The condition of education*. https://nces.ed.gov/pubs2013/2013037.pdf.

Noguera, P. A. (2012). Saving black and Latino boys: What schools can do to make a difference. *Phi Delta Kappan, 93*(5), 8–12. https://doi.org/10.1177/003172171209300503.

Patton, L. D., McEwen, M., Rendón, L., & Howard-Hamilton, M. F. (2007). Critical race perspectives on theory in student affairs. *New Directions for Student Services, 120*, 39–53. https://doi.org/10.1002/ss.256.

Perna, L. W., Gerald, D., Baum, E., & Milem, J. (2007). The status of equity for Black faculty and administrators in public higher education in the south. *Research in Higher Education, 48*(2), 193–228. https://doi.org/10.1007/s11162-006-9041-4.

Pope, M. L. (2002). Community college mentoring: Minority student perception. *Community College Review, 30*(3), 31–45. https://doi.org/10.1177/009155210203000303.

Oakes, J. (2005). *Keeping track: How school structure inequality* (2nd ed.). Yale University Press.

Rhodes, J. E., Reddy, R., Grossman, J. B., & Lee, J. M. (2002). Volunteer mentoring relationships with minority youth: An analysis of same-versus cross-race matches. *Journal of Applied Social Psychology, 32*(10), 2114–2133. https://doi.org/ 10.1111/ j.1559–1816.2002.tb02066.x.

Roberts, A. (2000). Mentoring revisited: A phenomenological reading of the literature. *Mentoring & Tutoring, 8*(2), 145–170. https://doi.org/10.1080/713685524.

Salami, T. K., & Walker, R. L. (2014). Socioeconomic status and symptoms of depression and anxiety in African American college students: The mediating role of hopelessness. *Journal of Black Psychology, 40*(3), 275–290. https://doi. org/10.1177/0095798413486158.

Sands, R. G., Parson, A. L., & Duane, J. (1991). Faculty mentoring faculty in a public university. *Journal of Higher Education, 62*(2), 174–193. https://doi.org/10.1080/ 00221546.1991.11774114.

Savas, G. (2014). Understanding critical race theory as a framework in higher educational research, *British Journal of Sociology of Education, 35*(4), 506–522.

Saufley, R., Cowan, K. B., Herman, J. (1983). The struggles of minority students at predominantly white institutions. *New Directions for Teaching and Learning, 16*, 3–15. https://doi.org/10.1002/tl.37219831603.

Schiraldi, V., & Ziedenberg, J. (2002). *Cellblocks or classrooms?: The funding of higher education and corrections and its impact on African American men.* http://www.justicepolicy.org/images/upload/02–09_REP_CellblocksClassrooms_ BB-AC.pdf.

Shabazz, R. (2015). *Spatializing blackness: Architectures of confinement and black masculinity in Chicago.* University of Illinois Press.

Sinanan, A. (2016). The Value and Necessity of Mentoring African American College Students at PWI's. Africology: *The Journal of Pan African Studies, 9*(8), 155–166.

Solórzano, D. G., & Yosso, T. J. (2002). Critical race methodology: Counterstorytelling as an analytical framework for educational research. *Qualitative Inquiry, 8*(1), 23–44. https://doi.org/10.1177/107780040200800103.

Smith, A. (2013). *Unsettling the privilege of self-reflexivity.* In F. Twine & B. Gardener (Eds.), Geographies of privilege (pp. 263–280). Routledge.

Steele, C. M. (1997). A threat in the air: How stereotypes shape intellectual identity and performance. *American Psychologist, 52*(6), 613–629. https://doi.org/10.1037 /0003–066X.52.6.613.

Steele, C. (2003). *Stereotype threat and African-American student achievement.* In T. Perry, C. M. Steele & A. G. Hilliard (Eds.). Young, gifted, and Black: Promoting high achievement among African-American students (pp. 252–257). Beacon.

Strayhorn, T. L., & Terrell, M. C. (2007). Mentoring and satisfaction with college for Black students. *The Negro Educational Review, 58*, 69–83.

Swartz, E. (1992). Emancipatory narratives: Rewriting the master script in the school Curriculum. *The Journal of Negro Education, 61*(3), 341–355.

Tate IV, W. F. (1997). Critical race theory and education: History, theory and implications. *American Educational Research Association, 22*(1), 195–247. https://doi.org/10.3102 /0091732X022001195.

Toldson, I. (2019). *No BS (bad stats): Black people need people who believe in Black people enough not to believe every bad thing they hear about Black people.* Brill/Sense Publishers.

Robertson, R. V., & Chaney, C. (2017). "I Know it [Racism] Still Exists Here": African American Males at a Predominantly White Institution. *Humboldt Journal of Social Relations, 39*(39), 260–282.

Wilder, C. S. (2013). *Ebony & ivy: Race, slavery, and the troubled history of America's universities.* Bloomsbury Press.

Willie, C., & Willie, S. (2005). Black, white, and brown: The transformation of public education in America. *The Teachers College Record, 107*(3), 475–495.

Yosso, T., & Lopez, C. B. (2010). Counterspaces in a hostile place. In L. Patton (Ed.), *Culture centers in higher education: Perspectives on identity, theory, and practice* (pp. 83–104). Stylus.

Yosso, T. J. (2002). Toward a critical race curriculum. *Equity & Excellence in Education, 35*(2), 93–107. https://doi.org/10.1080/713845283.

Zhang, P., & Smith, W. L. (2011). From high school to college: The transition experiences of Black and White Students. *Journal of Black Studies, 42*(5), 828–845. https://doi.org/ 10.1177/0021934710376171.

NOTES

1. The authors chose to capitalize "Black," "White," "People of Color," and "Students of Color" in order to reflect that we are discussing groups of people. By capitalizing Black and White, we are making necessary distinctions between colors and race—e.g., black hair versus Black hair.

2. In 2013, Dr. Ivory Toldson helped to expose the erroneous findings within Schiraldi and Ziedenberg's 2002 Justice Policy Institute report. Toldson used data from the U.S. Census Bureau, the Bureau of Justice Statistics' National Prisoner Statistics Program, and the Justice Policy Institute to show how Schiraldi and Ziedenberg's conclusions were incomplete with respect to the amount of Black men in federal prisons versus state institutions; those Black men who already finished college or served prison sentences; and those who had a life trajectory that did not involve college or prison attendance.

3. This 2019 legal case involves a dispute between a coalition of civil rights groups and students suing the state of New Jersey, calling into question the State's leadership to desegregate its public schools.

4. Swartz (1992) refers to the master script as pedagogy, theoretical paradigms, classroom practices and instructional materials that are grounded in White supremacist, European ideologies. Master scripts serve to "silence" (p. 341) marginalized groups by legitimating male, upper class, White dominant voices through the standardized knowledge that students are expected to know (Swartz, 1992).

5. Examples of microaggressions in classrooms and on campuses include using inappropriate humor in that degrades students from different groups; complimenting nonwhite students on their use of "good English"; making assumptions about students based on their backgrounds; expecting students of any particular group to "represent" the perspectives of others of their race, gender, etc. in class discussions or campus forums; or denying the experiences of students by questioning the credibility and validity of their personal stories and cultural histories.

Chapter Five

Exploring Mentoring and Faculty Interactions of Black Women Pursuing Doctoral Degrees

Marjorie C. Shavers, Jamilyah Butler,
Bettie Ray Butler, and Lisa R. Merriweather

BLACK WOMEN PHDS

As a whole, Black people (i.e., U.S. citizens or permanent residents) are underrepresented in terms of research doctoral degree attainment, attaining approximately 7 percent of doctoral degrees awarded within the United States (US) in 2020 (U.S. Department of Education. Institute of Education Sciences, National Center for Education Statistics [NCSES], 2021), the majority of which were in non-STEM related disciplines (NCSES, 2021). Black women, in particular, earned 62 percent of all research doctorates (NCSES, 2021) earned by Black people. While they are academically more successful than their male counterparts, Black women still represent a small proportion of all research doctorates (4.5 percent) (NCSES, 2021). Their numbers are dwarfed even when compared against women earning research doctoral degrees, who overall received 51 percent of all doctoral degrees (NCSES, 2021). Further, when looking at just the population of women, Black women earned just 8.6 percent of the degrees, while White women account for 66.9 percent (NCSES, 2021).[1] These startling numbers are discouraging and are symptomatic of the unique obstacles, rooted in racial and gender biases, faced by Black women in doctoral programs (Grant & Simmons, 2008; Ong et al., 2011; Pope & Edwards, 2016; Ramos & Yi, 2020).

Black women encounter a number of obstacles en route to the doctorate. A review of the extant literature suggests three broad categories: Climate (e.g., Grant & Ghee, 2015; Pope & Edwards, 2016, Ramos & Yi, 2020), identity and wellness (e.g., Dortch, 2016; Johnson & Scott, 2020; Pope & Edwards, 2016; Shavers & Moore, 2019), and support (e.g., Dortch, 2016; Grant & Simmons, 2008; Shavers & Moore, 2019). The campus climate was consistently found to impact persistence and success of Black women doctoral students. Campus climates perceived as unwelcoming (Dortch, 2016; Grant & Ghee, 2015) hindered degree completion and satisfaction. Welcoming climates were rare in the lives of Black women whose experiences were tinged with racialized and gendered discrimination, a characteristic often referred to as a double bind (Dortch, 2016; Malcolm et al., 1976; Ong et al., 2011). The double bind is described as "the unique challenges minority women faced as they simultaneously experienced sexism and racism" (Ong et al., 2011, p. 175). The double bind contributes to feelings of invisibility (Rasheem, et al. 2018) as their unique experiences are masked by shared racial identities with Black men and shared gender identities with White women.

Experiences of discrimination more often than not created environments in which they felt isolated and marginalized (Cartwright et al., 2021; Dortch, 2016; Johnson-Bailey, 2004) and faced microaggressive assaults (Ramos & Yi, 2020) such as having their intelligence questioned (Grant & Simmons, 2008; Johnson & Scott, 2020) and their experiences delegitimized (Ramos & Yi, 2020). These experiences described by Shavers and Moore (2019) as being a perpetual outsider "tend to be prominent at PWIs [predominantly White institutions] because of the discrepancy between students' personal culture and the culture of the university" (p. 221).

Shavers and Moore (2019) suggest that despite previous academic success and successful academic progression in their doctoral programs, the overall well-being of Black women and their identity are put at risk as they continue to feel like perpetual outsiders. Being an outsider contributed to feelings of invisibility (Johnson-Bailey, 2004; Rasheem et al., 2018), as well as hypervisibility (Cartwright et al., 2021; Shavers & Moore, 2019) and lack of sense of belonging (Ramos & Yi, 2020; Shavers & Moore, 2019). Black students are dehumanized in the process (Merriweather, 2019; Pope & Edwards; 2016), losing their sense of who they are in an effort to conform to who they are thought to be. The ability to understand and define their identity on their own terms are impacted by personal characteristics. According to Dortch (2016), Black women with lower self-efficacy, agency, and sense of self exhibit lower resilience in the face of adversity and challenges. When they struggle with navigating those identity terrains, they are predisposed to difficulties in both physical and emotional wellness (Cartwright et al., 2021; Rasheem et al., 2018), along with academics (Johnson & Scott, 2020). Lipson and colleagues

(2018) found that 61.9 percent of Black women in undergraduate and graduate programs reported needing mental health services to cope with anxiety and depression from their educational experiences.

Support is often cited as a necessary ingredient in the recipe for doctoral success. However, the lack of financial support, academic support, and social support are all known obstacles to success. When campuses are experienced as lonely places (Shavers & Moore, 2019), students are less likely to be engaged, invested, and happy with their doctoral education. Many students, including Black women, may need financial support but financial support alone in the form of scholarships, fellowships, and assistantships will not ensure conditions conducive to students thriving. The absence of meaningful campus-based relationships, with both peers and faculty, can leave students feeling unsupported (Cartwright et al., 2021; Johnson & Scott, 2020; Pope & Edwards, 2016). Having systems of support is important to combating negative experiences (Dortch, 2015; Patton, 2009; Shavers & Moore, 2019). Dortch (2016) addresses the role of peer support and others have indicated the role of family support (Ramos & Yi, 2020) in mitigating the challenges of racialized gendered illiterate populations of administration, faculty, staff, and students (Merriweather, 2015; Merriweather & Howell, in press). That is, environments that are anti-Black, antiwoman must have intentional efforts directed toward them. It seems in spite of a dearth of guidance and support, and outright hostility, Black women persist in pursuing the PhD (US Department of Education, 2019). These women use a variety of support systems and strategies to persist academically. One area of support that research consistently shows to be helpful for Black women doctoral student's success is mentoring (Johnson-Bailey, 2004; Patton, 2009; Robinson, 2013).

Within this context, this chapter explores how White faculty mentors impact the experiences of Black women pursuing doctoral degrees. To begin, this chapter explores the definition of mentoring and then delves into the unique experiences and needs for the mentorship of Black woman PhDs. Next, it introduces Black Feminist Thought (BFT) as the epistemological lens which frames and guides the present study. Then, drawing on the narratives of seven Black women at various stages within their doctoral program, this chapter uncovers stories of perseverance amidst abounding obstacles while in pursuit of their PhD. To conclude, recommendations for how White faculty mentors and others can recruit, retain, and sustain these women in their respective programs are discussed.

WHAT IS MENTORING?

There is a rapidly growing body of literature that explores the mentoring experiences of Black women in doctoral programs (e.g., Cartwright et al., 2021; Grant & Simmons, 2008; Howell, 2014; Pope & Edwards, 2016; Shavers & Moore, 2019) and the verdict is clear, mentoring is critical for Black women pursuing doctoral degrees. Because of the challenges Black women PhDs face, mentoring models should be implemented with care.

CHALLENGES

Research reports that Black women frequently lack opportunities for mentorship (Howell, 2014, Ramos & Yi, 2020) resulting in a lack of meaningful support through their doctoral experience. Many factors are at play that create these conditions. It comes as no surprise that Black women are underrepresented in the academy (Grant & Simmons, 2008; Ramos & Yi, 2020), leaving Black women students with fewer options to be mentored by a person whose culture may be more like their own. Doctoral mentorships are rarely mandated and therefore rely on self-selection. Black women are often not selected or they feel like they do not have faculty from which to select due to a lack of common research interest and backgrounds (Grant & Simmons, 2008; Ramos & Yi, 2020). Johnson and Scott (2020) refer to it as a lack of scholarly fit when the mentor is culturally different than the mentee. This phenomenon leaves Black women with few allies and even fewer accomplices (Isaac-Savage & Merriweather, 2021) to assist them toward degree completion.

Another challenge is that crosscultural mentorships, the form of mentorship that most Black women are relegated to having, have inherent weaknesses. Because of the lack of interest and limited knowledge of their mentees' topics—which often center race, gender, and culture; mentors are not as well equipped to guide their doctoral work. Further the lack of lived experiences with racialized gendered prejudice may result in greater insensitivity and less awareness of the discrimination Black women students confront. These manifestations of multicultural incompetence (Rasheem, et al., 2018) can prove detrimental and breed negative feelings about the doctoral experience, resulting in slow progress, ineffective support, and lack of confidence (Dortch, 2016).

MODELS OF MENTORING

There are several models of mentoring but it is the traditional model that is most often employed. This model focuses on role modeling, psychosocial needs, and professional development (Grant & Simmons, 2008). Johnson and Scott (2020) describe it as a process of:

> doctoral student socialization . . . largely focused on the faculty–student dynamic. This is described as a transmission of knowledge and sharing of academic culture, norms, and practices from faculty to student, while students build the skills necessary to engage in independent scholarship. (p. 2)

Contrastingly, Harris (1999) asserted that "by limiting the examination of mentoring based on one universal definition, the personal, complex nature of the mentoring experience by underrepresented groups, who do not fit into a male-oriented, competitive, individualist profile, will be excluded" (p. 230). Consequently, there has been a call for more culturally liberative mentoring models (Merriweather, 2012; Merriweather et al., in press) and strategies, models that look at race, gender, and their interstice (Pope & Edwards, 2016). Benefits for Black women include: opening opportunities; better psychosocial adjustment, such as, "being seen as a complete human being, . . . being seen by other students, and having professors who are politically and racially aware" (Rasheem, et al. 2018, p. 52); encouragement to be their authentic selves; and greater academic success (Johnson & Scott, 2020).

Ramos and Yi (2020) propose that spaces of resistance are needed. In many ways, culturally liberative mentoring relationships are spaces of resistance that help Black women to name and be aware of:

> structures and systems of marginalization and power and how these structures impact their lives in doctoral education programs . . . spaces of resistance [are defined] as contexts and opportunities that allowed doctoral women of color to thrive in academic spaces dominated by racist and sexist systems and ideologies. (140)

This is especially so with Black women mentors who were seen as better prepared to model how to weather discrimination based on race and gender (Cartwright et al., 2021), meet emotional needs (Rasheem, 2018), and build trust (Grant & Ghee, 2015). Grant and Ghee (2015) reiterate this in saying:

> Participating in a mentoring relationship with someone who looks like them, who has similar personal, professional, and scholarly interests, and is devoted to their holistic experience and personal success as a doctoral student in their chosen field, is keenly important for African American women. (p. 768)

Undoubtedly same-race/same-gender mentorships afford Black women with a plethora of benefits and consistently are preferred by Black women because the shared culture (Grant & Ghee, 2015; Rasheem, 2018), kinship connection (Pope & Edwards, 2016), and desire to see reflections of self in the academy (Pope & Edwards, 2016) offers an opportunity to be understood and respected (Johnson & Scott, 2020; Pope & Edwards, 2016; Rasheem et al., 2018). Pope and Edwards (2016) caution that maximum benefit may not be realized if the Black women mentors are reluctant to engage "vulnerable truth telling" (p. 770)—a willingness to openly discuss their personal challenges with racialized gendered oppression—and "homeplacing" (p. 770). Homeplacing occurs when:

> mentoring relationships . . . are informed by Black feminised cultural practices and communal commitments. Curriculum homeplacing places Black women and Black women's ways of knowing at the centre. It is first and foremost about asserting the humanity of Black women and consciously resisting institutional frames that would seek to invalidate their position as knowers, theorists, and scholars. (Pope & Edwards, 2016, p. 770)

Other forms of mentoring include peer mentoring, network mentoring, and crosscultural mentoring. Having a same-race/same-gender faculty mentor is the ideal, however in lieu of and sometimes in addition to that form of mentorship, Black women engage in peer mentoring (Cartwright et al., 2021; Grant & Simmons, 2008; Rasheem, 2018). Johnson and Scott (2020) noted peer "networks were sources of support in terms of navigating institutional policies, allowing students to learn indirectly from the experiences of others" (p. 11). Others (Cartwright et al., 2021; Grant & Ghee, 2015, Ramos & Yi, 2020) hail the virtues of network mentoring which draws support from external sources such as family, peers, other Black women who may not be in the academy, as well as, Black women who may not be in their field or academic units. According to Grant and Ghee (2015), "mentoring networks are vital support structures in a successful academic career, as scholars of color seek to navigate the complex and protean racial and gender dynamics of academic institutions" (p. 760). Cross-cultural mentoring (Cartwright et al., 2020) encapsulates any mentoring that is not same-race/same-gender. While it has challenges, it increases the number of potential mentors available to Black women and can be beneficial if the mentor is willing to engage practices of cultural sensitivity and cultural competency (Merriweather, 2012).

Mentoring provides vital support needed to thrive in doctoral education. Black women less often receive the effective mentoring that is necessary for navigating the tenuous terrains of doctoral programs which regularly mete out racialized gendered microaggressions and discrimination creating academic and psychosocial challenges for Black women. Delving into the lived experiences of Black women doctoral students can better inform strategies for recruiting, retaining, and sustaining them.

BLACK FEMINIST THOUGHT: AN EPISTEMOLOGICAL LENS

Black women in higher education have unique experiences as a result of their double bind status and resulting history of oppression. They experience academia in ways that differ from those who are not Black and woman. Thus, it was important to use an epistemological lens that would appropriately situate the herstories and testimonies of Black women. BFT describes how interlocking systems of oppression (i.e., racism, sexism, and classism) affect Black women. Though BFT acknowledges that Black people as a whole face similar challenges due to systemic racism, it stresses that Black women's experiences are distinct and nuanced (Collins, 2002). BFT is therefore used in the present study as a guiding framework for sharing and interpreting the lived experiences of Black women doctoral students at PWIs (Collins, 2002).

Grounded in Afrocentric and feminist methodology, BFT analyzes Black women's realities through the use of narrative. It creates a space and gives voice to Black women to tell their own truths—in contrast to having others tell stories about them—to be heard, seen, and better understood (Collins, 1989). BFT allows Black women the opportunity to exercise what Collins (2015) refers to as "epistemic agency" wherein they become the experts and authors of their own experiences and are viewed and valued as knowledge producers, rather than mere subjects of investigation or data points (p. 2350). Additionally, BFT emphasizes the importance of social justice as a form of collective resistance to oppression (Collins, 2015). For Black women, especially, Collins (2015) contends that "self" empowerment stems from fighting against, not apart from, larger social injustices that transcend but are still grounded within the context of Black women's struggles. BFT makes clear that self is not autonomous but instead an extension of human/group solidarity. This said, coalition building as understood by Collins (2002) is essential to intellectual transformation and social change—a significant aspect of BFT.

With these methodological considerations and principles in mind, BFT was used to guide the collection of data, identification of key themes, and interpretation of findings. This process is explained in greater detail next.

METHODOLOGY

This study was part of a larger project (Shavers & Moore, 2014) that investigated the broad experiences of Black doctoral students at PWIs. Both studies used a qualitative approach aimed at investigating the participants' subjective experiences (Collins, 2002). Data from the original study was collected over the span of a four-year period (2015–2019). The present study is slightly different in that it focuses specifically on the mentoring experiences of select (n=7) Black women PhDs. Using a combination of participant questionnaires and interviews the following research questions were addressed:

1. How do Black women doctoral students characterize their mentoring experiences and relationships?
2. How do their mentoring experiences and relationships impact their academic progression, psychosocial growth, and future career outlook?

PARTICIPANTS

For this study, the participants were selected using a criterion-based purposive sampling method (Lincoln & Guba, 1985). Participants were eligible if they were doctoral students who self-identified as women and African American and/or Black. All of the participants were enrolled in doctoral programs at major research PWIs. Participants were solicited through electronic communications (e.g., e-mail listserv) and snowball sampling (Patton, 2002). The sample size was determined throughout the data collection process, interviews were collected until redundancy occurred, and no more new information was gathered (Fossey et al., 2002; Lincoln & Guba, 1985). Redundancy emerged after seven interviews.

Detailed participant data is provided in Table 5.1. All personal information was deidentified and pseudonyms were used. The participants ranged in age from 23 to 42, with a mean age of 29 years. Each of the women were at various stages of their doctoral program. At the time of data collection, four participants were still engaged in doctoral coursework, while three had completed all degree requirements with the exception of their dissertation (i.e., ABD, all but dissertation). When asked about their first-generation background, three participants indicated that they were first-generation college students, but all of the women (with one exception) stated that they were the first in their family to pursue a doctoral degree. One participant declined to report her socioeconomic and first-generation status.

Table 5.1. Participant Demographic Data

"Name"	Age	Program status	Socioeconomic status	First-generation student	First-generation doctoral student
Stacey	35	ABD	middle-class	Yes	Yes
Breonna	24	1st year	low income	Yes	Yes
Patrisse	30	2nd year	middle-class	Yes	Yes
Cori	24	1st year	working-class	No	Yes
Opal	23	1st year	n/a	n/a	n/a
Mauree	28	ABD	middle-class	No	Yes
Kamala	42	ABD	middle-class	No	Yes

Note: Cells with n/a signify that this information was not obtained from the participant.

DATA COLLECTION AND ANALYSIS

The protocols used to collect the newer interviews followed the same procedures as set forth in the original study. Each participant engaged in a semistructured telephone interview that ranged from 45 to 90 minutes. The interviews were recorded and transcribed. A three stage, open and axial coding method was used to identify emerging themes as the data was being collected (Blaikie, 2000). During the first step, categories and subcategories were identified through an inductive process. The second-step of the coding process consisted of drawing relationships between the categories and subcategories to gain additional insight into the participants subjective experiences. The third step used BFT to interpret plausible themes which captured the unique experiences of the participants, taking into consideration the intersection of their racialized, gendered, and classed identities (Collins, 2002).

METHODOLOGICAL RIGOR AND TRUSTWORTHINESS

Methodological rigor and trustworthiness were established through credibility, transferability, confirmability, and authenticity (Lincoln & Guba, 1985). The data was triangulated using demographic questionnaires, participant interviews, research partner analysis, and member checking to increase credibility. In presenting the participant narratives, multiple stories and thick descriptions of participant interactions and encounters were used to maximize the depth of information provided so that readers could assess the findings and make informed decisions about transferability. Confirmability cautions against interpreting findings that are not supported by data, thus the data in this study was presented in a manner that was clear, consistent, and without bias. To demonstrate authenticity, the goals of the researchers were aligned with the needs of the participants. Through the process of member checking, participants were able to confirm or disconfirm the themes identified in the study to ensure that they accurately portrayed the participants' perspectives.

Finally, to ensure the consistency in the identification of themes the second author assisted the primary researcher (first author) in the process of evaluating the data to establish interrater reliability. In so doing, both the primary and secondary researcher (here on out referred to as "the researchers") identified themes and relationships independently and then met several times to discuss and finalize them (Lincoln & Guba, 1985). Any differences found between the researchers in relation to the identification of key themes and findings were discussed until perfect agreement was reached.

SUBJECTIVITY

It is always important to note that the researchers' subjectivity can impact the study. The first researcher, at the time of data collection, was a Black woman assistant professor at a PWI and former group facilitator for Black women at a college counseling center. The secondary researcher (second author) that assisted with the data analysis is also a Black woman and practicing clinician. The third and fourth authors both identify as Black women. The third author is an associate professor at a PWI and the fourth author is a full professor at a PWI. All four authors earned their PhDs from PWIs.

The experiences and identities of researchers have the propensity to impact the analysis and presentation of the data (Peshkin, 1988). Given the similarity in the researchers' and participants' background and experiences, the researchers had the capacity to "filter, skew, shape, block, transform, construe, or misconstrue what transpires from the outset of a research project to its culmination in a written statement" (Peshkin, 1988, p. 17). The researchers' roles naturally influenced the assumptions that guided the research process, analysis of the data, and the interpretation of the results. However, when researchers can identify and disclose where self and subject become joined it becomes advantageous to the research process. To elaborate further, Johnson-Bailey (1999) stated that when Black women interview other Black women, the interview can be more honest and intimate because there are fewer margins to mitigate. Therefore, shared racial and gender identities between the researchers and participants in fact helped the women in the study to feel less guarded allowing them to quickly develop a meaningful and positive rapport which led to open discussions of sensitive topics and more in-depth information being disclosed.

RESULTS

Theoretical constructs rooted at the intersection of race and gender are used to explain the varying phenomena in this qualitative study (Strauss & Corbin, 1998; Collins, 2002). BFT guided the interpretation of data and aided in the identification of key themes. BFT also situated the data in such a way that provided the necessary context and meaning needed to deconstruct how Black woman doctoral students were mentored at their respective PWI (Collins, 2002). Three primary themes were identified that were relevant to the lived experiences of Black women doctoral students and interactions with White faculty. These themes include: (1) the peculiarity of the predominately White institution as an unwelcoming environment, (2) advisor in title only, and (3) community motivation.

THE PECULIARITY OF THE PREDOMINANTLY WHITE INSTITUTION AS AN UNWELCOMING ENVIRONMENT

Black women in graduate programs face a variety of challenges that can negatively impact their pursuit of a doctoral degree (Johnson-Bailey, 2004; Turner & Thompson, 1993). Race and gender bias experienced by Black women in doctoral programs often includes inadequate mentorship and a strong impact on one's mental health (Dortch, 2016; Shavers & Moore, 2019). This finding was consistent with the participants' narratives in this study. Many of the women that were interviewed shared instances where they believed that the intersection of their race and gender, but predominantly their race, led to unwelcoming behavior that sometimes caused their environments to feel hostile. When asked how her experience was impacted by her race and gender, Patrisse stated:

> Well, the most obvious for me will be the racial piece, obviously being at a PWI and being of a minority group. You definitely sense your feeling . . . of one of few, especially even more so within classes where you find yourself all the time being the only black person.

All of the participants reported being in programs where they were one of a few, if not the only Black person in their program. The awareness of being "the only one" caused students to feel hypervisible and often heightened stereotype threat. Stereotype threat is the risk and fear that members of marginalized groups have because they are worried that anything that they do that is perceived to be negative could be misconstrued as confirmation of a negative stereotype about the larger group (Steele & Arnoson, 1995). Patrisse shared how this threat impacted her on a regular basis, saying:

> We are so few represented. Sometimes I've been the only [Black] person in my class and not wanting to, or not wanting to let me . . . be representative of Black individuals as a whole. I didn't want my shortcomings to be attributed to the larger group so sometimes that would cause me to maybe not speak up, not say things, not share my ideas, cause I didn't want to sound less intelligent and I didn't want that appearance of less intelligence to be attributed to, you know, [being] Black in general.

Kamala added:

> As a Black female, you always have to be prepared to answer any questions that your faculty may ask. You always have to appear knowledgeable of the subject. You must be on top of it, can't appear to be slacking at all.

While the desire to reflect positively on one's race was important, Kamala also shared that being a Black woman in her program also required additional work when trying to interpret feedback from faculty. She mentioned, "We have to be able to take criticism and try to separate it out like real criticism, because the quality of my work needs to be criticized at that level, but not criticisms of my race and my gender."

Particularly in a doctoral program, where students are often asked to interpret and analyze information, one's race has an effect. Kamala discusses how difficult it can be when a faculty member doesn't know much about the student. She stated, " . . . [Professors] don't understand the background. So, your space of understanding . . . is very different than mine." This dissonance can be frustrating and add another layer of challenge to students throughout their doctoral work.

The women also discussed instances where they were left feeling unwelcomed because of their race, even when they believed their gender was not a factor. Breonna shared, "With my [White] advisor, I felt that one of our tensions might have been because of my race." Breonna went on to discuss a time when she was walking with a faculty member and a White classmate who was not the faculty's mentee. She reported being aware of how differently the faculty member treated this classmate. She said she was "warm, friendly, offered encouragement and [told] her it would be okay. She asked questions about her personal life and her home life." This was dramatically different from what she experienced with this faculty member and was even more striking because the faculty member did not have the same relationship that she had with her White peer. All seven participants discussed experiencing similar interactions when seeing other White faculty members and professors interact with their White classmates.

While the unwelcoming environment was challenging, the most problematic part may have been the impact the environment had on the women's overall mental wellness. When Opal was asked how the environment impacted her, she wanted to have a more positive response but said, "It's mainly, I guess, negative, which with me being the positive person I want to be, I don't want it to be, I don't, I'm always looking for the other side, but like no this is actually detrimental."

Participants identified a variety of coping strategies. The need for these strategies and the mental toll of the environment was evident. Kamala stated that it was "exhausting having to always know and understand the rules of the majority culture and to try to bring my bits of my culture into the space without making them feel threatened." She said that it is a "fine line you have to walk." The participants outlined a variety of experiences that should provide context for the general feeling that many of these women faced. While the role of faculty mentor is one that should help participants navigate the space, this was not typically the case.

ADVISOR IN TITLE ONLY

Mentoring is not the only component of successful persistence in a graduate program, academic advising (e.g., assessing students' areas of weakness and strength; fostering professional growth; and helping students negotiate projects, doctoral committees, professional conferences, and publishing) is equally important (Barnes & Austin, 2009). When coupled together, both play a vital role in one's success (Brunsma, Embrick, & Shin, 2017). The pursuit of a doctoral degree is unique and includes complex social and academic processes that must be navigated by the student (Gardner & Barnes, 2007; Lovitts, 2001; Tinto, 1975). A faculty mentor who also advises students can help them to navigate these complex systems. Unfortunately, the participants discussed instances where they were often not provided appropriate advising and suggested that their faculty members held those roles in "title only."

Some participants shared relationships with faculty that were not inherently bad, but lacked the true advising and mentoring a doctoral student would need. For instance, when asked about her relationship with her advisor, Stacey reported:

> I think my advisor sees me as capable and I think she trusts that I would call on her if I need her. Instead of taking the approach of checking in on me, she knows I'll check in with her.

While it is encouraging that Stacey believes her advisor sees her as capable, she also expresses the need for more guidance and support. Stacey stated, "Sometimes, I wish I looked a little more fledgling in her eyes so maybe she would give me a little more support." This highlights a general need for more direction and support during her doctoral studies. Similarly, Kamala shared, "There was no real guidance from my advisor on what classes to take, how to map out things, no kind of end goal planning so . . . I didn't like that." The advisors of the participants may have incorrectly assumed that the women did not need guidance; or worse, withheld valuable wisdom from them. Ultimately, they left the women to figure out the socialization and academic processes of their studies on their own.

While it may be easy to assume that all graduate students had similar experiences, this was not the case with the participants interviewed. Breonna shared that while she was not offered research opportunities in her program, her White colleagues were. Because of the lack of advising Breonna received, she often had to rely on peers for important advising information. When Black doctoral students are forced to rely on their White peers for information because their advisors are not helping them, it often leaves students feeling inadequate and shakes their confidence. When asked about her relationship with her advisor, Patrisse shared, "I would say that he thinks that I'm a worry-wart, but I'm always preoccupied with comparing myself to others who were in their programs and trying to measure myself against kind of where they are, what they've done as part of their program." The lack of guidance and mentoring left participants feeling insecure and questioning their competence despite their ability to progress without the appropriate support.

Even when participants directly asked for help from their advisor, they often did not receive what they needed. Breonna shared:

> I was in a grant proposal class last year and a part of my grant was for a qualitative study, I had never had to write a proposal for a qualitative study . . . I asked her if she had an old qualitative grant proposal that I could look at and make sure that I am thinking of all the right [things]. And her response was that she was not going to give it to me because she didn't want me to copy and paste her work, which [would have been] really impossible.

The [White woman] advisor's response hints at the discriminatory beliefs this advisor held about her student. One, that she would cheat, and two, that she was incapable of the work that was required. Advisors are supposed to help students navigate the academic and social landscape, but in most cases, the advisors became roadblocks; which, in this interaction, ultimately had a negative impact on the participants' mental health. Stacey referred to the microaggressions (i.e., everyday, commonplace, subtle messaging that directly—but often indirectly—reflects biased views toward marginalized groups) that took place in her doctoral programs as "confidence shakers." Kamala put her interactions with her advisor bluntly stating, "I don't think anybody in my program, including my advisor and program director, gives a shit if I finish or not."

The microaggressions, blatant discrimination, and lack of advising that participants experienced took a toll on their mental health, if they were not careful. Mauree shared that "[in her] first semester [she] was getting stressed and felt like [her] body was going haywire." She stated that while sharing her stress with her advisor, "She looked [at her] and said . . . You're not a mom. You're out here by yourself," insinuating that she had no reason to be stressed. Mauree reported that she never shared how she was doing with her advisor again. When a student felt comfortable to share her concerns, her feelings were often not validated. This was mentioned specifically by three of the seven participants without being asked. Participants discussed varying health concerns that arose based on the overall unwelcoming setting and their interactions with faculty members. Patrisse discussed how stress began to impact her. She said, "maybe I just had never had this level of stress that I'm having right now . . . I oftentimes felt like something was wrong with my brain, and I was wanting to go to the doctor, getting an MRI because . . . my brain would be on the verge of exploding from my head." Each participant discussed the impact that this stressful climate had on their mental health and five of the seven participants discussed using therapy or recommending therapy for other Black women considering the pursuit of a PhD.

The findings from the data suggest that the advising relationship for many of the women was not very helpful, oftentimes leaving them on their own— alone and in isolation. Even more disturbing are the relationships and interactions with faculty that undermined the participants' confidence and overall progress and health.

COMMUNITY MOTIVATION

Despite the challenges that these women faced, they were continuing to persist and determined to complete their doctoral studies. When asked about their motivations the participants generally highlighted something bigger than themselves which often reflected their communities. The Afrocentric worldview often places emphasis on communalism or focusing on the interest of the group over a more individualized perspective that focuses on the interest of individuals (Randolph & Koblinsky, 2003); a concept known as "linked fate" (Dawson, 1994). Shavers and Moore (2014) found that many Black women in pursuit of doctoral degrees saw their pursuits as something that was bigger than them and part of their shared identity with their larger racial group; that is, Black people as a whole. This suggests that Black women often view their pursuit of a doctoral degree as an accomplishment that they share with their families and communities or as way to eventually serve their communities (Shavers & Moore, 2014).

Similar findings were uncovered when participants were asked directly about what motivates them to stay in their doctoral programs. Participants typically spoke about their communities either in terms of their own families or the greater community of which they were a part. When participants discussed how their families motivated them, the discussion often focused on the pride their families would feel, the sacrifices their families had made to support them, and the lessons they wanted members of their families to take with them by seeing them reach their goals. When asked what motivates her to continue in her program, Kamala shared:

> That the 16-year-old living in my house told me, mom, let's finish. Cause really, I can walk away right now and be content, but she would never let me live it down. So now I'm just like, okay. I'm going to push through.

Kamala went on to explain the importance of her daughter seeing her overcome challenges and finish something that she had begun.

Participants not only saw their family members as their community, but also linked to their broader community. When asked about motivation, Cori said:

> My family first and foremost and their belief in me and what I tell them about myself and [the students] that I work with [is my chief motivation]. The grounding and belief that the work I'm going to do matters to them and . . . other students that are similar to them . . . gives me the opportunity to produce something that will matter and hopefully make a difference.

Cori is motivated by her family's belief in her, but also the impact that she can have on students that are similar to her own family. She sees her family and others, like her, as her extended community and that helps to ground her and give her a sense of a greater purpose. Similarly, Opal reported that she was motivated to stay in the program when she thinks about the impact of her work. When asked what motivates her, she said, "relevant issues that I'm dealing with in [my] field of study." When further probed, she went on to share that "it goes beyond the actual literature, to actually implementing change." Opal stated that in her courses they "talk about change on the ground and how to make impact and then how that shows up in the literature. So [she is] realizing slowly that . . . what [she] write[s] is actually something that can impact the field and that motivates [her] too, to stay in the program and really value what [she's] doing." The participants were able to identify a purpose in their work grounded in the idea of community and being part of something that improved and transformed the lives of those from within their community.

The community motivation was enough to make these women stay despite the unwelcoming environments they experienced. Two participants also discussed how faculty at their institutions had an impact on them staying in their programs. Patrisse shared that she had considered transferring to a program close to home, but stated that her funding and her advisor cemented her decision to stay. She stated:

> My advisor played a part in that because I think that I've developed somewhat of a relationship with him and . . . he, is a really good advisor in terms of knowing his stuff and, you know, being resourceful and being able to kind of take me to that next level and wanting to work with him.

Patrisse is a second-year student that shared about an "okay" relationship with her advisor. She had not really developed a relationship with him yet, but highlighted her advisor's resources and ability to help her be successful as the reason she decided to stay. At the time of the interview, Patrisse believed that her advisor would provide better support as she got further along, but admitted that she had not had much help up to that point.

Kamala also identified faculty that helped motivate her to stay. While she shared that she did not believe that her advisor cared about her, she had developed relationships with two Black male faculty members in different programs that she referred to as her "mentor team" and believed they were invested in her success. When asked about the two Black mentors and how they impacted her motivation, she responded:

> Gosh. I feel like I don't want to let them down. I feel that they have invested so much in me and they believe in me. I will not let them down. I feel like they are all in my community.

She also shared a time she needed to step away from her doctoral work because of some family issues that she needed to address. She shared that her advisor was not supportive and expressed her "displeasure" with her situation. In contrast to that reaction is the reaction from her "mentor team," which was much more supportive saying, "You've got to take care of family first and then we can finish this degree." The difference in responses highlight how her mentors had become part of her community. Additionally, it shows that they understood and valued her family ties. The emphasis that Black women doctoral students put on community can also provide some insight into how faculty, especially White faculty at PWIs, can better support Black women in doctoral programs.

RECOMMENDATIONS FOR CULTURALLY RESPONSIVE MENTORING

The experiences shared by the participants highlight the disconnect that colleges and universities have between their written statements of diversity, equity, and inclusion and the practice of those principles (Bush, 2011). This disconnect is evidenced in the actions and inactions of the faculty members that the participants spoke about in their narratives. To best address these concerns, a serious overhaul is required of faculty to address the discrimination that exists on predominantly White campuses and within White faculty interactions with Black students. Scholar and activist, Angela Davis, was quoted as saying, "in a racist society, it is not enough to be non-racist, we must be anti-racist" (Kendi, 2016, p. 429); meaning that a verbal denouncing of racism means nothing if it is not coupled with fighting against racist policies, institutions, and practices.

Antiracism acknowledges that structures and systems are founded in racism and White supremacy. As shared by Wolf-Wendel (2016) in a recent Association for the Study of Higher Education (ASHE) report, Whites who are dedicated to making campus more inclusive may end up helping to sustain racist structures without a true commitment to antiracism. While antiracism work is important on the policy and structural level, White faculty can also engage in antiracism on a personal and professional level to help recruit, retain, and sustain Black women in doctoral programs. The strategies that follow are a starting point for White faculty—and by extension PWIs—to begin actively engaging in the larger social justice work of antiracism.

STRATEGIES TO RECRUIT, RETAIN AND SUSTAIN

Using a Black feminist approach to mentoring, Jones and colleagues (2013) build on the work of Barnes and Austin (2009) who discuss the roles and responsibilities of doctoral advising. According to Barnes and Austin (2009), effective faculty mentors should give attention to the: 1) research development of students, 2) students' overall development as professionals, and 3) intellectual and affective dimensions of mentoring which encompasses providing knowledge, suggestions, and feedback, in addition to, offering care and support while remaining friendly. In expanding on these ideas, Jones and colleagues (2013) developed a Black feminist approach to effectively advising Black women in doctoral programs. They suggest that decoding the curriculum, acknowledging scholar activism, and encouraging activity in identity-based professional organizations and associations were particularly integral to the success of Black women PhDs.

Using both approaches—presented by Barnes and Austin (2009) and Jones and colleagues (2013), the recommendations hereafter offer culturally responsive practices that center the mentoring needs and expectations of Black women doctoral students. These strategies address how White faculty (and others) can recruit, retain, and sustain this group more effectively.

Recruit

In order to best recruit (i.e., to intentionally identify, attract, and enroll) Black women, faculty must assume that the strategies identified to retain and sustain Black women are connected and these strategies must be used and addressed holistically. It is unwise to separate recruitment and retention because Black women often learn about the climate at a university by "word-of-mouth." Additionally, it is unethical to recruit students without a focus on one's obligation to also retain and sustain these students. Because participants in our study discussed the peculiar environment of their programs, it would be important for potential students to be aware of the environment. White faculty and others should talk about that environment during the recruitment process with emphasis on how their programs and their faculty are addressing those peculiarities from an antiracist stance.

Jones and colleagues (2013) purport that a function of an advisor is to develop awareness about Black women and their experiences in the academy by reading literature. "This awareness undergirds all of the other advisor functions and will assist the advisor in understanding the student's experiences with racism, sexism, and classism in academe, without discounting them" (p. 333). White faculty and mentors should do this before attempting to recruit Black students to their programs. White faculty can be the voice of initiatives and invite Black experts into their universities to help increase the awareness and understanding of Black women amongst colleagues. However, "in this rush to become anti-racists or abolitionists, it is imperative to self-reflect and determine if we are riding performative waves rather than pushing for substantive change" (Rudham et al., 2020, para. 2). This will require genuine, and at times uncomfortable, introspection and reflection. While faculty must address their own biases, the work of an antiracist requires that they also address policies and the environment in which they exist.

Retain

Once a Black woman begins a doctoral program, this is when faculty and mentors must begin the real work. Faculty "need the intentional mindset of 'Yep, this racism thing is everyone's problem-including mine, and I'm going to do something about it'" (Singh, 2019, p. 87). This mindset is required as faculty members work to retain (i.e., to intentionally support and successfully guide from admission through graduation) Black women in their doctoral programs. Based on the participants' experiences, there are many things that faculty can do to enhance their experiences. The most obvious thing that White faculty can do is to have a more hands-on and supportive approach in advising.

The participants in our study identified a variety of instances where their faculty members were more hands off and left them to *fend for themselves* while needing to rely on their peers for information. Barnes and Austin (2009) stated that advisers should commit to assessing the students' needs, helping them to identify researchable (realistic and manageable) dissertation topics, and aiding them in the selection of committee members. This assistance is a very important part of the doctoral process and Black women need this support, but will also need help navigating the institutional and cultural norms of which many Black women are not aware. Learning these norms is something that Kamala thought was needed in order to be a part of her department.

Faculty mentors can also promote Black women and protect Black women against the harmful environment and interactions that can take place (Jones et al., 2013). First, faculty must be willing to engage in work to address their own stereotypes and biases about Black women, along with their own discomfort. Breonna discussed a faculty member who did not help with a grant proposal because her advisor did not want her to copy and paste. Faculty members must assess their own biases and behavior. Additionally, faculty must call out their peers if and when they hear comments that hint at biases and stereotypes. The protection from these deficit views that others have of Black women must be a part of the advising functions that faculty undertake (Jones et al., 2013), particularly because the deficit view is wholly inaccurate.

Finding ways to connect the work with the student's community is also a very important part of retention for Black women. The results showed that all of the participants were motivated to stay in their programs by their own desires to make their families proud and give back to their families and communities. These findings highlight the importance of supporting and encouraging work and research that the students see as valuable, which often ties to their own identities and communities. Milner (2004) stated, "to attempt to advise African American students without considerations of their whole person would be to understand and advise in a fragmented and disconnected manner" (p. 28). This act was acknowledged by participants who also shared that their advisors did not get to know them. Advisors must take time to develop trust and know their students, so that they can advise in a connected manner.

Sustain

While all of the participants in this study were progressing academically, Opal more than the other women was intent on trying to find the positives when she was being interviewed. Ultimately, she was forced to admit that the overall toll of her experience was "detrimental." Faculty can play an important role in sustaining (i.e., to intentionally prepare, or provide ongoing support, for postgraduation success) Black women by looking critically at oppression and making a concerted effort to disrupt it (hooks, 1994). Some of this work can be done through intentional observation and reflection of one's own behaviors. Breonna discussed an instance where she witnessed a White faculty member treat a White student in a warmer and more encouraging way than she had ever experienced that faculty member. The realization of that served to shake her confidence, but also left her to feel undervalued. Faculty could gain some insight by just auditing their interactions and relationships with White students and asking difficult questions about how they differ from their relationships with Black women in their programs. This inventory should highlight behaviors that are different, but also should spotlight more subtle things like how faculty are going about building relationships with those students.

Simply acknowledging students and taking an interest in them can go a long way. Kamala discussed the challenges of existing in an environment where she worried that "bits of her culture" would not be accepted. Other participants discussed instances where their advisors rarely asked about their lives outside of the department. While it is understandable that advisors would want to have boundaries with students that do not intrude into their personal lives, asking them about their family and lives can help to build a relationship that makes the different dynamics of the relationship easier and more fruitful. Jones and her coauthors (2013) highlight the importance of "a holistic advising relationship that considers the academic, personal, and community responsibility of the advisee" (p. 331). They maintain that providing "a holistic advising relationship will serve the 'whole' person, not just one part of [her] identity" (Jones et al., 2013, p. 331).

CONCLUSION

Black women face a variety of experiences during their time in doctoral programs that can impact their overall well-being (Patton, 2009; Shavers & Moore, 2014). Additionally, Black women's double bind status creates a variety of barriers to their overall success (Minnett et al., 2019). White faculty and others can become forces that overhaul the environment and adjust their relationships with Black women in a way that serves to recruit, retain, and sustain them. While this chapter identifies some practical things that each faculty member can do, it is also the responsibility of these faculty members to critically evaluate their own role in sustaining oppression and redirecting that energy to dismantle it (hooks, 1994). While doing this, faculty members must ground themselves in the belief that "Black women are inherently valuable" (Combahee River Collective, 1983, p. 3). This belief requires personal reflection that will be uncomfortable, but necessary if faculty want to make any true change not just in the lives of Black women, but other marginalized groups as well.

REFERENCES

American Psychological Association. (2019, September). *Racial and ethnic identity*. APA. https://apastyle.apa.org/style-grammar-guidelines/bias-free-language/racial-ethnic-minorities.

Barnes, B. & Austin, A. (2009). The role of doctoral advisors: A look at advising from the advisor's perspective. *Innovative Higher Education, 33*, 297–315.

Blaikie, N. (2000). *Designing social research*. Polity Press.

Brunsma, D. L., Embrick, D. G., & Shin, J. H. (2017). Graduate students of color: Race, racism, and mentoring in the White waters of academia. *Sociology of Race and Ethnicity, 3*(1), 1–13. https://doi.org/10.1177/2332649216681565.

Bush, E. M. L. (2011). *Everyday forms of Whiteness: Understanding race in a "post-tracial" world* (2nd ed.). Rowman & Littlefield Publishers, Inc.

Cartwright, A. (2021). Black female doctoral students' mentorship experiences in counselor education. *Journal of Counselor Leadership and Advocacy, 8*(2), 87–99. https://doi.org/10.1080/2326716X.2021.1961642.

Combahee River Collective. (2000). The Combahee River Collective Statement (pp. 264–274). In B. Smith (Ed). *Home girls: A Black feminist anthology*. Rutgers University Press.

Collins, P. (1989). The social construction of Black feminist thought. *Signs, 14*(4), 745–773.

Collins, P. (2002). *Black feminist thought: Knowledge, consciousness, and the politics of empowerment* (2nd ed.). Taylor and Francis.

Collins, P. (2015). No guarantees: Symposium on Black feminist thought. *Ethnic and Racial Studies, 38*(13), 2349–2354. http://dx.doi.org/10.1080/01419870.2015.105 8512.

Dawson, M. C. (1994). *Behind the mule: Race and class in American politics.* Princeton University Press.

Dortch, D. (2016). The strength from within: A phenomenological study examining the academic self-efficacy of African American women in doctoral studies. *The Journal of Negro Education, 85*(3), 350–364. https://doi.org/10.7709/ jnegroeducation.85.3.0350.

Fossey, E., Harvey, C. McDermott, F., & Davidson, L. (2002). Understanding and evaluating qualitative research. *Australian and New Zealand Journal of Psychiatry, 36*, 717–732. https://doi.org/10.1046/j.1440-1614.2002.01100.x.

Gardner, S. K., & Barnes, B. J. (2007). Graduate student involvement: Socialization for the professional role. *Journal of College Student Development, 48*(4), 369–387. https://doi.org/10.1353/csd.2007.0036.

Grant, C. M., & Ghee, S. (2015). Mentoring 101: Advancing African American women faculty and doctoral student success in predominantly White institutions. *International Journal of Qualitative Studies in Education, 28*, 759–785. https://doi. org/10.1080/09518398.2015.1036951.

Grant, J. M., & Simmons, J. C. (2008). Narratives on experiences of African American women in the academy: Conceptualizing effective mentoring relationships of doctoral student and faculty. *International Journal of Qualitative Studies in Education, 23*, 501–517. https://doi.org/10.1080/09518390802297789.

Harris, F. (1999). Centricity and the mentoring experience in academia: An Africentric mentoring paradigm. *The Western Journal of Black Studies, 23*, 229–235.

hooks, b. (1994). *Outlaw culture: Resisting representations.* Routledge.

Howell, C. (2014). *Black women doctoral students' perceptions of barriers and facilitators of persistence and degree completion in a predominately White university* (Publication No. 3721043). University of North Carolina at Charlotte. Proquest Dissertation Publishing.

Isaac-Savage, E. P., & Merriweather, L. R. (2021). Preparing adult educators for racial justice. *New Directions for Adult and Continuing Education, 2021*(170), 109–118. https://doi.org/10.1002/ace.20430.

Johnson, J., & Scott, S. (2020). Nuanced navigation: Narratives of the experiences of Black "all but dissertation" (ABD) women in the academy. *International Journal of Qualitative Studies in Education.* https://doi.org/10.1080/09518398.2020.1852485.

Johnson-Bailey, J. (1999). The ties that bind and the shackles that separate: Race, gender, class, and color in a research process. *Qualitative Studies in Education, 12*, 659–670. https://doi.org/10.1080/095183999235818.

Johnson-Bailey, J. (2004). Hitting and climbing the proverbial wall: Participation and retention issues for Black graduate women. *Race Ethnicity and Education, 7*, 331–359. https://doi.org/10.1080/1361332042000303360.

Jones, T. B., Wilder, J., & Osborne-Lampkin, L. (2013). Employing a Black feminist approach to doctoral advising: Preparing Black women for the professoriate. *The Journal of Negro Education, 82*(3), 326–338. https://doi. org/10.7709/jnegroeducation.82.3.0326.

Kendi, I. (2016). *Stamped from the beginning: The definitive history of racist ideas in America.* Nation Books.

Lincoln, Y. S., & Guba, E. G. (1985). *Naturalistic inquiry.* Sage.

Lipson, S. K., Kern, A., Eisenberg, D., & Breland-Noble, A. M. (2018). Mental health disparities among college students of color. *Journal of Adolescent Health, 63*(3), 248–356. https://doi.org/10.1016/j.jadohealth.2018.04.014.

Lovitts, B. E. (2001). *Leaving the ivory tower: The causes and consequences of departure from doctoral study.* Rowman & Littlefield Publishers.

Malcolm, S., Hall, P., & Brown, J. (1976). *The double bind: The price of being a minority woman in science.* American Association for the Advancement of Science. https://web.mit.edu/cortiz/www/Diversity/1975-DoubleBind.pdf.

Merriweather, L. (2012). A need for culturally responsive mentoring in graduate education. *All About Mentoring, 42,* 103–108.

Merriweather, L. (2015). Literacy as dangerous practice: Black women, capital, and discursive formation. In D. Ntiri (Ed.), *Literacy as gendered discourse: Engaging the voices of women in global societies* (pp. 171–184). Information Age Publishing.

Merriweather, L., Howell, C., Sanczyk, A., Douglas, N., Villanueva, K., & Casey, S. (in press). Lifting the veil: Toward the development of culturally liberative STEM faculty doctoral mentors. In S. Linder, C. Lee, & K. High (Eds.), *Handbook of STEM faculty development.* Information Age Publishing.

Merriweather, L., & Howell, C. (in press). On seeing academics who are Black and woman: Understanding the Ontological We. In B. Turner Kelly & S. Fries-Britt, *Building mentorship networks to support Black women: A guide to succeeding in the academy.* Routledge.

Merriweather, L. (2019, January). *Racialized gendered literacy: A racial realist reading of museum space of the African American female* [Paper]. Feminists and feminisms in museums and art galleries: International knowledge exchange and engagement with common research issues SSHRC Connections Workshop, Lisbon, Portugal.

Milner, H. R. (2004). African American graduate students' experiences: A critical analysis of recent research. In D. Cleveland (Ed.), *A long way to go: Conversations about race by African American faculty and graduate students* (pp. 19–31). Peter Lang.

Minnett, J. L., James-Gallaway, A. D., & Owens, D. R. (2019). Help a sista out: Black women doctoral students' use of peer mentorship as an act of resistance. *Mid-Western Educational Researcher, 31*(2), 210–238.

Ong, M., Wright, C., Espinosa, L. L., & Orfield, G. (2011). Inside the double bind: A synthesis of empirical research on undergraduate and graduate women of color in science, technology, engineering, and mathematics. *Harvard Educational Review, 81*(2), 172–208. https://doi.org/10.17763/haer.81.2.t022245n7x4752v2.

Patton, L. (2009). My sister's keeper: A qualitative examination of mentoring experiences among African American women in graduate and professional schools. *The*

Journal of Higher Education, 80(5), 510–537. https://doi.org/10.1080/00221546.2 009.11779030.

Patton, M. Q. (2002). *Qualitative Research and Evaluation Methods* (3rd ed.). Sage.

Peshkin, A. (1988). In search of subjectivity: One's own. *Educational Researcher, 17,* 17–22. https://doi.org/10.2307/1174381.

Pope, E., & Edwards, K. (2016). Curriculum homeplacing as complicated conversation: (re)narrating the mentoring of Black women doctoral students. *Gender and Education, 28*(6), 769–785. http://dx.doi.org/10.1080/09540253.2016.1221898.

Ramos, D., & Yi, V. (2020). Doctoral women of color coping with racism and sexism in the academy. *International Journal of Doctoral Studies, 15*, 135–158. https:// doi.org/10.28945/4508.

Rasheem, R., Alleman, A., Mushonga, D., Anderson, D., & Vakalahi, H. (2018). Mentor-shape: exploring the mentoring relationships of Black women in doctoral programs. *Mentoring & Tutoring: Partnership in Learning, 26*(1), 50–69. https:// doi.org/10.1080/13611267. 2018.1445443.

Randolph, S. M., & Koblinsky, S. A. (2003). Infant mental health in African American families: A sociocultural perspective. In G. Bernal, J. E. Trimble, A. K. Burlew, & F. T. L. Leong (Eds.), *Handbook of Racial and Ethnic Minority Psychology* (pp. 307–326). Sage Publications, Inc.

Robinson, S. J. (2013). Spoke tokenism: Black women talking back about graduate school experiences. *Race Ethnicity and Education, 16*(2), 155–181. https://doi. org/10.1080/ 13613324.2011.645567.

Rudham, G., Beale, T., McCunney, D., & Hilton, A. A. (2020, November 6). Doing the real work in higher education amidst two pandemics. *Diverse Issues in Higher Education*. https://diverseeducation.com/article/195460/.

Shavers, M. C., & Moore III, J. L. (2014). The double-edged sword: Coping and resiliency strategies of African American women enrolled in doctoral programs at predominately White institutions. *Frontiers: A Journal of Women Studies*, *35*(3), 15–38.

Shavers, M. C., & Moore III, J. L. (2019). The perpetual outsider: Voices of Black women pursuing doctoral degrees at predominantly White institutions. *Journal of Multicultural Counseling and Development*, *47*(4), 210–226. https://doi. org/10.1002/jmcd.12154.

Singh, A. A. (2019). *The racial healing handbook: Practical activities to help you challenge privilege, confront systemic racism, and engage in collective healing.* New Harbinger Publications.

Steele, C. M., & Aronson, J. (1995). Stereotype threat and the intellectual test performance of African Americans. *Journal of Personality and Social Psychology, 69*(5), 797–811. https://doi.org/10.1037//0022-3514.69.5.797.

Strauss, A., & Corbin, J. (1998). *Basics of qualitative research: Techniques and procedures for developing grounded theory.* Sage.

Tinto, V. (1975). Dropout from higher education: A theoretical synthesis of recent research. *Review of Educational Research, 45,* 89–125. https://doi. org/10.3102/00346543045001089.

Turner, C. S. V., & Thompson, J. R. (1993). Socializing women doctoral students: Minority and majority experiences. *The Review of Higher Education, 16*(3), 355–370. https://doi.org/10.1353/rhe.1993.0017.

U.S. Department of Education. Institute of Education Sciences, National Center for Education Statistics. (2021). *Survey of earned doctorates: Doctorate recipients from U.S. universities: 2020.* National Science Foundation. https://ncses.nsf.gov/pubs/nsf22300/data-tables.

Wolf-Wendel, L. E. (2016). Foreword. In N. L. Cabrera, J. D. Franklin, & J. S. Watson (Eds.). *Whiteness in higher education: The invisible missing link in diversity and racial analyses* (pp. 11–13). Wiley Periodicals, Inc.

NOTES

1. Racial and ethnic groups are designated by proper nouns and are capitalized. Therefore, we use of "Black" and "White" instead of black and white (colors) when referring to human racial and ethnic groups. Source: *Publication Manual of the American Psychological Association* (2019).

Chapter Six

Don't Let Them Break You Down

Mentoring Young Black Women in College

Torie Weiston-Serdan

In my experience, I have seen many college mentoring programs dedicated to Black men and boys of color. While I was happy that they existed and even happier to support them; in my fifteen years of work as a mentoring expert, I noticed that there were very few mentoring programs on college campuses exclusively established for young Black women and women of color. I understand, firsthand, what it is like to navigate college as a young, Black woman. Even on the most diverse campuses, many of the professors, administrative staff, and student support personnel are white.[1] Given this context, I suspected that my protégé would be exposed to various forms of euro-centrism and white supremacy; and this concerned me deeply.

My protégé was a participant in my Youth Mentoring Action Network (YMAN) organization, a grassroots nonprofit that I founded in 2007 and that operates in the Inland Empire of Southern California, so I knew that she engaged in critical conversations about race, class, gender, sexuality, ability, and other socially conscious topics. She was what some would call "woke,"a term that describes a critical consciousness about a range of social and political issues. Young people often use this term to describe people who are constantly challenging the status quo and who are thinking deeply about issues of equity and justice. Because my protégé was "woke" it might make it harder for her to thrive at a predominately white institution (PWI). Still, my concern for her socioemotional well-being, coupled with my doubts about whether she could thrive within a potentially toxic environment, did not keep me from encouraging her to attend college. For many youth coming from marginalized backgrounds, like my protégé, going to college is what some consider a "catch-22." Upward mobility for Black folks and folks of color often means higher education degrees, but earning those degrees often come at a cost as we struggle to deal with institutions that are often hostile to Black minds, Black bodies, and particularly Black women.

This chapter intentionally centers young Black women because this group is often misunderstood, misread, and marginalized; which has in turn, led to their high rates in race-gendered inequities. In the carceral system, "Black girls [and young women] receive more severe sentences when they enter the juvenile justice system than do members of any other group of [women and] girls [making them] the fastest-growing population in the system" (Crenshaw, 2014, p. 6). In K-12 education, young women and girls of color are disproportionately impacted by disciplinary processes in their schools (Blake et al., 2011), which increase their risk of being pushed into the school-to-prison pipeline (Morris, 2016). Despite these findings, in many ways, girls and women of color continue to be ignored and silenced (Crenshaw, 2014; Hurd & Zimmerman, 2010). It is no surprise then, that very little attention has been paid to Black women in higher education, and even less attention has been given to their mentoring relationships.

Utilizing BFT and Black feminism, this chapter explores the mentoring experiences of young Black women and the unique challenges they face in college. It emphasizes the importance of mentors and the necessity of culturally sustaining mentoring processes in supporting Black womens' entry and completion of college. Culturally sustaining mentoring is a term derived from the concept of culturally sustaining pedagogy. In Ladson-Billings's seminal (1995) work, she describes culturally relevant pedagogy as being a theoretical framework that supports the academic achievement of Black, Indigenous, youth of color (BIYOC) by affirming their cultural identities in academic spaces and ensuring that curriculum was made relevant to them (Ladson-Billings, 1995). The "re-mix" to that original comes from two of her academic proteges who developed the concept of culturally sustaining pedagogy, Django Paris and Samy Alim (Paris, 2012; Paris & Alim, 2014). They posit that the educational experiences of BIYOC must be more than relevant, they must do the work of helping them to sustain their ways of being, particularly as it relates to language, practices, etc. (Paris & Alim, 2014). "The term culturally sustaining requires that our pedagogies be more than responsive of or relevant to the cultural experiences and practices of young people—it requires that they support young people in sustaining the cultural and linguistic competence of their communities while simultaneously offering access to dominant cultural competence" (Paris, p. 95, 2012). I use the term culturally sustaining mentoring in the same way but instead of applying it to traditional educational experiences, I am applying it to mentoring relationships, especially those that happen in community spaces rather than educational ones. Applying this frame to mentoring helps community organizations and others doing youth work understand that these frames are not only useful when situated in academic spaces, but can be powerful tools when leveraged in community. Because YMAN utilized a culturally sustaining mentoring process, particular focus is given to how Black women engage in the mentoring process, how they benefit from it, and what that means for our work as mentoring and youth development scholars and practitioners.

This chapter begins with a brief overview of the literature on mentoring and Black women. This is followed by a discussion of BFT—the epistemological lens used to guide this work. Next, I chronicle the college experiences of two young, Black, queer women in college to demonstrate the transformative power of critical youth mentoring. To conclude, I provide recommendations for engaging in responsive mentoring practices when working with Black women in college.

MENTORING AS (RE)MEMBERING
FOR BLACK WOMEN

In her seminal book on (re)membering, Dillard (2012) describes memory as "an awakening, an opening to the spirit of something that has, until that moment, been asleep within us" (3). This chapter is about (re)membering. It is about (re)calling, decolonizing and documenting the work of Black women who have been engaged in the ancient art and act of mentoring. While it is generally understood that mentoring is a tool useful for positive youth development (DuBois & Karcher, 2014), mentoring is rarely recognized as a cultural tool used for teaching and healing in communities of color and even less so as central to the way in which Black women survive and thrive. In fact, much of the mentoring done by Black women is not necessarily being identified as mentoring. For example, "other-mothering," a concept born out of necessity, is when Black women provide maternal support to children becoming an "other-mother" for them (Case, 1997). Since the violent institution of slavery did not respect family bonds or connections, other-mothering has always been at work in Black communities. Black women in particular, have a history of helping to mother entire communities when there have been a lack of familial resources in underresourced centers. Sistah Circles have served as another community level resource. Sistah Circles are groups of Black women who form to support, network, and resource one another (Neal-Barnett et al., 2011). Both of these processes are often informal and neither of them have been deeply researched as mentoring praxis for Black women. However, both of these processes have a rich tradition and are essential to understand when looking at the way Black women provide informal mentorship.

RACE, GENDER, AND MENTORING RESEARCH

Youth mentoring research has been a monolith—focusing primarily on data sets from formalized programs, and by proxy, the young people attracted to those programs (Herrera et al., 2008; Jucovy and Herrera, 2009). Many of these early briefs and reports took data from one major national program and used the findings to make generalized assumptions about mentoring praxis and outcomes.

The knowledge about mentoring, how it works, who it works for, and why it works stems from these foundational studies and has informed sets of standards and training curricula that continue to guide the field. As a result, the field has been guided by standards and curriculum limited in scope and ability to serve diverse and marginalized youth populations. Black and Afro-Latina researchers have highlighted the importance of naturally occurring and informal mentoring among young people of color (Sanchez et al., 2008; Hurd & Zimmerman, 2010; Hurd et al., 2012).

As more attention is paid to issues of equity and mentoring, the researchers who study it require a more nuanced understanding of what mentoring is and how it operates in the lives of different groups of people. Mentoring has evolved to become a popular and mainstream youth development strategy (DuBois & Karcher, 2014). It is defined as a caring relationship focused on the consistent support and positive development of a child or young adult (Keller, 2010). It has been studied to harness its empirical significance and impact (DuBois et al., 2002; Keller, 2010; Rhodes & DuBois, 2006). Because youth mentoring has a long and relatively positive social history, it is accepted widely and is said to "resonate with mainstream cultural values" (Keller, 2010, p. 23). The fact that youth mentoring resonates so strongly with the mainstream may, in fact, be one of its problems, especially when it comes to the context of marginalized youth. Sanchez et al. (2014) explained that,

> despite evidence that race and ethnicity play an important role in mentoring relationships, there are limited research-based guidelines in the practice field regarding how race/ethnicity should be considered. Some of the essential resources in the field, such as Elements of Effective Practice (MENTOR/ National Mentoring Partnership, 2009), pay little attention to the role of race and ethnicity in mentoring programs (p. 147).

A recent survey of mentoring service programs, asked whether mentors felt equipped to deal with issues of race, gender, class, and sexuality. Interestingly, a large number of the survey respondents reported feeling underprepared (Garringer et al., 2017).

In higher education, biochemistry and molecular biology scholar, Beronda Montgomery, has done extensive research and writing on what mentoring should look like in higher education programs. Montgomery's work, while connected to her area of science research, is also very much tied to her experiences as a Black woman and professor in higher education (Montgomery, 2020). Tying together her scientific studies of plants with her mentoring experiences in higher education, Montgomery (2018) sees mentoring as "environmental stewardship" and highlights six mentoring lessons (p. 2). These lessons include: 1) probing the environment in which protégés do not fare well, 2) recognizing that resources and relocations are sometimes necessary to encourage growth, 3) recognizing that mentors' skills and preparation are essential to the persistence of protégés, 4) seeking external expertise when mentor efforts fail, 5) recognizing mentor failures as caretakers rather than blaming protégés, and 6) refusing to attribute a protégé's lack of growth to a protégé's failure to thrive (Montgomery, 2018). All of these mentoring "lessons from plants" are essential, especially for programs and mentors serving Black women in higher education.

CRITICAL MENTORING

The most viable approach for culturally sustaining mentoring is a practice called *critical mentoring* (Weiston-Serdan, 2017). Critical mentoring is not a new concept. It has been newly defined and newly named, but the practice itself has existed as long as marginalized peoples have. Like many other things, it is a practice that has not been formerly named because the power to name it has been historically unavailable to the marginalized peoples who developed and own the practice (Weiston-Serdan, 2017). Critical mentoring is not confined to a traditional passing down of knowledge; it is a space for mentor and protégé to engage in critical conversations and work collaboratively toward change (Weiston-Serdan, 2017).

In theory, critical mentoring focuses on using essential components of critical frameworks, particularly critical race theory (CRT), to inform crucial elements of mentoring. In this paradigm, mentoring begins with a critical understanding of the context youth exist in and then uses components of CRT and other critical theories to inform mentoring activities. Albright, et al. (2017) conducted a review of mentoring literature with a social justice frame. They examined over fifty empirical articles, and found that justice-oriented mentoring emphasized critical consciousness and social capital. From this, the authors suggest that mentoring done within a social justice framework has the potential to "yield more favorable youth outcomes, and help facilitate social change" (Albright et al., 2017, p. 15).

In practice, critical mentoring is being utilized as a means for the critical interrogation of youth context and as a process for providing culturally sustaining support in relationships that have often been rendered colorblind and postracial in traditional mentoring circles (Weiston-Serdan, 2017; Weiston-Serdan & Daneshzadeh, 2017). Combating the neoliberal approach to mentoring that focuses on individualism and assimilation (Hillman, 2016), critical mentoring challenges the notion of anti-Blackness and centers youth, youth voice, and youth choice in the mentoring relationship (Weiston-Serdan & Daneshzadeh, 2017).

Overall, there has been a general lack of response to race, ethnicity, culture, and class in mentoring in both theory and practice (Sanchez et. al., 2014). While deficit-based approaches to mentoring have traditionally dominated the discourse, scholars and practitioners are starting to find ways to improve the cultural relevance and the lack of action in mentoring practices through critical mentoring (Liang et al., 2013). Weiston-Serdan (2017) acknowledged the need for a critical, justice-oriented approach to mentoring. As an advocate of this approach, she issued a call to action that continues to challenge mentoring and youth development researchers and professionals to not only change the way mentoring is being done with marginalized youth, but to change how it is being studied when it concerns them. The establishment of YMAN is a clear example of current, ongoing efforts to improve mentoring for marginalized groups.

THE YOUTH MENTORING ACTION NETWORK (YMAN)

YMAN is a grassroots nonprofit founded by two queer, women educators in 2007. It was founded in the Inland Empire region of Southern California and focused on providing mentorship opportunities to marginalized youth. The organization's focus on serving marginalized populations meant it was constantly grappling with which youth required the most support and why. While the organizations has served the spectrum of genders, abilities, sexualities, and racial backgrounds, it narrowed its focus on young Black women with a special initiative called Black Girls (EM) Power. The initiative centered young Black women in their own mentoring work and worked to increase the education and mentoring opportunities for Black girls in the region. In its initial conception, YMAN strategically focused on academic outcomes, particularly high school graduation, college attainment, and college retention.

The program found success, boasting a 100 percent high school graduation rate, a 95 percent college acceptance rate, and 100 percent college graduation rate. Serving approximately 182 high school students annually, these percentages were impressive but also very concentrated. These rates were across all demographics served by the program which included Black, Latinx, Queer, low-income and first-generation. The program's success is credited to YMAN's laser focus on serving the holistic needs of students, especially those that pertain to culture and identity, while providing intensive, personalized academic support.

Leading the evidence-based charge on critical mentoring work, YMAN has facilitated powerful discussions with other mentoring and youth development organizations in the field about critical ways to engage in mentoring praxis. YMAN has also developed impactful, replicable programs in support of young people who are often underresourced and marginalized. YMAN's laser focus on closing the resource gap for underserved populations yields the success it does because it is co-created with the very students who will benefit from the initiative. The blend of strategy, innovation, collaboration, and mentorship provides a multipronged development offering that not only meets students where they are, but gives them the opportunity to teach. Those who educate and support young people, learn how to do so in a meaningful, relevant way that will resonate with youth.

YMAN's history of work is the backdrop for the Black Girls (EM) Power program. While always rooted in equity and social justice, Black Girls (EM) Power work centered Black women and girls and their mentoring experiences in particular. The Black Girls (EM) Power program has a dual focus—education and mentoring. Ultimately, the program aims to improve the material conditions of Black women and girls by creating culturally sustaining mentoring and educational programs that enrich them personally and professionally. Like the other work done at YMAN, the Black Girls (EM) Power initiative centers the voices and experiences of Black women and girls in the work and provides opportunities and resources informed by them.

This chapter focuses on two young, Black, queer women that were mentored through the Black Girls (EM) Power program. I unpack their experiences, interactions, and struggles during their college experience in hopes of filling a void within the mentoring research and practice.

BLACK FEMINIST THOUGHT

Utilizing Black Feminist Thought (BFT), this chapter explores how young Black women navigate college. BFT is an epistemology, or way of knowing, that emphasizes the importance of Black women and girls being independent knowledge constructors, purveyors of their own truths and understandings (Hill-Collins, 1989). To that end, this chapter positions Black women and girls as experts in their own work and seeks to grasp their knowledge about the inner workings of mentoring and its impact on their lives. Evans-Winter (2019) speaks to the importance of disrupting the "linear" ways in which qualitative research is done and shared and focuses on centering the voices and lived experiences of Black women and girls in ways that make sense for this group.

What is important to note about BFT is that it centers the voices of Black women. With no apologies or particular need for affirmation, BFT is a space for Black women and girls to explore their ideas, needs, and lived experiences. First, it is a space where Black women talk about oppression in its various forms. BFT does this honestly and without intimidation, speaking truth to power is core to the tradition (Hill-Collins, 2015). Second, BFT takes epistemological space. It does not wait for permission from white supremacist philosophies for its voice (Hill-Collins, 2015). BFT recognizes that validation will not come from traditional philosophies and does not ask for a seat at the table. BFT creates its own table. Third, BFT is committed to justice. Black women's voices are key in the struggle for justice and liberation and BFT carries that mantle by centering Black feminist thinkers in that struggle (Hill-Collins, 2015). Finally, BFT addresses the unique and particular oppression facing Black women as both raced and gendered beings (Hill-Collins, 2015). Long before the term *intersectionality* was popularized, Black Feminist thinkers were exploring the notion that to be both Black and woman denotes a level of oppression often unseen, and therefore, unrecognized.

In an effort to disrupt the eurocentric approach to mentoring and conducting research on mentoring, this chapter creates a space for a Black women researcher to discuss Black women and girls in a way that centers our knowledge, processes and stories around mentoring relationships.

CONTEXT OF STUDY

Black Girls (EM) Power Program

The Black Girls (EM) Power program served seventy young Black women and girls in its first year, twelve of which were college-aged. YMAN the organization in which this program is housed, is a youth-centric organization. Young people drive the work of the organization by working within it as employees, serving on its board of directors and carrying out research projects. This approach is even more tailored in the Black Girls (EM) Power program as Black women informed and co-created the program. A small and intimate program for the college going youth, the program connected participants with Black women in professional positions, met with participants biweekly, and provided scholarship support for each participant as well. Each mentoring meeting and biweekly check-in was planned in collaboration with participants and included professional job talks, wellness and self-esteem workshops, resume writing, hair braiding workshops, and more. Before launching the program, YMAN spent one full year learning from Black women and girls. Asking them to participate in focus groups, pilot events, and building relationships with the community in intentional ways. The first step to co-creating, that year not only provided significant data, but helped to earn the trust of the population YMAN was attempting to serve via the program. YMAN made special invitations to two young Black women who stood out in that year and hired them to work alongside them in the creation of the Black Girls (EM) Power program. This meant that each of them was able to examine the data with us, make recommendations about what each program should look like, help design the program and organize and lead events for the program. By partnering with the community centered in the programming, the purpose was twofold: to ensure the community had voice power and choice when it came to their own services and to provide the platform and resources the community needed to do their own work. Young people, particularly young Black women thrived utilizing this model and process.

Each participant in the college-aged portion of the program had already been in the general YMAN program. They were not handpicked in any special way, there were no specific criteria by which they were chosen for the program. This detail is important to note as many higher education mentoring programs and even community-based pipeline programs have basic grade point average requirements, application processes, and interviews to participate. Whether knowingly or unknowingly, these processes either invite or disinvite certain students, and these programs are often filled with middle class youth whose parents have middle class sensibilities and who understand these processes.

For YMAN, a critical and justice-oriented framework meant intentionally working with youth who might not otherwise seek out the resources and opportunities being provided. Of the twelve college-aged youth participating, three were attending local community colleges, five were attending local state colleges and universities, two attended local private colleges, and two were enrolled in out-of-state private universities. Most of the students had scholarships in some form, as the program staff at YMAN worked with them on college application and college scholarship opportunities. Half of the participants had taken out loans in some form to help finance their education and were working a part-time or full-time job to help pay the cost of college tuition. Two of the college-aged youth were employed by YMAN to

help facilitate the programming. They were responsible for organizing program events, reaching out to participants regularly to keep communication
open between them and program leads, and serving as ambassadors during
program meetings and decision-making processes. Those two young women
were Ebony and Aaliyah.

PARTICIPANTS

Ebony

Ebony, born to Jamaican immigrants, was a young high school student. She
graduated early in her seventeenth year and earned a full scholarship to a
prestigious New England university as a science major. This university, a
PWI, is an elite, private research university. Ebony's parents owned a small
insurance agency and were raising two girls only three years apart. Ebony's
sister Shanice was in the high school version of the program. Ebony maintained a 4.0 GPA throughout high school, was involved in high school clubs,
and took advanced placement courses. Equally artist and scientist, she wrote
about the physics of sound for her college essay and impressed the university
admissions representatives in an online interview. Her acceptance to this
elite institution was an important milestone for her coming of age process
as it would be the first time she would be far away from her parents and her
home. For Ebony, this distance would also prove important as she identified
as queer and needed space to mature and develop in the ways that made most
sense to her. At the time, she was not "out of the closet" to her family and
felt she would have the freedom to be herself in a city where she did not
know anyone.

Aaliyah

Aaliyah lived with her grandmother all through high school. She was an only
child and both of her parents were in the entertainment field and spent most
of their time on the road traveling, so Aaliyah lived with her grandmother
for the stability that it offered. Aaliyah was a reluctant academic, she earned
mostly Cs throughout high school and did not like the notion of school at all.
However, Aaliyah was a naturally talented musician and worked hard in the
piano and music appreciation classes at school. One of her mentors taught
those classes and worked closely with Aaliyah to help her hone her musical
skills. Between Aaliyah's junior and senior year of high school, she participated in a summer college program at a local public university that inspired
her to attend college. She was accepted into that same university as a music

major and earned a full ride scholarship through Michael Jordan's WINGS program. Aaliyah, very comfortable in her identity as a queer girl, was happy to stay close to home and connected to family.

COLLECTION OF NARRATIVES

Both Ebony and Aaliyah's narratives were captured utilizing various processes. I utilized interviews, observations, and text exchanges. The data was collected over the course of a year during the Black Girls (EM) Power programming. Observations were made as they interacted, spoke and engaged in the programming. Informal interviews happened in biweekly mentoring meetings when I was able to check in with each of them. Formal interviews were conducted at the beginning, middle and end of the program year. I also kept text message exchanges that were related to the study as data and evidence.

Only formal interview data was collected in a linear way. All other forms of data collection happened as the mentoring relationship and program progressed throughout the year. Both Ebony and Aaliyah were actively involved in shaping the data. Their awareness of and participation in the study meant they were intentional in sharing as they wanted others to be able to understand their lived experiences.

CRITICAL MENTORSHIP OF TWO YOUNG, BLACK, QUEER WOMEN IN COLLEGE

Mentoring Relationship

As a mentor to both Ebony and Aaliyah, I was challenged at every level. My own background as a queer, Black woman was pivotal to my ability to support each of these young women. They expressed seeing me as a model, they saw my life as something they desired to have for themselves. My professional qualities and skillset were important to them as well, but they were heavily impacted by the idea that they could see their future selves happy and thriving as queer, Black women too. In addition, our shared identities as Black women was a key component of our connection and mentoring relationship. Both in individual meetings, as well as joint meetings, we often discussed the particular ways in which our Blackness and woman-ness impacted how we were perceived, what we had access to, and how we showed up in academic and professional spaces.

My experiences, as both an academic and professional, were also critical to the mentoring relationship. Both protégés viewed me as someone who had successfully navigated higher education, so successfully that I had earned a PhD. Equally important was my experience navigating professional spaces, networking, and building a social enterprise. Each of them leaned on my various expertise in vastly different ways, but the capital these experiences provided were essential to the mentoring process. My mentoring relationships with each of these young women were long-term. I had been engaged in a mentoring relationship with Aaliyah since her freshman year of high school. I mentored Ebony starting in her junior year in high school. It is more than fair to say that we had established trust and open communication. These young women are still my protégés; I speak to each of them on a regular basis and still provide ongoing support. I have mentored Aaliyah for over 6 years and still actively work with her, supporting her budding music career and helping her to learn the ins and outs of running a business. I have been mentoring Ebony for over seven years now and recently helped her to navigate graduate school applications as she applies to literature programs. She wants to be a writer and culture critic now. Each of these young women faced different obstacles along their college path, some that would prove to be detrimental to college retainment, but none that impacted our mentoring relationships.

EBONY'S COLLEGE EXPERIENCE

Ebony eagerly began her first year of college. She was excited to begin, excited to explore New England, and excited to begin her academic career. She jumped in headlong, taking advanced science courses, participating in research field trips outside of classes, and applying for research travel programs. Our biweekly sessions were often about her lack of sleep, her classmates' antics, and how she was adjusting to college life outside of the state. As Ebony's first year continued, she began to experience a number of challenges. Ebony disliked the competitive nature of the science degree programs at her elite research university. She expected a level of camaraderie in the program but, instead, found a lack of community among her colleagues, and she often felt disconnected. She complained that many of the students were often comparing scores and grades, and she did not feel comfortable doing the same. She was thriving in her classes, but did so studying independently and had very little success finding a study group with which to work.

In addition to the competitive nature of her program, Ebony was also continuing to wrestle with her queerness and gender identity. She began a relationship that year and that led her to begin exploring who she was in terms of her gender identity. This exploration was not only complicated on a personal level, but began to create complications with her professors and her college advisor. As her physical appearance began to change and became more center-of-masculine, her professors and advisor misgendered her. Ebony was still thriving academically, so on the surface, her freshman year seemed to be going well, but Ebony was beginning to rethink her degree program all together. She felt she had abandoned the part of her that was an artist and that her classes were generally unfulfilling. She began exploring other degree program options and looking for job opportunities that might support her in finding her path.

AALIYAH'S COLLEGE EXPERIENCES

Aaliyah was also excited about starting her first year of college. She was not the eager academic, but she was a social butterfly, and she was excited about the opportunity to study what she loved—music. Aaliyah hit institutional barriers almost immediately. She received very little advice as to what to take in terms of classes. Her schedule was almost dictated to her, and she felt very limited in terms of the classes she could take. As a music major, she was very disappointed with the degree program options at her school. Her music classes were primarily taught by white professors and did not give Aaliyah the comprehensive music education she was looking for. Prior to even graduating high school, Aaliyah had vast experience as a music engineer and producer. She had participated in and even facilitated a music mentoring program for high school students. She spent two months becoming Apple certified in Logic music software. Aaliyah had written music, released music professionally, and performed in venues. Her college music classes disappointed and failed to stimulate her since she already had vast experiences as a musician. When she asked her advisor about access to campus studios and music engineering classes, she was steered away from them. Aaliyah had a hard time keeping up academically. She was smart, yes, but was disinterested in her classes and failed to fully engage.

By the end of her first semester in college, Aaliyah wanted to drop out. She was convinced that her career in music would be made via experience in the field, not in the classroom. She did not feel connected to her university at all and felt the guidance and degree program were lacking. Even in the midst of a music degree program, Aaliyah would leave her dorm to work in her father's Los Angeles music studio every night. This nightly studio work was proving to be much more fulfilling to Aaliyah than her degree program. While Aaliyah was disappointed by her coursework and by her experiences with professors, she also had a negative experience with another music student who made a racially insensitive statement, using instruments, in a common music student area. Aaliyah reported this incident to the appropriate personnel, but received very little support or advocacy and this caused her to feel even more like an outsider on her campus. She ended her final semester of college taking classes online during the COVID-19 quarantine. Already feeling disconnected, COVID-19 exacerbated Aaliyah's issue with school. She dropped out of college after completing her first year.

CRITICAL MENTORING IN ACTION

As mentor, my primary role for both of these young women was to provide love, support, and resources. As suggested earlier in this chapter, I utilized a critical and culturally sustaining mentoring approach which meant my role was to ensure that each of these young women were affirmed and had the tools they needed to sustain their own identities and cultural tools while still learning to navigate the spaces and processes of the dominant culture. I was meant to nurture them, affirm their brilliance and help them extend their networks in ways that would be useful for them. I was also focused on ensuring that they were supported in their various forms of resistance. If they identified opportunities to challenge these systems my purpose was to support them in thinking through that process and also supporting them as they took action. The mentoring process for each of these young women, while rooted in some specific strategies, varied depending on their individual needs during the course of their college experience. Ebony needed academic guidance, a focus on what degree programs would offer her, some help exploring possible career paths. She was becoming stronger in her identity and required a level of encouragement in support of her identity development. Aaliyah was talented in terms of her music, but had trouble finding the information and experiences she needed in college. My primary role was to help her make an important decision about whether or not to remain in higher education, to help her understand what her alternative options were, and to support her as she processed what she thought was failure. Each young person, even though one was more academically inclined, had similar experiences in that they both lacked a sense of belonging on their respective campuses. Each struggled to find a community, a space that made sense to them and for them. Neither of them had a Black female mentor they could access on their campus and depended heavily on their mentoring relationship with me to garner the support that they required. In addition, the long-term relationship we had built gave them a sense of stability as they worked through the uncertainty of college. Each of them needed to feel anchored and our biweekly meetings provided that for each of them.

Ultimately, Ebony ended up shifting from a science major to an English major. She took more time working on her undergraduate degree, but she found the right path for her and my job was to support her in that. Aaliyah ultimately decided that college was not right for her or the career she wanted. This decision was difficult enough to make without having to navigate my expectations or disappointment. My role as a mentor was to provide support without conditions.

LESSONS LEARNED

Connecting to BFT

Central to our mentoring relationship was shared identity. As Black women we all saw ourselves as connected and we all understood our relationship to the Black Feminist tradition. In some ways it was explicit, as we processed our experiences together, in other ways it was unspoken because our shared experiences made naming it unnecessary. We understood though, as a collective that our mentoring relationship was a reflection of age old Black Feminist thought and processes. In the same way that BFT is an unapologetic space for Black women, so too was our mentoring relationship. We were free to be us, we normalized individual liberation and gave ourselves permission to exist.

Each of my proteges experienced various forms of oppression on their perspective campuses. Our mentoring relationship created a space for them to unpack that oppression and to learn to navigate and resist it. Being rooted in the BFT tradition meant that it was our constant work to grapple with the oppression that we faced. Within the context of mentoring, it meant that many of our mentoring meeting discussions would be focused on identifying oppression and learning how to make sense of how it impacted their daily lives on campus.

However, while this oppression as being processed, each of my proteges were actively encouraged to utilize their voices, their ways of being, their knowing both on and off campus. I actively encouraged them to see themselves as intellectual beings and as creators of knowledge and challenged them as often as possible to leverage this on campus and in classroom spaces. Actively citing BFT as an example, I encouraged Ebony, through her writing and Aaliyah, through her music, to see themselves as creators of new ways of thinking and being. I encouraged them to extend beyond the ideas posited by their predominately white institutions and to value their own cultural production.

As suggested in the concept of critical mentoring, mentoring is not passive. As BFT centers resistance to oppression, I also encouraged my proteges to resist the active oppression they were experiencing on campus. Many of our biweekly meetings included active brainstorming sessions on ow to best address some of the challenges they were having within these oppressive institutions. Often, much of the resistance included rest. Armed with an understanding that these institutions would not go anywhere quickly, I often cautioned them that some of their resistance to oppression needed to include radical rest, caring for themselves, loving themselves, and giving themselves space to heal.

Finally, we often discussed the intersectionality of the oppression they were experiencing. Especially as each of them were in fields of study that often centered white men, they had to recognize that their positions as both Black and woman would present constant challenges for them. In Ebony's case, her initial science major was full of white male students and faculty who likely doubted her ability as a scientist because she was a woman and her general intellect and ability because she was Black. For Aaliyah, her field of study did not center Black music and when Black music was discussed, typically centered Black men. In this way her experiences as a musician were erased and the history of Black and woman musicianship missing from her education as a model of what was possible.

The four basic aspects of BFT were always at the forefront of our mentoring work and much of what we all learned as a result came from centering a BFT process.

As each of these young women navigated higher education and as I worked to advocate for them and provide them with guidance and resources, some essential mentoring lessons emerged.

ACADEMIC GUIDANCE

Mentors providing academic guidance without actual support means very little. Since I had experience navigating higher education institutions, I was able to provide my proteges with a lot of advice about where to access resources on campus, what to consider as they chose a degree program, and what kind of exploratory classes to take. But all of this advice could have also been provided by an advisor or college counselor. The key component to my academic guidance was the relationships we had established and the support they both knew I was aiming to provide. My guidance stemmed from their needs, their wants, and their desires for themselves, not in checking a box or improving my diversity data. Because fully supporting them was my purpose, my academic guidance was ancillary to my caring. Higher education mentoring programs that are designed with academic outcomes in mind and that focus on improving data will fail if they do not genuinely support and care for protégés.

WELLNESS

Mentors must continually consider emotional wellness. Emotional wellness was a topic we discussed often. The stress that accompanies earning a higher education degree is well documented. Some students fare better than others, but Black women and girls have unique challenges because they must navigate these institutions as both raced and gendered beings. The toll that the daily stress of school takes on students is only one aspect of what these young people have to deal with. If those providing mentoring and guidance are not thoughtful and intentional about centering emotional wellness, young Black women may see success as only working and often lose sight of the regular healing and trauma repair that is necessary as a marginalized identity navigating white supremacist institutions. All too often individuals and institutions alike depend on the labor of Black women. In addition, part of the work of Black women has been to provide rest and respite for other sisters in our care. Being intentional about suggesting rest, play, joy, therapy, physical exercise, and good nutrition can make the difference between surviving and thriving for protégés.

CAPITAL

As experienced professionals, extending our social capital can make all of the difference for young Black women navigating higher education spaces. I worked tirelessly to extend my social capital to each of my proteges. Understanding that networks are essential to navigating new spaces and to being successful in them, I leveraged my relationships with individuals within and adjacent to their institutions to connect them with additional support. While these connections looked different for each of my proteges, I made a concerted effort to link them with people in my network who could help them to access internships, special research and study opportunities, and any connection that would help them to reach their personal, academic and professional goals. Many of their white counterparts had existing networks and came into higher education with these networks available to them. As a mentor, it was my job to ensure that my protégés had access to the same and that they knew how to utilize this capital to its fullest potential. Ensuring that my protégés had every opportunity possible to fulfill their academic and professional dreams was the goal. Networks are an essential part of that.

DEMYSTIFYING HIGHER EDUCATION

Demystifying processes rooted in class and whiteness help young Black women to understand that they belong in these institutions and that their processes and lived experiences are of equal value to their peers. A significant part of the mentoring work I had to do with my proteges was supporting them as they navigated white supremacy. Both whiteness and class are at play on college campuses and too often they present obstacles for students without many of us even knowing that they do. Sometimes, these obstacles are simple processes put in place to streamline entry; in other cases, these processes are intentionally used as a "weeding out" to ensure only certain students have access. Either way, a lot of my responsibility as a mentor was to demystify these processes as often as possible to ensure that my proteges understood their purpose and how to navigate them. Advising my students to meet with their professors during office hours even if they did not feel the need to do so was an example of this. I encouraged my students to show professors that they had a good work ethic, that they were interested in the subject matter, and that they were open to taking extra time to meet their professor. It is a formality, but it is one of those hidden processes that often elude first-generation college students. This demystification process also served an important role in building up self-esteem. It let my protégés know that there was nothing particularly special or outstanding about their white peers; they just knew how to play the game and navigate these hidden expectations.

UNCONDITIONAL SUPPORT

Mentors need to provide unconditional support despite each protégé's individual processes. One of the most important lessons learned was that my role as a mentor was to provide unconditional love and support. While each of my proteges walked their own path and navigated college in their own ways, they needed to know that I was there and that I would be there whether they changed majors, failed classes, or even dropped out of school. Mentoring is not about the mentor's expected outcomes, it is about what the young person wants and needs for themselves and for their future selves.

RECOMMENDATIONS FOR CULTURALLY RESPONSIVE MENTORING

Black women and girls are undercounted and often underresourced in higher education programs. On one end, statistics say we are the most educated group in America, those data lead people to believe we are thriving in these institutions and do not require help or additional support. While those data may speak to general degree attainment, much of the data within higher education institutions themselves tell a different story. Black women tend to be underrepresented in degree programs and underfunded in them as well. The fact that Black women are among the most educated people in American speaks to their resilience and hard work. In addition, our willingness to help one another, to mentor one another, and to provide networks of support for one another also speaks to our resilience. Mentoring is part of our effort to decolonize, clear spaces, and open doors for one another. We learn how to survive, even thrive, with the help of a sister here, and other-mother there. We conquer and then we throw a lifeline to the next one and next one after her. Our mentoring is not often formalized; it does not follow the rules; it is not to be strategically written down for a formal process; it is the way we speak life into one another; it is in the way we understand the joint struggle, nod in agreement when we see one another, and do the invisible labor of supporting one another even when we too are struggling to fight. Each of these young women learned lessons in their college process, each of them gained an understanding of how these institutions work and how they must work to survive them. Each of these young women also learned how to mentor, how to provide support for other young Black women and girls working trying to fulfill a promise to themselves and to their ancestors.

One of the central principles of critical mentoring is that mentors must engage in a critical interrogation of context. While we too often focus on "fixing" young Black women, we miss that they exist in and must navigate toxic contexts. Contexts in which white supremacy, racism, ableism, homo-antagonism, cisgender preference, and more are allowed to run rampant. These issues impact the material conditions of folks from marginalized identities daily. The goal of good mentoring—that is critical, justice-oriented mentoring—is not to help young people adapt to these toxic contexts but to partner with and provide resources to aid them in the process of resisting and changing those conditions. To that end, the recommendations provided below are less about mentoring directly and more about improving the higher education context for young Black women.

1. Black women and girls need to see themselves on campus. They need to see themselves at every level of the university, in every department, in the lecture halls, etc. This representation is especially important for mentoring. While cross-race matches are possible and can be effective, the importance of connecting with someone who looks like you is necessary. Hire Black women and include their mentoring labor as part of their service toward tenure or provide them with flexible schedules to accommodate the time they will spend supporting the young Black women within the institution.

2. Listen to Black women as they voice their wants and needs. Good mentors do a lot of listening and great mentors do more than listen, they act in partnership with their protégé. As Black women and girls talk about what they need from you and from the institution, listen and listen with the intention to act. Understand what can be done to support them as they navigate and affirm their daily lived experiences. Nothing is more harmful and frustrating than having a protégé's experience minimized, especially in institutions where they may feel disconnected already. Mentors must listen, affirm, and be ready to act in partnership.

3. Become a co-conspirator. Co-conspirators, different from allies, move beyond knowledge of the ism's and become willing to act on this knowledge by putting "their privilege on the line for somebody else" (CSPAN, 2019). The latter part of the listening strategy is about being prepared to act. Mentors must become good co-conspirators. Mentors must collaborate and partner with their proteges to make change in the institution. This action means making what privilege you have available to protect Black women and girls and to leverage the power and respect that privilege brings you to hold space for Black women and girls to speak in spaces where they may not otherwise have been able to speak. This process is about mentoring in action and knowing that mentoring will not be a passive passing down of advice but a relational and collaborative endeavor.

Meeting the needs of young Black women in higher education spaces is about partnership, community, connection, and support. That is what every student on campus requires to thrive. If higher education institutions can effectively recruit and retain Black women and girls by creating healthy campus cultures, providing critical mentoring, and centering the lived experiences of Black women, they will have improved the institution for every single student.

REFERENCES

Blake, J., Butler, B. R., Lewis, C. & Darensbourg, A. (2011). Unmasking the inequitable discipline experiences of urban Black girls: Implications for urban educational stakeholders. The Urban Review, *43*, 90–106.

Blake, J. J., & Epstein, R. (2019). *Listening to Black Women and Girls: Lived Experiences of Adultification Bias*. Retrieved from https://genderjusticeandopportunity. georgetown.edu/wp-content/uploads/2020/06/Listening-to-Black-Women-and-Girls.pdf.

C-SPAN. (2019, March 19). We want to do more than survive: An interview with Bettina Love [Video]. CSPAN https://www.c-span.org/video/?458837-1/ we-survive.

Case, K. I. (1997). African American Othermothering in the Urban Elementary School. *The Urban Review, 29*, 25–39.

Coles, A. (2011). *The role of mentoring in college access and success.* Pathways to College Network, Institute for Higher Education Policy.

Crenshaw, K. (2014). Black girls matter: Pushed out, overpoliced and undeprotected. *African American Policy Forum*, 1–53. Retrieved from http://www.aapf. org/recent/2014/12/coming-soon-blackgirlsmatter-pushed-out-overpoliced-and-underprotected.

Dillard, C. B. (2011). Learning to remember the things we've learned to forget: Endarkened feminisms and the scared nature of research. In N. K. Denzin & M. D. Giardina (Eds), *Qualitative inquiry and global crisis* (pp. 226–243). Taylor & Francis Group.

Dubois, D. L., Holloway, B. E., Valentine, J. C., & Cooper, H. (2002). Effectiveness of mentoring programs for youth: A meta-analytic review. *American Journal of Community Psychology*, *30*(2), 157–197.

Dubois, D. L., & Karcher, M. J. (2014). Youth mentoring in contemporary perspective. In D. L. Dubois & M. J. Karcher (Eds.), *Handbook of youth mentoring* (2nd ed., pp. 3–13). Sage Publications.

Evans-Winters, V. (2019). *Black feminism in qualitative inquiry*. Routledge.

Garringer, M., Kupersmidt, J., Rhodes, J. E., Stelter, R., & Tai, T. (2015). *Elements of effective practice for mentoring.* http://www.mentoring.org/new-site/wp-content/ uploads/2016/01/Final_Elements_Publication_Fourth.pdf.

Garringer, M., McQuillin, S., & McDaniel, H. (2017). *Examining youth mentoring services across America: Findings from the 2016 national mentoring program survey*. Mentor The National Mentoring Partnership.

Herrera, C., Grossman, B., McMaken, J., Cooney, S., & Kauh, T. (2008). *High school students as mentors: Findings from the Big Brothers Big Sisters school-based mentoring impact study*.

Collins, P. H. (1989). The social construction of Black Feminist Thought. *Signs*, *14*(4), 745–773.

Collins, P. H. (2015). No guarantees: Symposium on Black Feminist Thought. *Ethnic and Racial Studies*, *38*(13).

Hillman, M. (2016). Youth mentorship as neoliberal subject formation. *International Journal of Child, Youth and Family Studies, 7*(3/4), 364–380.

Hurd, N., & Zimmerman, M. (2010). Natural mentors, mental health, and risk behaviors: A longitudinal analysis of African American adolescents transitioning into adulthood. *American Journal of Community Psychology, 46*(1–2), 36–48. https://doi.org/10.1007/ s10464-010-9325-x.

Hurd, N. M., Sánchez, B., Zimmerman, M. A., & Caldwell, C. H. (2012). Natural mentors, racial identity, and educational attainment among African American adolescents: Exploring pathways to success. *Child Development, 83*(4), 1196–1212. https://doi.org/10.1111/j.1467-8624.2012.01769.x.

Jucovy, L., & Herrera, C. (2009). High school mentors in brief: Findings from the Big Brothers Big Sisters school-based mentoring impact study.

Keller, T. E. (2010). Youth mentoring: Theoretical and methodological issues. In T. D. Allen & L. T. Eby (Eds.), *The Blackwell Handbook of Mentoring: A Multiple Perspectives Approach handbook of mentoring: A multiple perspectives approach* (pp. 23–47). Blackwell Publishing.

Ladson-Billings, G. (1995). But that's just good teaching! the case for culturally relevant pedagogy. *Theory Into Practice, 34*(3), 159–165.

Liang, B., Spencer, R., West, J., & Rappaport, N. (2013). Expanding the reach of youth mentoring: Partnering with youth for personal growth and social change. *Journal of Adolescence, 36*(2), 257–267.

Montgomery, B. L. (2018). From deficits to possibilities. *Public Philosophy Journal, 1*(1), 1–12.

Morris, M. W. (2016). *Pushout: The criminalization of Black girls in schools.*

Neal-Barnett, A., Stadulis, R., Murray, M., Payne, M. R., Thomas, A., & Salley, B. B. (2011) Sister Circles as a Culturally Relevant Intervention for Anxious African American Women. *Clin Psychol (New York), 18*(3), 266–273.

Paris, D. (2012). Culturally sustaining pedagogy: A needed change in stance, terminology, and practice. *Educational Researcher, 41*(3), 93–97.

Paris, D., & Alim, H. S. (2014). What are we seeking to sustain through culturally sustaining pedagogy? A loving critique forward. *Harvard Educational Review, 84*(1). https://doi.org/10.17763/haer.84.1.982l873k2ht16m77.

Rhodes, J. E., & Dubois, D. L. (2006). Understanding and facilitating the youth mentoring movement. *Social Policy Report, 20*(3), 3–19.

Sánchez, B., Esparza, P., & Colón, Y. (2008). Natural mentoring under the microscope: An investigation of mentoring relationships and Latino adolescents' academic performance. *Journal of Community Psychology, 36*(4), 468–482. https://doi.org/10.1002/jcop.20250.

Sanchez, B., Colon-Torres, Y., Feuer, R., Roundfield, K., & Berardi, L. (2014). Race, ethnicity, and culture in mentoring relationships. In *Handbook of youth mentoring* (Second, pp. 145–158). Sage Publications.

Weiston-Serdan, T. (2017). *Critical mentoring: A practical guide.* Stylus.

Weiston-Serdan, T. & Daneshzadeh, A. (2017). You can't call that mentoring: The fallacy of mentoring in Obama's My Brother's Keeper. In L. J. Walker, F. E. Brooks,

& R. B. Goings (Eds.), *How the Obama presidency changed the political landscape* (pp. 122–141). Praeger.

NOTES

1. While APA guidelines recommend that all racial identities be capitalized, this chapter has intentionally chosen to lowercase white as a way to dismantle anti-Blackness in academia.

Chapter Seven

The Rage of Whiteness and the Hindrance of Black Mentorship

A Critical Race Perspective

Cleveland Hayes and Issac M. Carter

COLONIZATION, HIGHER EDUCATION, AND BLACK STUDENT SUCCESS

Due to the incestuous nature of colonialism, there is no U.S. institution void of oppressive toxins, the education system included. Knowledge production has always been of a binding domain to the colonizer, for knowledge is power. Thus, limiting or preventing the *Other* (nonwhite people) from reading, writing, and any form of education was the original colonial design (Hayes, 2006). Over the last two centuries, the colonizer has slightly acquiesced to the restrictions (the removal of colored only signs on restrooms and drinking fountains) due to landmark legal decisions such as *Brown v. Board of Education* (1954). Nevertheless, access, matriculation, and completion rates among people of color are enduring problems within all levels of education, especially when these statistical trends are disaggregated by race and gender.

Higher education, as a representation of the hegemonic structures and intuitions imported from colonial design, is also a colonization site. Black male students' racialized and stereotypical treatment in the academy by faculty, staff, and their peers is evident in classrooms, campuses, and communities (Gaskins, 2006). The access and "achievement gaps" for Black college students, when compared to their White[1] counterparts, are often explained away by disparities in wealth and preparation or deficit models, emphasizing a lack

153

of ability (Harper & Davis, 2012). Relatedly, diverse faculty and staff hiring initiatives are scrutinized, and questions of qualifications are among the core concerns. Student initiatives are treated similarly, and notions of deficits stigmatize students of color. Consequently, too often campus climate issues receive compassionate and sympathetic window dressing without any intent to dismantle the systems generating continued opportunity gaps.

SETTING THE STAGE

In this chapter, in an autoethnographic performance, we share our experience of the two years we tried to get the Men of Color Initiative (MOCI) instituted. Building on the counterstorytelling and personal narrative traditions, we bring various data sources to help us construct the counterstories share in the subsequent performances. These sources include our respective personal and professional experiences, along with literature from outside the formal educational research realm (Solorzano & Yosso, 2002). To present our performative autoethnography (Park-Fuller, 2000), we use the device of a narrated collegial conversation of Issac and Cleveland meeting for lunch and spending the afternoon in conversation about their work as mentors trying to establish a retention initiative for Black and Brown students at a Latino Serving Institution[2] (LSI). There was resistance from several stakeholders on the campus, including Black, Latin@, and White members of the campus community due to the entrenchment of Whiteness within the campus citizenry. It is essential to understand that Whiteness is protected (stereotypes, status quo, rage, etc.) by People of Color and White people. Each of the performative autoethnography vignettes observes tension between dominant forces and critical race counternarratives opposing the White colonial hegemony of the institution.

In employing autoethnographic performance, we call on the work of Park-Fuller (2000). Park-Fuller defines autobiographical narrative performances and specifically states:

> the performer often speaks about acts of social transgression. In doing so, the telling of the story itself becomes a transgressive act—a revealing of what has been kept hidden, speaking of what has been silenced—an act of reverse discourse that struggles with the (re) conceptions borne in the air of dominant politics. (p. 26)

An autoethnographic performance is when the authors, in the case of this chapter, opens up a space of resistance between the individual (auto-) and the collective (-ethno-) where the writing (-graphy) of singularity cannot be foreclosed. The authors simultaneously appeal to and debunk the cultural traditions that help to redefine. Through the performative writing of our personal stories, we choose to literally give our bodies to the narrative both internally and externally by connecting the inquiry, process, and product (Buzard, 2003; Danzak, Gunther, & Cole, 2021; Juárez & Hayes, 2010; Upshaw, 2016).

Dialogues on issues of race, class, gender, sexual orientation, and the "Other" are informed and insulated by dominant hegemonic forms of discourse that frame and articulate the experiences of people of color in a limited, deficit framework. Building on the counterstorytelling tradition, we bring a variety of data sources to help us construct the counterstories share in the following narrative. These sources include our respective personal and professional experiences, along with literature from outside the formal educational research realm (Solórzano & Yosso, 2002). Counterstorytelling in this chapter, deconstructs dominant racial stereotypes and myths and offers a critique by normalizing and centering voices of color. Though our project reveals the essence of White rage (Anderson, 2016) as a hindrance to Black mentorship, our examination also offers further insight into the conflicts and opportunities for a coalition between Black and Latin@ populations in higher education.

REVIEW OF RELEVANT LITERATURE

The U.S. Department of Education, National Center for Education Statistics projects that enrollment of U.S. residents in postsecondary institutions will increase slightly between 2016 and 2028. In 2028, it is projected that 52 percent of U.S. residents enrolled in postsecondary institutions will be White, 21 percent will be Hispanic, 15 percent will be Black. According to the Hispanic Association of Colleges and Universities 2020 Fact Sheet, by 2029, Hispanic enrollment in higher education is estimated to be 4.2 million or nearly 25 percent of all students. The shifting demographics mirror society at large. The Latin@ population nationally has displaced Black as the largest minority in the United States.

Due to these changing demographics, political, social, linguistic, and economic conflicts have emerged, and stereotypes created by White supremacy culture are enforced. For instance, some Latin@ seek to adopt a stance that they are more closely in approximation to Whites than Blacks, and often the Black response to this anti-Blackness is an antiimmigration stance, especially in the job market. There is growing body of research detailing colorism and the racialized anxiety within the Latin@ community (Aja et al., 2014; Andrade, 2020; Lacoya, 2019). The racial tensions create a complex relationship in higher education. According to Literte (2011), although Black and

Latin@ face similar obstacles, preparation access, retention, and graduation, White and Black often perceive the increase in Latin@ students as threatening. Black and Latin@ professors and students often find themselves at odds over limited resourses such as office space, department and program chair positions, program titles, funding priorities and more. The complexities of identity, sociopolitical-economic landscape, and the color caste system affirm that CRT is necessary in explaining social inequities, convergence and contradictions.

Critical Race Theory

CRT is essential in situating Black males' voices and their racialized experiences. This theoretical framework allows engagement with the complexities of individual, institutional, and structural racism and the variance in power in proximity to certain social and cultural identities. Critical race theory in education is defined as a theoretical and heuristic framework that challenges the ways race and racism oppress, marginalize, invalidate, and decenter the experiences of people of color.

CRT is conceived as a social justice project that works toward the liberatory potential of schooling (Freire, 1970, 1973; hooks, 1994). Further, CRT assumes that race and racism are hegemonic and normalized through a variety of individual and institutional practices (Adams, 2002; Crenshaw et al., 1996; Ladson-Billings, 1995; Grzanka & Grzanka, 2014). As a methodology, Solórzano and Yosso (2002) assert that there are five general characteristics foundational to CRT methodology: (a) promotes understanding of the intersectionality of race and racism with other forms of oppression based on the subordination of Other identities; (b) challenges and deconstructs dominant ideological frameworks; (c) seeks transformation in our society and is expressed through commitment to social justice; (d) centers experiential knowledge and counternarratives of people of color in opposition to neutrality and claims of objectivity; and (e) draws from transdisciplinary and critical theories such as Black feminist thought, women's studies, cultural studies, and queer studies.

Whiteness

To further understand the critical methodologies of CRT, comprehending the pervasive nature of Whiteness in the Academy is a priority. Often dialogues pertaining to inequity on college campuses engage in strategic moves to innocence, where overrepresented White individuals in leadership attempt to alleviate their feelings of responsibility or guilt associated with racial inequity without giving up power and privilege (Hayes & Juárez, 2009). In other words, Whites have built antiracist understandings that construct the racist as always someone else, the problem residing elsewhere in other Whites. In some instances, this alibi is a White subject's former self. In a recuperative logic, "whiteness is able to bifurcate whites into 'good' and 'bad' subjects, sometimes within the same body or person during public race dialogue" (Leonardo 2009, p. 151). Critical scholars Ladson-Billings and Tate (1995) assert that Whiteness is not a culture but a hierarchical and hegemonic racial, social concept privileging and empowering those aligned with the normalcy of White supremacy.

STUDY CONTEXT

University of Inland

The University of Inland (pseudonym) is a small private Latino Serving Institution (LSI) located in the country's western region, nestled in a sub-urban city. Over 75 percent of Inland residents are White, while more than half of the students attending the University are students of color, with Black students comprising 6 percent of the diverse student population. The Latin@ students comprise make up 40 percent of the population at the University. However, the graduation rates for male subgroups are much lower than their female-identified counterparts. The data at the University of Inland does not disaggregate by gender and race. Still, at the time of this conversation, there was a dialogue on campus and up to the president of the United States attempting to address the lack of representation of Black and Brown males in higher education.

The Actors and Their Positionalities

The concept of positionality acknowledges the complex and relational roles of race, class, gender, and other socially constructed identities (Hayes, 2020; Milner, 2007). Positionalities may include identity—race, class, and sexuality—and the personal experience of research and research training. For example, telling minoritized stories is one of the premises of this research. The idea that individuals construct an understanding of the world and perceive themselves to occupy a particular location within the reality they construe is one of the critical premises of positionality. Positionality for our argument is a significant aspect of how we have interacted together in the development of this chapter as well as how we individually interacted with the characters in the composite story. We offer our positionalities as our identities are instrumental in accurately capturing our truth, and our performative autoethnographic counternarratives (Milner, 2007; Zarate & Conchas, 2010).

Similar to Ladson-Billings (1994), we write this chapter in multiple voices and from multiple positions. Cleveland self-identifies as a Black radical cis-queer scholar from the South. He researches the lived experiences of Black male teachers. His research, more recently, has been centered on the experiences of Latin@ male teachers. Cleveland employs various methodologies such as autoethnographic and critical race counternarratives to draw on the personal and professional experiences of Black teachers from the past to provide a historical and contemporary analysis of how their experiences and pedagogical practices can inform the present. By examining the transformative pedagogy of past teachers, Cleveland juxtaposes their experiences with contemporary teachers to celebrate our education successes with students, especially those labeled "hard to teach." Cleveland spent ten years at the University of Inland, the research site.

Issac self-identifies as a Black feminist male, cisgender from the Midwest, with close Southern roots. He grew up in a very Afrocentric home and community that emphasized service and support of each other. Issac is a critical educator, organizer, musician, and scholar. He has led many initiatives throughout his career to broaden educational access and success for Black male students. Issac possesses over twenty-five years of higher education experience, and his scholarship incorporates Critical Race Theory, intersectionality, and decolonizing methodologies. His pedagogical praxis connects knowledge production with social justice action. The goal of his education and training is to support individuals in becoming engaged citizens and radical subjects. Issac spent five years at the University of Inland.

How to Read This Chapter

Methodologically as we constructed this chapter, the stories happen at different points in the development of the MOCI. This chapter is a mixture of composite story, counternarratives, counterstories, personal narratives in order for Issac and I to tell our stories. In this chapter, we are concerned with the ongoing failure of predominantly White institutions (PWIs) to provide the necessary support for the success of men of color in general and Black men more specifically. The frustration level is even higher when the institution has a label as a Minority Serving Institution (MSI) and receives millions of dollars to provide support to students. Using a CRT methodology of counterstorytelling (Solorzano & Yosso, 2002), we create a performance of actual events in the spirit of a composite story/critical race counternarrative/critical race counterstory to highlight our experiences. Our experiences and perspectives explore the continued White rage students and faculty of color face at PWIs. Our experiences are what Juárez and Hayes (2014) term academic lynching.

Academic lynching, while not physically violent like the lynchings of the nineteenth and early twentieth century, are attacks centered on race and shrouded in postracial discourse. It represents a type of emotional lynching—attempting to kill the personality, soul, and spirit of people of color. Harris (1995) describes the "valorization of [w]hiteness as treasured property in a society structured on racial caste," arguing that Whiteness confers tangible and economically valuable benefits and is consequently highly guarded as a valued possession. Fasching-Varner (2009) argues that people vested in Whiteness experience a high sense of value, demonstrating a certain absoluteness. However, those who have and continue to benefit from Whiteness feel threatened by those who challenge this highly guarded commodity—subsequently, those who challenge and question become victims of academic lynching.

As our narratives will illustrate, later in the chapter, when faculty and senior university leadership saw this MOCI as a threat to this valued commodity of Whiteness, Issac and Cleveland were academically lynched. Of course, academic lynching can take many forms. However, its foundation centers on eliminating any threat to the White social order, just as Jim Crow era lynching worked to eliminate any physical threat to Whiteness as perceived by Whites. As Fasching-Varner (2009) argues, Whites often attempt to determine what kind of Blackness is acceptable to them, how that Blackness should be expressed, and how one gets disqualified or excluded from Whiteness through one's Blackness—tame versions of "Blackness ONLY allowed!" reminiscent of Jim Crow segregation (Hayes, 2015; 2016).

The chapter will demonstrate how the privileging of White interests, values, experiences, and beliefs and the Whiteness of the university is underscored by the emergence of conversations about and calls for equitable access and success for Black male students at Inland. The primary focus of our chapter is to demonstrate how we created a space where men of color could gather and face the challenges of Whiteness and White supremacy at the university in a space somewhat free from Whiteness. Contending that Whiteness serves as a hidden referent structuring interaction and activity within university spaces, the authors draw on narratives to highlight and analyze moments to show how Whiteness obstructs the establishment of the MOCI.

The Setting: The Need to Get Started

The performance for this chapter starts at the Provost Retreat. The provost and chief academic officer bring together every year their direct reports, which include the deans of the four colleges (education, arts and sciences, business and public administration, and the law school), associate provost and chief diversity officer; vice president for student affairs; the dean of students; the athletic director; the faculty senate president and vice president and other university management council members. Cleveland was at the retreat because, at the time, he was the faculty senate vice president and Issac was there because of the work he was doing on campus around the MOCI, which was a retreat agenda item. The theme for the retreat was Inland becoming a Hispanic Servicing Institution (HSI), and as an organization, how should the University respond and one of those responses was the MOCI.

This chapter begins with a dialogical script that recounts the associate provost and chief diversity officer at the University of Inland (pseudonym) conversation around the change in the student population at the institution. The following occurs after a presentation at the Provost retreat.

Associate Provost: The University of Inland has become a Hispanic Serving Institution. What this means for those of you in the room is that the University has reached a threshold of students that self-identify as Latino. With this designation, the University can receive federal dollars to increase the academic achievement of these students. As a university, we should be thinking about how to embrace this identity and what it means for so many of our students.

Black Faculty Member: Well, what does this mean for the Black and White students?

Cleveland: Having the label as an LSI does not change anything for the Black and White students at Inland. I think this is an excellent opportunity for the University (all students regardless of how they identify). In reality, Inland is a Hispanic-enrolling institution. There are not services for Latino students on this campus. This is interest convergence at its worst.

White School Administrator: What is interest convergence? And you talking over our heads, Cleveland, doesn't make the situation any better. Also, what do you mean by "Hispanic-enrolling"?

Cleveland: Well, that is not my intent to talk over anyone's head. But interest convergence is when Whiteness benefits at the expense of people of color. One of critical race theory's (CRT) most important topics of the continued discussion revolves around its challenge to dominant ideology or interest convergence. Interest convergence is the notion that judicial progress towards racial equality is only pursued when it converges with the interests of Whites. That is to say that no matter the injustices of slavery, segregation, exclusion, miseducation, and violence faced by nonwhites (or non-Europeans) in U.S society, policy change only comes when policymakers recognize that such relief will in some way accommodate the interest of Whites. CRT argues that traditional claims toward colorblindness, meritocracy, and race-neutrality act as smokescreens for self-interest, power, privilege, and ultimately the maintenance of Whiteness in the U.S.

Also, I don't use the term "Hispanic" because that is the colonizer's language, and none of my Latin@ academic hermanos y hermanas use that term. But I will use the term "Hispanic" in the context of what happens on this campus as it relates to the success of our Black and Brown students. "Hispanic-enrolling" basically means this campus takes these students' money and doesn't provide any space for them to be Black and Latin@. As a matter of fact, the Black males and the Latino students have the worst graduation rates of any population on campus.

This campus does not have a Latin@ Studies major or minor. There is no African American history or Latin American history course offered in the history department. So, yes, Inland is a Hispanic-enrolling institution! This campus just wants these students for the tuition dollars they pay.

I think we should model ourselves as a University after HBCUs and strive to become the premier Latin@ Serving Institution in the country.

Dean of Students: Well, what about the other students? This may appear that we are favoring one group over the other.

Issac: If I can echo what Cleveland is saying. Establishing a MOCI not only helps the Latin@ male students but also the Black males on this campus. Here are some stats showing the lack of success that many Black men experience on this campus. So, looking at the data from the cohort of Black men that started four years ago, less than 10 percent of them graduated in 6 years. And when you look at the data for Black men over the last 4 or 5 years, only a total of fourteen graduated, and you all are worried about if it is going to offend someone. You all should be offended and upset by the number of Black men that are not graduating, but they are good enough to be on your football team.

The meeting continued with other conversations about Inland's change in demographics. These conversations included every excuse as to why Inland could not modify its strategic planning to really pursue the goal of becoming a LSI in the tradition of HBCUs. One good thing, so we (the authors of this chapter) thought, that came out of the meeting was the start of a MOCI that the associate provost wanted us to lead. The intent of the MOCI was to increase the retention of Black and Brown male students, which included mentorship for those two populations. We think we were selected to lead this initiative because of our identities as Black men, as well as the fact that we were the most outspoken about the need for change on the campus as it related to men of color in general, and Black men specifically.

PROCESSING THE PROVOST RETREAT:
THE BIRTH OF THE MOCI

Background and the Intersectional Nature of the MOCI

The program design used evidence-based data to improve the graduation rates and retention of men of color across all sectors of the university. The work of increasing the graduation rates of men of color could not be done by student affairs alone; therefore, it was important to have partnerships and collaborative efforts with academic affairs, student affairs, and administration. The MOCI was a way of engaging male students of color with issues of social justice, race, racism, and educational equity (Leonardo, 2009; Stovall, 2004), threaded through their academic and other forms of learning. The intersections between the research, the participants and mentors were an enactment of critical race praxis coming together to produce transformative pedagogies; a pedagogy that bridges theoretical concepts of oppression, liberation, and schooling success from freedom to everyday practice (Hayes, 2020).

Intermission: The Meeting after the Meeting

After the Provost Retreat, Issac got together for lunch to process the meeting and begin to strategize together as we knew he had an uphill battle to get the MOCI launched. We met in the late spring semester 2015 and the Provost Retreat had happened early January 2015. We waited so long to meet because we needed to get official notification that the MOCI was going to happen and between my teaching schedule and his schedule this was the first time we could meet. But the trauma from the meeting a couple of months later was still very fresh and plus I had taken copious notes from the retreat to help guide our conversation. During our time together, we attempted to work through the logistics of establishing the MOCI.

This meeting occurred at one of our favorite places, off-campus. We chose to meet off-campus because we did not want anyone from the university to overhear our conversation, specifically as it concerned why we believed an initiative like MOCI was needed in the first place. Having this type of collegial conversation helped us to process the often daily microaggressions we were subjected to in our fight for social justice and inclusion at Inland.

Issac: What did you think about the Provost Retreat?

Cleveland: As usual, these meetings are a waste of my time. I sit in meetings, and they [administration and faculty] talk about student retention and success and how much they love our students. They begin the colonization of their minds as freshmen, and when the students realize it, it is too late they are either graduating or leaving the University.

Issac: I kept thinking to myself, why are they so focused on the wrong things? There is a national trend that Black men are not graduating from college at the same rates as their Black female counterparts, and they are worried about if this is going to offend someone.

Cleveland: See, this is the problem I have with White liberals. White liberals have a strong and longstanding commitment to ethnic integration. They believe in the general ideas of civil rights and justice for people of color. Many believe in general antidiscriminatory principles, that "color makes no difference," "people are people," and "there should be one human race." Importantly, White liberal forms of helping have historically helped the helper more than those being helped.

Issac: There is a deep-seated distrust of the institution of policing and the legal system, due to a lack of social, political and economic accountability. Such as the horrific and unconscionable injustices against Rodney King, Emmet Till, and Medgar Evers. Acquittals paid leaves, retirements with pensions, and reassignments to neighboring districts have not garnered the trust of the Black community. One reason there are movements like *#BlackLivesMatter is* because universities, and other institutions, refuse to see the humanity of the Black lives. This applies to our campus and our treatment as Black faculty.

Issac: I am telling you; I don't see how you have lasted at this place for as long as you have. I would have been gone a long time ago.

Cleveland: I stay because of the students. We work at a university that is 52 percent students of color. However, at Inland, there are only three Black male professors. Those three Black professors are me, Professor Stevens (pseud-onym), and Professor Napoleon (pseudonym) who are faculty members in the College of Arts and Science. However, in the College of Education, I am the only Black male professor and the first Black male in the history of the College to earn tenure and promotion to associate professor. I also stay because of the MOCI and that we are trying to get a Black male student mentorship program off the ground. It is important and exciting work. So, yes, to answer your question about co-chairing the MOCI with you, it is an honor and a privilege.

Issac: Good, there are several things that we will need to do to get started, like developing the curriculum and developing the theoretical framework.

Intermission: Tasks after the Lunch

The lunch ended with me and Issac planning our next course of action. During the lunch meeting, regarding the potentiality of the Men of Color initiative, we identified a few key strategic priorities necessary to successfully launch the MOCI. Some of these key strategic priorities were: (1) the incorporation of curricular components in the general education, (2) buy-in from board members of color, and support from faculty of color, and (3) the establishment of an advisory committee that included faculty and staff from student affairs. The members of the advisory council as a start would include: the chief diversity officer, the associate dean for retention, the director of institutional research, the director of housing and residential life, and the director of multicultural services and the advisory committee was set. Each of the members had key responsibilities that we needed to launch the MOCI. However, we knew these priorities were complicated due to the lack of representational equity at every level of the institutions, though each is essential to influence equitable decision making and resource education.

We left the meeting with tasks that needed to be completed and people we needed to engage with. This plan was a university effort and we needed faculty support which we both knew was going to be difficult because while the student body population was 50 percent BIPOC, the faculty was 82 percent White and White liberals who often make diversity initiatives very difficult to move forward. As the chapter progresses, we problematize Whiteness as a hinderer to developing a Black male student mentoring program.

THE CONVERSATIONS: NO SUPPORT FROM FACULTY

Professor Stevens (the senior Black professor of Color at the University of Inland)

Professor Stevens: I would like to talk with you about your plans for the MOCI, especially the 1-unit course that cohorts all men of color into single-sex cohorts.

Issac: Sure! What do you think about our idea of creating a safe space for our men of color?

Professor Stevens: I don't like the idea at all; we need to help these kids to learn how to integrate into the system, not isolate them from it.

Issac: The students have already told us that they feel isolated in the classroom and on campus and what efforts are you trying to do to create a space where the Black male students specifically and the men of color in general feel included on this campus.

Professor Stevens: Into the campus, it feels like the men of color initiative is trying to separate them from the other parts of the campus where they would, may feel better engaged.

Issac: You are basing this off what? There is plenty of empirical evidence in higher education, where I have spent twenty-five years working in Student Affairs in order to make that claim, were affinity groups along gender and race increase student achievement. To me, it sounds like you are more interested in our kids accepting second class citizenship, rather than empowering them and having the University take responsibility for their well-being.

General Education

One of our strategies was to create a one-unit course that counted for a required general education elective for men of color. This one-unit course would cultivate students' cultural knowledge and leadership skills by examining a variety of social, political, cultural and leadership theories. Specially, this course would cultivate a space for students to dialogue and support each other's multiplicity of identities to affirm self and others. Topics to be explored are the processes of social and cultural construction; differential statuses and roles; socialization and stereotypes; institutional power and conflict; economics and labor; health and wellness.

This course would be the mentoring part of the MOCI. To get the course approved, we were required to present at the General Education Committee. During their presentation, there was one faculty member who expressed concern over their proposal. Professor Pallid is a member of the undergraduate academic programs (UGAP). The committee approves all new courses at the undergraduate level. Professor Pallid was not the only one who voiced her nonsupport for this one-unit course, but we singled her out for the purpose of this chapter because she consistently professed how liberal she is and her concern for student success. Bottom line, she was upset because she was excluded from the planning (Hayes & Juárez, 2009).

Professor Pallid (assistant professor, cisgender woman, who identifies as a White and Queer)

Professor Pallid: I like the idea and plans you have, but I have concerns about the 1-unit course.

Cleveland: What are your concerns?

Professor Pallid: I think it is dangerous to have a course with only men of color.

Cleveland: What do you mean, "dangerous?"

Professor Pallid: Well, for example, I went to a program once where a group of women resident assistants were trying to teach men about the effects of catcalling on women. To support their claim, they [the women in the group] created a simulation where men were surrounded by women and began doing "catcalls" to simulate the harassment that women experience daily.

Cleveland: I don't understand your example, it doesn't have anything to do with our one-unit class we are proposing.

Professor Pallid: Yes, it does, it shows how when men are placed together, they are going to ignore women.

Issac: The fact that you are saying that groups of men of color are dangerous proves why we need the one-unit course. Men of color should have one space on campus where they are not stereotyped and targeted.

INTERMISSION: THE PURPOSE OF THE VIGNETTES

Issac and I have laid out the complexities that male students of color in general and Black male students specifically face when it comes to providing mentorship in meaningful ways. We started the chapter laying some foundation. This foundation was the Provost Retreat where the provost and the associate provost recognized there was a problem with Black and Latin@ men and graduation rates. Out of the Provost Retreat, the MOCI was born. The associate provost then asked Issac and I to lead the efforts. We then developed a mission and vision and strategic goals. One of the strategic goals was the development of this one-credit course where we could be deliberate with the mentorship that many of these young men needed that they were not getting informally. We recognized that there needed to be a formal process established, the one-credit leadership course.

However, I had spent ten years at Inland, and I knew the challenges that this program was going to present and the battle we were going to face because of the entrenchment of Whiteness at Inland. The provost had us jump through hoop after hoop to get this course approved. However, the point of the above vignettes is to show the difficulties that we faced trying to develop something that would benefit male students of color. We make the argument that there cannot be mentorship on a campus if there is no mentoring program and the MOCI never became because of White rage.

The Ways Whiteness Manifests as a Hindrance to Black Students' Success

The premise of this chapter was to lay out a context where we interrogate Whiteness and Black success, interconnected concepts that have a long historical context (Anderson, 2016; Ortiz, 2018). As we conclude, we follow Camper's (1994) format to explain how Whiteness is a hindrance to Black student success. This discussion below not only applies to White folks but also people of color who are complicit in maintaining Whiteness and White supremacy. Like Dr. Martin Luther King Jr. (1958), among others, we have found that the problem of Whiteness is not a problem of evil, but a problem of good! For example, Professor Pallid does not think she is doing anything bad and would consider herself a good White person. So, this chapter is not about folks who clearly do not want Black students to succeed as they are verbal about it, and we know where they stand. This chapter is for folks like Professor Stevens who is complicit in maintain White supremacy and Professor Pallid who is maintaining Whiteness through "good."

For Folks Complicit in Maintaining Whiteness and White Supremacy

These folks proudly pointed to traditions of inclusion and democratic education in our university, college, and department while the syllabi, teaching practices, and curricula of our programs are indicative of education that is by, for, and about White people; these folks casually dismiss questions about why we have no courses on the history of Black, American Indian, or Latino education. Whiteness hinders Black male student success.

These folks put together diversity hiring committees and then ask us if we know any potential applicants of color who teach *just science* or *just literacy methods*, but not all that political business because they get tired of "*White people bashing.*" Yes, they "want very much to have a Black person in [their] department as long as that person thinks and acts like [them], shares [their] values and beliefs, [and] is in no way different" (hooks, 1989, p. 113; emphasis in the original). Nothing new here, Whites have been deciding for the past 500 years what kind and how much "diversity" they will tolerate. Whiteness hinders Black male student success.

These folks are offended, saying we are moving too fast in bringing a scholar from another university to talk about White racism and on being Black in historically White institutions. Certainly, White people are regularly offended—as demonstrated by *an appalling oppressive and bloody history known all over the world* (Baldwin, 1985). Yet, after 244 years of slavery, 100 years of lynching, and 40 odd years of formal civil rights, we are moving too fast for whom? And why is it White people always decide how fast we should be going? Whiteness hinders Black male student success.

These folks are afraid your feelings will be hurt if we keep talking about the pernicious and pervasive educational and other social inequities still running along U.S. society's enduring colorline. They don't like being continually *beat over the head* with White racism and feeling guilty about being White. Whiteness hinders Black male student success.

These folks indignantly protest, saying we have made so much progress (just look at the city's Black and Latino leaders, you say) charging us with *reverse racism*, when we tell them that we deliberately and explicitly put the perspectives and experiences of minoritized peoples at the center of our research, teaching, and everything else we do in the university, in the community, and at home. We have made progress because "[a] few well-screened, well-scrubbed Negroes have been allowed into previously all-White classrooms" (Lomax, 1962 as cited in Westin, 1964, p. 22). Indeed, it is not progress until these folks admit that it was them who stabbed me in the first place. Whiteness hinders Black male student success.

Finally, these folks are astonished, even indignant and outraged, that we dared to question and criticize their many efforts and awards for helping the *Other* and working in the *Other's* neighborhoods and schools. Why should they have to keep proving that they are one of the [good] Whites who *get it*? When *well-behaved* (Juárez et al., 2008) people of color do indeed serve as a marvelous means of helping White people to fulfill "*the obligation of nobility to the ignoble*" (DuBois, 1920 as cited in Lewis, 1995, p. 554).

> So long, then, as humble Black folk, voluble with thanks, receive barrels of old clothes from lordly and generous [w]hites, there is much mental peace and moral satisfaction. But when the Black man begins to dispute the [w]hite man's title to certain alleged bequests of the Fathers in wage and position, authority and training; and when his attitude toward charity is sullen anger rather than humble jollity; when he insists on his human right to swagger and swear and waste—then the spell is suddenly broken, and the philanthropist is ready to believe that Negroes are impudent, that the South is right, and that Japan wants to fight America. (DuBois, 1920 as cited in Lewis, 1995, p. 455)

WHITE RAGE AND NO MOCI AT INLAND

We do not apologize for our blunt indictment of Whiteness at the University of Inland or any institution of higher learning for that matter. After all, racism is a correlate of democracy (Cone, 2004; Delgado, 1999). When the immensity and depth of the physical and psychological violence continually committed against minoritized peoples is considered, the majority of it by *nice* people, we realize that the cost in suffering and lost lives are too high to keep tiptoeing around Whiteness and trying to appease and placate White people with velvet gloves. We also realize that

[w]hat societies really, ideally, want is a citizenry which will simply obey the rules of society. If a society succeeds in this, that society is about to perish. The obligation of anyone who thinks of [herself or] himself as responsible is to examine society and try to change it and to fight it—at no matter what risk. This is the only hope society has. This is the only way societies change. (Baldwin, 1962/1963, as cited in Wise, 2005, p. 61)

Hence, for democratic education for Black and Brown students to be realized, we must work together to abolish, rather than ignore, Whiteness.

Issac and I spent two years trying to get this MOCI up and running. Keep in mind, this experience is an example of Black tax where faculty of color spend hours above and beyond their duties to create a space where students of color and in this case males of color can reach their full academic achievement. In my time at Inland, I have seen programs that were grounded in Whiteness move through the approval process in weeks.

RECOMMENDATIONS FOR CULTURALLY RESPONSIVE MENTORING

Checklists and theories to practice only serve one purpose and that purpose is to put the blame and responsibility of success on the persons who did not create the situation. For us this creates anger and resentment. We used the term Black tax, and the burden of this work falls under the category of Black tax. Extra burden on faculty and staff of color to create programs for Black and Brown student success and when the checklist fails, or the items are written in ways so others cannot hear then the academic lynching begins. So, against our better judgement and drawing on our experiential knowledge of checklist development and execution, here are some implications. The exhaustion of anger, fear, being accused of being argumentative, deliberate silence and withdrawal from stress-inducing situations takes away from the work that needs to be done to improve the educational experiences of students of color in general, and Black and Brown male students in particular. Again, this is why we struggle with checklist in cases we have illustrated in this chapter, but here are things that could be considered.

These recommendations are what university administrators should consider when developing mentoring programs for the success of Black and Brown students. Informally, mentoring can be one way of providing help but that places the burden on faculty members like Issac and myself which is not sustainable. Our thoughts below encompass outline recommendation for university leadership.

1. Do not allow the faculty member of color who are complicit in Whiteness to circumvent decisions after they are made.
2. Be intentional about building a base for activism at the workplace even for folks whose privilege does not require them to think about having to be an activist. Create a culture of co-conspirators and not allies (Love, 2019; Smith, 2007).
3. Take a survey of your inner circle. Be sure you are intentional about understanding the racially hostile experiences of Black faculty and students. Consider what you understand—and don't—and how your narrative of Black faculty and students may be incomplete as a result.
4. Lastly, higher education leaders, if they are committed to providing support to Black and Brown students to paraphrase Malcolm X here—If you, as a higher education leader, are not posing a very serious threat to Whiteness and saying something that seriously threatens Whiteness, regardless of the phenotype, then you are probably not saying much anyway; Whiteness only responds to threats deemed serious enough to challenge its dominance and at the end, the students are not getting the support they need especially at universities that have in their mission statement to provide support for all students but ignore Black and Brown students and block programs that support those students.

PARTING THOUGHTS

Narratives, storytelling, and counterstories can be transformative and empowering for educators and those who write policy. According to Fernandez (2002), these methods can make public what many already know but have not spoken out loud and, through the use of critical methodologies incorporating grounded analysis, the perspectives and voices of a community come alive (Zarate & Conchas, 2010). Lastly, using experiential knowledge, challenging dominant ideologies, and acknowledging the centrality of race in American life will help us uncover that which has been covered. Our hope is to use these cultural experiences as a means to challenge, transform, and help Black and Brown male students navigate the oppressive nature of American education (Fernandez, 2002; Irizarry & Nieto, 2010).

REFERENCES

Aja, A. A., Bustillo, D., & Wallace, A. (2014). Countering "Anti-Blackness" Through "Black-Brown" Alliances and Inter-Group Coalitions: Policy Proposals to "Break the Silence." *Journal of Intergroup Relations*, *35*(2), 58–57.

Anderson, C. (2016). *White rage: The unspoken truth of our racial divide.* Bloomsbury.

Andrade, S. (2020). Y yo no me voy a quedar callado: Anti-Blackness and Colorism in Miam's Latinx Community. *Harvard Political Review, 51*(3), 37–39.

Baldwin, J. (1985). *The price of a ticket: Collected non-fiction 1948–1985.* St. Martin's Press.

Baldwin, J. (1962/1993). *The fire next time.* Vintage Books.

Buzard, J. (2003). On auto-ethnographic authority. *The Yale Journal of Criticism, 16*(1), 61–61+. http://ulib.iupui.edu/cgibin/proxy.pl?url=http://search.proquest.com. proxy.ulib.uits.iu.edu/scholarly-journals/on-auto-ethnographic-authority/ docview/205459331/se-2?accountid=7398.

Camper, C. (1994). To White feminists. *Canadian Woman Studies, 14*(2), 40.

Crenshaw, K., Gotanda, N., Peller, G., & Thomas, K. (Eds.). (1996). *Critical race theory: The key writings that formed the movement.* The New Press.

Cone, J. H. (2004). *Martin and Malcolm and America: A dream or a nightmare.* Orbis Books.

Danzak, R. L., Gunther, C. B., & Cole, M. A. (2021). Someone else's child: A co-constructed, performance autoethnography of adoption from three perspectives. *The Qualitative Report, 26*(3), 637–651.

Delgado, R. (1999). *When equality ends: Stories about race and resistance.* Westview Press.

Fernandez, L. (2002). Telling stories about school: Using critical race theory and Latino critical theories to document Latina/Latino education and resistance. *Qualitative Inquiry, 8*(1), 45–65.

Freire, P. (1970). *Pedagogy of the oppressed.* Bloomsbury.

Freire, P. (1973). *Education for critical consciousness.* Seabury Press.

Fasching-Varner, K. J. (2009). No! the team ain't alright! The institutional and individual problematic of race. *Social Identities, 15*(6), 811–829. https://doi. org/10.1080/13504630903372520.

Gaskins, A. (2006). Putting the color in Colorado: On being Black and teaching ethnic studies at the University of Colorado-Boulder. In C. E. Stanley, (Ed.). *Faculty of color: Teaching in predominantly White college and universities* (pp. 139–152). Bolton: Anker Publishing Company.

Grzanka, P., & Grzanka, P. R. (Eds.). (2014). *Intersectionality.* Routledge.

Harper, S. R., & Davis, C. (2012). They (Don't) care about education: A counternar-rative on Black male students' responses to inequitable schooling. *The Journal of Educational Foundations, 26*(1), 103–120.

Harris, C. (1995). Whiteness as property. In K. Crenshaw, N. Gotanda, G. Peller, & K. Thomas (Eds.). *Critical race theory: The key writings that formed the movement* (pp. 276–291). The New Press.

Hayes, C. (2020). The salience of Black mentors on the teaching praxis of Latino Male Teachers. *Race, Ethnicity and Education, 23*(3), 413–431.

Hayes, C. (2016). Unhooking from whiteness and the assault that follows: Lynching in the academy. In N. D. Hartlep & C. Hayes (Eds.). *Unhooking from whiteness: Resisting the esprit de corps* (pp. 13–26). Sense Publishers.

Hayes, C. (2015). You wonder why I am an angry Black man. In K. J. Fasching-Varner, N. D. Hartlep, L. L. Martin, C. Hayes, R. W. Mitchell, & C. A Allen-Mitchell, (Eds.). *Assaults on communities of color: Exploring the realities of race-based violence* (pp. 10–25). Rowman and Littlefield.

Hayes, C., & Juárez, B. G. (2009). You showed your Whiteness: You don't get a good White people medal. *International Journal of Qualitative Studies in Education, 22*(6), 729–744. https://doi.org/10.1080/09518390903333921.

Hayes, C. (2006). *Why we teach: Storying the lives of Black family of Mississippi educators.* [Unpublished dissertation]. Education Culture and Society, University of Utah.

hooks, b. (1994). *Teaching to transgress: Education as the practice of freedom.* Routledge.

hooks, b. (1989). *Talking back: Thinking feminist, thinking Black.* South End Press.

Irizarry, J. G., & Nieto, S. (2010). Latino/a theoretical contributions to educational praxis. In E. G. Murillo, S. A. Villenas, R. T Galvan, J. S. Munoz, C. Martinez & M. Machado-Casas (Eds.), *Handbook of Latinos and education: Theory, research and practice* (pp. 108–123). Routledge.

Juárez, B. G., & Hayes, C. (2010). Social justice is not spoken here: Examining the nexus of knowledge and democratic education. *Power and Education,2(3),* 233–252.

Juárez, B., Smith, D. T., & Hayes, C. (2008). Social justice means just us White people: The diversity paradox in teacher education. *Democracy & Education, 17*(3), 20–25.

King Jr., M. L. (1958). Letter from Birmingham jail. In E. P. J. Corbett & R. J. Connors (Eds.). *Classical rhetoric for the modern student* (4th ed.)(pp. 301–307). Oxford University Press.

Ladson-Billings, G. (1994). *The dream keepers: Successful teachers of African American children.* Jossey-Bass.

Ladson-Billings, G. & Tate, W. (1995). Toward a critical race theory of education. *Teachers College Record, 97,* 47–68.

Literte, P. E. (2011). Competition, conflict, and coalitions: Black-Latino/a relations within institutions of higher education. *The Journal of Negro Education, 80*(4), 477–490.

Lewis, D. L. (1995). *W. E. B. DuBois: A reader.* Henry Holt and Company.

Love, B. (2019). *We want to do more than survive: Abolitionist teaching and the pursuit of educational freedom.* Beacon Press.

Leonardo, Z. (2009). *Race, whiteness and education.* Routledge.

Milner IV, R. H. (2007). Race, culture, and researcher positionality. Working through dangers seen, unseen, and unforeseen. *Educational Researcher, 36*(7), 388–400. https://doi.org/10.3102/0013189X07309471.

Ortiz, P. (2018). *An African American and Latinx history of the United States.* Beacon Press.

Park-Fuller, L. (2000). Performing absence: The staged personal narrative as testimony. *Text and Performance Quarterly, 20,* 20–42.

Smith, C. (2007). *The cost of privilege: Taking on the system of White supremacy and racism.* Camino Press.

Solórzano, D. G., & Yosso, T. J. (2001). Critical race methodology: Counter-storytelling as an analytical framework for education research. *Qualitative Inquiry*, *8*(1), 23–44. https://doi.org/10.1177/107780040200800103.

Stovall, D. (2004). School leader as negotiator: Critical race theory, praxis, and the creation of productive space. *Multicultural Education*, *12*(2), 8–12.

Upshaw, A. (2016). Arias to academia: An academic malpractice suite in three movements. *Qualitative Research Journal*, *16*(3), 263–273.

Westin, A. F. (1964). *Freedom now! The civil-rights struggle in America.* Basic Books.

Wise, T. (2005). *White like me: Reflections on race from a privileged son.* Soft Skull Press.

Zarate, M. E., & Conchas, G. Q. (2010). Contemporary and critical methodological shifts in research on Latino education. In E. G., Murillo Jr., S. A. Villenas, R. T. Galván, J. S. Muñoz, C. Martínez, & M. Machado-Casas (Eds.), *Handbook of Latinos and education: Theory, research and practice* (pp. 90–108). Routledge.

NOTES

1. Racial and ethnic groups are designated by proper nouns and are capitalized. Therefore, we use of "Black" and "White" instead of black and white (colors) when referring to human racial and ethnic groups.

2. In this chapter we use the terms LSI Hispanic Servicing Institution (HSI). When we use HSI, those are usually someone else's words or the Department of Education Language, politically we do not use HSI because that is the Hispanic is a colonizer term. A Hispanic Enrolling Institution is one that just enrolls Latin@ students without providing any real services. Once again HEI is a term that the authors use.

Chapter Eight

Mentoring and Planning Transition for Black Students with Diverse Abilities in Postsecondary Education

Edwin Obilo Achola

Effective mentorship relationships represent an important component of academic, career, and personal success for many students enrolled in postsecondary education (PSE). In its broadest form, mentoring is framed as a formal or informal relational process in which a more knowledgeable person facilitates the growth, maturation, and development of another person with less experience (Booker & Brevard, 2017; Brooms et al., 2021; Coles, 2011). Within PSE settings, such relationships play an important role in academic guidance and social support as well as in recruiting and retaining students from traditionally underrepresented communities. Despite these clear and measurable benefits, many institutions of higher learning struggle to develop effective mentoring relationships, particularly those that benefit Black students with diverse abilities (BSWDA). The increased enrollment rates suggest that these institutions succeed at recruiting BSWDA yet fail to leverage strategies such as mentorship to foster positive campus experiences, higher retention rates, timely graduation, and postcollege success.

In general, evidence suggests that, though access to PSE has increased for individuals with diverse abilities, BSWDA remain underrepresented (Banks, 2014). Many BSWDA in postsecondary institutions face a plethora of barriers, including institutional and personal ones. According to the National Longitudinal Study-2 (NLTS2), Cohort 2 contained 17 percent more young adults with diverse abilities enrolled in PSE than Cohort 1 (in 1987). During the same period, 12 percent more BSWDA enrolled in four-year colleges

(NLTS2, 2005). Unfortunately, many BSWDA experience difficulty accessing disability support services and appropriate accommodations (Banks, 2013). In addition, these students are confronted with institutional barriers, most notably faculty attitudes, lack of awareness, and few support resources (Harper & Kuykendall, 2012; Harris et al., 2016). Some of the barriers, such as lack of awareness, may be linked to students' inadequate secondary to postsecondary transition planning, the stigma of accessing resources, and their lack of college readiness (Abott & Martinez, 2018). Consequently, college degree attainment for BSWDA remains less than half that for European American students with diverse abilities (Wagner et al., 2005).

Researchers such as Stumbo et al. (2011) have asserted that mentorship represents a critical component of a multipronged solution to address these complex barriers. These scholars have noted that students could be identified and mentored in a number of ways, such as when they collaborate on faculty research projects (especially those that have an African American focus or that provide direct contact with children with special needs); join student organizations such as African Americans in Education or the Student Council for Exceptional Children; or obtain work-study positions that give opportunities to teach or aid youth with disabilities (Cartledge et al., 1995).

This chapter aims to do the following: (a) explore the complex identities, assets, and needs of BSWDA; (b) reveal gaps in mainstream mentoring relationships for BSWDA; (c) discuss a multicultural and feminist framework relevant to understanding effective mentoring relationships with BSWDA; and (d) present promising mentorship practices for faculty and staff.

THE (DIS)ABILITIES CONTEXT

In the context of the Americans with Disabilities Act, "disability" is a legal term used to refer to a person who has a physical or mental impairment that substantially limits one or more major life activity (e.g., learning, walking, speaking). This includes people who have a record of such an impairment, and those who do not have a (dis)ability but are regarded as having a (dis)ability. For this chapter, we focus on three broad groups of students with diverse abilities namely; (a) those with significant support needs (b) those with nonapparent diverse abilities and, (c) students who are identified as both gifted and have some form of impairments.

BSWDA, like their peers without disabilities, share the group identity of being in transition, a phase characterized by the onset of new roles and responsibilities in such interconnected life domains as education, employment, and adult living. Evidence shows that BSWDA can be successful in school and prepared for PSE opportunities, especially when learning environments embrace and celebrate their cultural backgrounds and utilize strengths-based perspectives (Trotman et al., 2015); however, these students face a unique set of complexities during adolescence and are deeply affected by events stemming from their marginalized and intersectional attributes, which include varied abilities. This set of complexities can magnify the discrimination and marginalization they might experience, especially for young adults with significant support needs that seriously limits one or more functional capacities, such as mobility, communication, self-care, self-direction, interpersonal skills, work tolerance, and work skills. For many BSWDA with significant support needs, everyday youth experiences related to transitioning from school to postschool life, (dis)ability disclosure, sexuality, and identity development manifest in unique ways as a function of their multiple minoritized identities. For example, students with diverse abilities in college are generally less likely to disclose their disabilities to access necessary supports in PSE (Pearson, 2019). However, BSWDA are even less likely to disclose their disabilities due to competing cultural identities and deficit ideologies that undermine their attempts at self-determination (Banks, 2014). Consequently, compared to their peers from dominant racial communities, BSWDA are more likely to experience difficulty accessing disability support services and appropriate accommodations necessary for college success.

Many of these challenges also apply to youth with hidden or nonapparent disabilities, such as mental health or emotional disorders, specific learning disabilities, attention-deficit/hyperactivity disorder, and attention-deficit disorders. Nonetheless, because such disabilities often have few visual identifiers, they may remain hidden to those interacting with the individual peripherally, thereby reifying the outward social construction of disability. Though having an "invisible" disability might seem like a privilege, students with such disabilities often confront challenges related to the deficit perceptions of their disabilities (Mullins & Preyde, 2013; Olney & Brockelman, 2003). Some students with hidden disabilities choose not to disclose them in order to mitigate stigmatization and, as a result, receive less academic support from their academic institution (Grimes et al., 2017).

In light of the challenges experienced by young adults with disabilities, Congress mandated a transition planning process for all students receiving special education services who have an Individualized Education Program (IEP). This process must begin no later than the first IEP in effect when the child turns 16 years of age. The Individuals with Disability Education Act (2004) provided specific guidelines for transition planning, focusing on identifying and developing goals to facilitate the student's transition from secondary school to postsecondary activities, including employment, PSE, and independent living. The law further mandated that transition planning must be results oriented, individualized, and based on a student's needs, strengths, and interests. In all, the underlying purpose of transition planning for youth with diverse abilities was to prepare students for successful life after secondary school (Cameto et al., 2004).

Though the research literature related to postsecondary transition for African American students remains limited, it is clear that racial differences exist in transition planning (Harris et al., 2016; Landmark & Zhang, 2012). Evidence from the NLTS2 study shows that a smaller percentage of African American students (40.2 percent) had transition goals related to attending a two-or four-year college compared to White[1] students (47.8 percent); however, a larger percentage of African American students (46 percent) had transition goals related to attending a vocational school compared to their White peers (37.4 percent). The NLTS2 data further reveal that, even though more parents of African American students voiced a desire for greater involvement in this process than the parents of White students, far fewer of the parents ultimately participated in the transition planning process (Cameto et al., 2004). These findings are hardly surprising, given that young adults from predominantly nonmainstream ethnic and cultural communities are more likely to receive transition plans that fail to meet compliance requirements and less likely to experience satisfaction with the transition experience (Geenen et al., 2003; Landmark & Zhang, 2012; Rueda et al., 2005; Schuster et al., 2003). As such, these students' opportunity to transition successfully into and through PSE is significantly decreased.

Mentorship for young adults with diverse abilities is considered especially important during times of transition (Powers et al., 2001; U.S. Department of Labor, 2006; Weir, 2004) to ease anxieties, improve social competence, and strengthen the (dis)ability-related skill set and motivation needed for postschool success (Burgstahler, 2008; Stumbo et al., 2008). Additionally, through mentorship, young adults might develop strong cultural identities, self-understanding, an awareness of campus resources, and navigational skills—all of which serve as a buffer against negative experiences (Tovar-Murray et al., 2012). Navigating the academic and social landscape at PSE institutions may be particularly challenging for gifted Black boys with diverse abilities, who are often unaware of cultural offices, offices of disability support services, and academic support offices (Mayes & Moore, 2016). In addition, gifted Black boys with disabilities might be interested in multiple areas of study, which could make it more difficult for them to decide on a career (Greene, 2006); consequently, they may need support in narrowing down their options and planning their specific postsecondary educational pathway.

MULTICULTURAL FEMINIST MENTORING MODEL

Numerous models of mentoring have been proposed in the last couple of years, such as Fassinger's feminist mentoring model and Kram's model; however, concerns remain about how well these traditional mentoring models can be applied to diverse groups of individuals (Benisheck et al., 2004). These concerns center on power dynamics between mentors, who often share privileged identities, and their mentees from marginalized communities, who may have more unique talents and needs than the White male mentees. In addition, many of these models, though informative, are not directly applicable to the context of global learning, in which learners interact with emerging and possibly cross-cultural situations across multiple disciplines (Prasad et al., 2019).

Fassinger's feminist mentoring model (Fassinger, 1997), however, represents a significant development in the conceptualization of mentoring in that it focuses both on the relational component of mentoring and on issues related to power and empowerment. This framework has two central attributes. First, the mentor recognizes the existence of power differences between themselves and the mentee and responds appropriately to mitigate the impact of the power dynamics. Second, the mentor strives to use power as a means to empower the mentee. Ultimately, the mentor and mentee relationship aim to minimize the impact of socially defined power dynamics to achieve the mentee's goals.

In the context of students with diverse abilities, Fassinger's model is unique in that it explicitly identifies diversity as a salient aspect of the mentoring relationship that deserves attention within that relationship. Mentoring attuned to issues of diversity, power, and privilege may be particularly salient to scholars who embody multiple marginalized identities. Fassinger's feminist model of mentoring represents a concerted effort to better understand and place greater value on diversity and power dynamics, even highlighting multicultural issues and respect for cultural differences; however, as Benisheck et al. (2004) argued, it is problematic in one significant respect: It fails to integrate these priorities throughout the model.

The multicultural feminist mentoring model (MFMM) proposed by Benishek et al. (2004) addresses that central weakness of Fassinger's model. The MFMM explicitly infuses multicultural considerations into the mentoring dimensions identified by Fassinger (1998). Specifically, the MFMM proposes that important differences regarding cultural identity, power, and privilege between mentor and mentee should be explicitly identified, explored, and valued. In acknowledging and responding to their differences, the mentors and mentees recognize that full equality in the mentoring relationship is impossible, and the pursuit of this unattainable utopia only serves to create "an atmosphere of denial and oppression" (Benishek et al., 2004, p. 437). This perspective creates opportunities for mutually beneficial hierarchical relationships to occur. Some of the central dimensions of the MFMM approach that are most salient to BSWDA include the following:

- Valuing collaboration between mentor and mentee, integrating self-knowledge with abstract knowledge, and incorporating a political analysis into mentorship (Benishek et al., 2004)
- Recognizing that most mentorships are reciprocal in nature, and thus have implications for both mentor and mentee. Consequently, the MFMM offers a useful theoretical base for developing promising practices for BSWDA.
- Promoting the practice of transparency (an open dialogue about one's thoughts and feelings) to balance personal and political power in relationships with mentees and to provide guidance otherwise unavailable to mentees with underrepresented identities (Benishek et al., 2004; Fassinger, 1997). If not adequately anticipated and managed, power disparities can lead to mentee exploitation, oppressive dynamics, ineffective mentoring, and the perpetuation of unhealthy systemic practices (Arczynski et al., 2019).
- Creating a relationship built on mutuality, which implies mutual empathy, mutual empowerment, mutual caretaking with a healthy degree of reciprocity, equality, respect, authenticity, and role flexibility

The expanded theoretical foundation of the MFMM approach is useful in a number of ways for programs seeking to create mentorship supports for BSWDA. First, the explicit focus on diversity, power, and privilege may encourage an intersectional approach to mentorship, in which mentors are trained to consider the needs of students with multiple minority identities that include varying levels of ability. Furthermore, in this model it is the mentor's responsibility to initiate conversations about multicultural issues (that have implications for the success of the student with a disability). In doing so, mentors gain a more complete understanding of their mentees' talents and needs, which they can use to challenge the status quo (especially regarding ableism) and support mentees as allies. Second, because of its emphasis on transparency, mutuality, reciprocity, and tolerance toward ambiguity, the MFMM model could be used to understand the context of mentor–mentee interactions, whether the mentor and mentee are from similar or vastly different ability backgrounds. Such attributes (e.g., reciprocity) allow both mentors and mentees to share information about lived experiences with disabilities and gain an increased understanding of how the experiences define mentee's needs and strengths. Ultimately, however, the goal of the PSE mentoring programs grounded in the MFMM model is to achieve expected outcomes specific to the BSWDA in light of their unique identities and contexts.

IDENTITIES, ASSETS, AND EXPERIENCES OF BSWDA

Daymond John is a distinguished American entrepreneur of African descent who turned a $40 budget into a $6 billion fashion empire. John is not only a *New York Times* best-selling author but also a pioneer in the fashion industry, an investor on the four-time Emmy Award-winning television series *Shark Tank*, and a highly sought-after motivational speaker. Over the last couple of years, John has supported and invested in many businesses owned by young people of African descent; his primary focus in doing so is on mentoring and nurturing talent within communities of color. John was diagnosed with dyslexia and benefited from numerous educational opportunities in a variety of settings, such as his immediate cultural space at home, his community, and the expanded networks of his workplaces.

Haben Girma, another successful American of African descent (Eritrean), currently works as a human rights lawyer advancing disability justice. Not only is Girma the first Deaf-Blind person to graduate from Harvard Law School, but she has also won the Helen Keller Achievement Award, earned a spot on the *Forbes* 30 Under 30 list, and spoken in a TIME100 Talk. Haben has been recognized and honored by renowned world leaders, including President Bill Clinton, Prime Minister Justin Trudeau, and Chancellor Angela Merkel. Born and raised in the San Francisco Bay Area, Girma greatly benefited from civil rights laws, including the Individuals with Disability Education Act (2004); as a result, she had access to assistive technology and other supports that her elder brother in Eritrea, who is also Deaf-Blind, did not. In addition to her long track record of success in the field of disability rights, Girma has received acclaim for her volunteer work in minoritized communities, such as when she traveled to Mali at age 15 to build a school.

At first glance, these stories clearly portray two remarkable young people of African descent who have disabilities and have been successful in a variety of ways. However, beyond these commonalities lie the diverse cultural–historical contexts that inform the experiences of young people of African descent in America, which are characterized by success, diversity, adversity, and identities constructed largely in relationship to the history of slavery and colonialism. Indeed, descendants of Africans in America are both culturally similar and varied in ways that people outside their communities rarely acknowledge in full. The variations within these communities may be attributed to regional, urban, and rural differences, as well age, language, education, immigration status, country of heritage, belief system, socioeconomic status, and history of contact with other communities. In fact, the community of people of African descent and consciousness residing in America comprises individuals who do not comply with the heteronormative standards of mainstream society, who espouse politically conservative beliefs, participate actively in faith communities, speak languages other than English, have disabilities, and descend directly from enslaved Africans.

A key unifying factor that often draws limited attention in the literature is the long history of contributions that members of this community have made to America and the shared sense of pride that radiates from these successes. This litany of accomplishments not only creates a culture of success but also engenders a sense of pride, helps young people see their potential, and inspires school success. Consequently, many successful individuals of African descent frequently assume mentorship roles within their communities, not only to sustain these traditions of success but also to resist, in their own way, pejorative narratives that emphasize deficit themes (Mayes et al., 2019).

The successes of these individuals flow from a wide variety of sources. This includes, but is not limited to, distinctive educational contexts at historically Black institutions; highly educated middle-class parents; strong cultural identities; a plethora of cultural assets; a deep desire to overcome challenging obstacles; acts of resistance; a desire to disprove dominant narratives; proactive messages to offset larger society ideology; efforts of family members to develop counteridentities; positive role models; self-advocacy; and the support and mentorship of a village of people: community mentors, faculty, administrators, staff, and peers who understand and care about these individuals' experiences (Komarraju et al., 2010; Lewis et al., 2004; Solorzano et al., 2000).

A secondary unifying factor, which arguably receives the most attention, is the long history of legal, social, economic, and political discrimination faced by persons with known African ancestry, coupled with a general prejudice toward these individuals and the violence associated with anti-Black racism. People of African descent have endured centuries of systemic racism and other acts of prejudice intended to subordinate, marginalize, and exploit Black communities for the benefit of communities that have held maximal power and privilege in America. Unlike acts perpetrated against other structurally marginalized groups, the acts of racism and prejudice against people of African descent have deep roots in that community's unique history of slavery and colonialism, with consequences that often span multiple generations. These acts are generally applied differently to, and become even more consequential for, people of African descent who claim additional marginalized identities, such as those who have a disability, identify as queer, or are undocumented—a phenomenon often referred to as double marginalization

(Shawanda, 2018). Even within the Black community, double-marginalized individuals are generally invisible, tend to be more isolated, experience double-consciousness, and often feel compelled to prioritize one component of their marginalized identities over the others (Harris et al., 2016). Miles (2020) succinctly captured this experience as follows:

> So, it's strange and somewhat cruel when I'm asked as an adult, which ones do I pick over the others. However, what's really being asked of me is, "Whose side are you on?" The answer of course is, "Mine." I'm on my side. Hence, to be more of one aspect of me and less of another would suggest that I should be at war with some part of myself, and I am not doing that. There are too many people and systems seeking to destroy bodies like mine, and I am not going to help them.

Despite evidence of success, many young BSWDA struggle to navigate the cultures and spaces they encounter in institutions of higher learning, in part because of the challenge of affirming to themselves the integrity of their disability and cultural identities while confronting the norms of educational systems that have historically been hostile to those identities (Bans & Hughes, 2013). These systems are generally replete with ableism, pejorative cultural narratives that emphasize themes of personal tragedy, perceptions of disability as likely acquired through acts of violence, and pedagogies that seek only to highlight what students lack and to disregard the cultural wealth they bring to bear (Lynn et al., 2010). In addition, interventions designed to respond to these problems often fail to account fully for the ways in which race, gender, economics, culture, and disability intersect to contribute to schooling contexts that often result in lowered academic expectations, segregation in self-contained classrooms, and "othering" by peers and educators (Banks, 2017).

GAPS IN MAINSTREAM MENTORING RELATIONSHIPS FOR BSWDA

Many BSWDA have been exposed to the formalized mentorship structures common in institutions of higher learning (Mayes et al., 2019; Niblet, 2019). These formal mentoring relationships are generally initiated as organizational efforts for a specific duration and feature mentor–mentee matching, goal setting, and structured activities (Ehrich et al., 2004; Erickson et al., 2009). These relationships seldom attend to the intersectional experiences of BSWDA (Mayes et al. 2019). Because these relationships occur as part of strategic organizational interventions to achieve a particular goal or outcome, they rarely capture the true experiences and priorities of many BSWDA. Dolmage (2017) asserted that this may be in large part because the college campus was designed as a training ground for the ableist notion of the most "capable, hyper-able students." To the extent that ableism is understood as the appraisal of ablebodiedness—making disability invisible while reinforcing able-bodied supremacy—academic institutions have a long history of excluding body–minds marked as "other."

In fact, the formal nature of these relationships do not mirror the successful mentoring relationships formed organically among BSWDA. The formalized relationships follow a curriculum structured by weekly or monthly goals to guide activities. Often, the curriculum topics are predetermined based on "universal" challenges experienced by students with disabilities, such as access to instructional materials and campus facilities. Other topics covered include socializing on campus, peer pressure, time management, communicating with peers and professors, classroom etiquette, study skills, and seeking help and campus resources (Hillie et al., 2019).

Because these mentorship relationships are often focused more broadly around the needs of the "quintessential college student," they are likely to be grounded in harmful color-blind and nonintersectional strategies. Research shows that the majority of mentors in STEM fields, for example, are more likely to hold color-blind views of their students and to dismiss the idea that social identities shape their students' academic experiences (Brunsma et al., 2017; McCoy et al., 2015; Prunuske et al., 2013). Using race-neutral, color-blind language (i.e., language in which racial terms are implied but not stated explicitly) allows White faculty mentors to describe their students as academically inferior, less prepared, and less interested in pursuing research and graduate studies while the mentors potentially ignore structural causes (McCoy et al., 2015). BSWDA's combined marginalized racial–ethnic and disability statuses create distinct college experiences and needs that demand an intersectional approach to mentoring.

The mainstream approach to mentorship creates a number of challenges for BSWDA. First, the colorblind and nonintersectional (Byars-Winston & Dahlberg, 2019) aspects of this approach marginalize BSWDA, particularly those who claim multiple minoritized identities, such as first-generation students and female students, who are less likely to have satisfactory professional mentorships in undergraduate and graduate school (Noy & Ray, 2012). Forms of dissatisfaction and exclusion in mentorship often emerge at the intersections of marginalized identities. Intersecting oppressions, such as those faced by an undocumented transgender person of color, for example, create less supportive mentoring situations for these individuals than the situations experienced by privileged students (Noy & Ray, 2012; Strayhorn & Saddler, 2008).

A shared intersectional identity and lived experience is critical to the success of mentor–mentee relationships (Hurd & Sellers, 2013; Noy & Ray, 2012). Current research indicates that when a student has a mentor of a similar background, the student's views of the quality of the relationship improve (Hurd & Sellers, 2013; Noy & Ray, 2012), which can aid the development and increase the utility of the mentoring relationship. LGBT youth, for example, benefit significantly from mentoring relationships, in particular with a fellow member of the LGBT community (Bird et al., 2011; Russell & Horne, 2009). The importance of similar identity and shared experiences between the mentor and mentee is well established in the literature; however, there is a structurally based shortage of mentors of various marginalized backgrounds (Graham, 2019). Therefore, it is crucial for institutions to create and sustain a pipeline of mentors with intersectional experiences and identities. In addition, institutions must train allies who can help students feel safe and validated in their identity, become critically conscious, advocate for BSWDA, understand disability laws and rights, demonstrate a deeper connection to disability support services, and commit themselves to long-term change in systems.

Because of their systematic exclusion from higher education institutions, BSWDA rarely encounter mentors of similar backgrounds (Ortiz-Walters & Gilson, 2005; Schueths & Carranza, 2012), with whom they are more likely to be culturally compatible—a shortage that often means those invited to mentor BSWDA do not feel competent to do so, in part due to a lack of shared lived experiences or limited training. This reality magnifies the ethical concerns that could manifest in mentor–mentee mentorships, including (a) issues of power, (b) multiple and/or inappropriate relationships, (c) boundary problems, and (d) competence to mentor (Schlosser & Foley, 2008). It is no surprise, therefore, that BSWDA face disparities in their mentoring experiences, particularly within predominantly White institutions. In contrast, Black students within the historically Black college and university (HBCU) system often experience higher levels of support from faculty mentors (Hirt et al., 2006). Recent findings suggest that Black students at predominantly White institutions feel as though faculty attempt to "weed them out" of specific disciplines such as STEM, whereas students at HBCUs reported feeling encouraged and well socialized to enter such disciplines (McCoy et al., 2017). Attention to student success in these fields is particularly urgent given that enrollment rates in undergraduate STEM programs are approximately 2 percent lower for students with diverse abilities than they are for students who do not report any disabilities (Alexander & Hermann, 2016; NCSES, 2013).

It is also important to note that while cultural compatibility due to shared lived experiences and identities is crucial, it alone does not constitute mentorship competence, nor does it represent a basic requirement. Culturally compatible mentors who are not well trained have the potential to create unsuccessful mentoring relationships. For example, Banks (2019) noted that because many faculty at HBCUs are not experts in the area of disability services, their good intentions do not often translate to effective support for BSWDA. In some cases, faculty have routinely been found to question students with less visible disabilities, such as a learning disability, to ensure that the student is not using the disability to avoid difficult assignments (Beilke & Yssel, 1999). Culturally compatible mentors and allies from other communities may still be successful if they undergo continual training, consultation, and supervision required to ensure they are providing competent mentoring.

NEW DIRECTIONS FOR MENTORSHIP PRACTICES FOR BSWDA

The experiences of BSWDA in college paints a picture of young people entering a new and challenging environment with a vast array of skills, gifts, and talents—many of which go unrecognized in institutions that remain hostile to BSWDA. Another picture also emerges of young adults who are dealing not only with the typical difficulties of academic demands and inaccessible campuses, but also the unique pressures of ableism, racial discrimination, and the pressure to represent well not just their family and community of origin, but Black culture more generally. Thus, in addition to their talents and gifts, BSWDA bring into their early college experiences the cultural–historical context of marginalization in education, suggesting that—for this group of students—effective mentoring requires more than extra advising: It requires the creation of transformative mentoring relationships attuned to this culturally and historically embedded reality that extends from early childhood to college. This transformative approach must also recognize how PSE systems frequently reproduce this history of exclusion and contribute to a general expectation that the students will be marginalized, which furthers trepidation and mistrust among BSWDA. Ultimately, progress requires institutions and leaders to grapple with the inherent tensions between organizations' desire for equilibrium and the need for systems to change so the success of students from diverse cultural backgrounds can be fostered.

RECOMMENDATIONS FOR CULTURALLY RESPONSIVE MENTORING

The complexity of BSWDA's experiences and the effect on their success of chronic racially motivated behaviors demands a deep understanding of BSWDA's priorities and needs that can be addressed through culturally responsive and sustaining mentoring relationships (CRSMR). These needs and priorities include but are not limited to:

- developing critical consciousness and racial identity and affiliation
- decoding the hidden curriculum (Golden et al., 2020)
- living successfully after college
- accessing culturally responsive disability services and classroom instruction
- infusing, promoting, and sustaining Black culture in mentorship
- acknowledging intersectional experiences
- accessing a network of mentors
- intentionally distributing counterhegemonic stories of BSWDA (Banks & Hughes, 2013)
- nurturing cultural assets
- building a sense of history and community of possibility
- promoting culturally responsive self-determination
- increasing mentoring competence
- challenging students to be agents of social justice change in their programs (Green et al., 2017)
- fulfilling social–emotional, cognitive, and spiritual needs

Mentoring BSWDA is an intensive and multifaceted process that reflects both formal and informal acts of mentoring (Esposito et al., 2017; Jones et al., 2018; Spaulding & Rockinson-Szapkiw, 2012). Whereas informal mentoring happens naturally and serendipitously through unstructured interactions (DeAngelo et al., 2015; Wanberg et al., 2006), formal mentoring may occur within structured programs developed by institutions. In both cases, the mentors and mentees explicitly identify, explore, and value important differences regarding cultural identity, power, and privilege between mentors and mentees. In this way, mentors and mentees seamlessly forge a mutually beneficial relationship (hierarchical or not) in concert with the application of culturally relevant pedagogies. Mentors and mentees recognize that full equality in the mentoring relationship is neither possible nor a universal goal. In many cases, the mentees enter these relationships expecting clear hierarchies even as they anticipate a reciprocal learning process between themselves and their mentors.

In outlining culturally appropriate mentoring strategies, Watkins (2015) identified concepts such as spirituality, harmony, movement, verve, affect, communalism, expressive individualism, orality, and social time perspective as central features of CRSMR. Watkins noted that these ways of knowing and understanding provide additional guidance and strategies that mentors may employ in mentoring students, keeping in mind that all students are unique and their affinity to these domains can vary. Additionally, CRSMR must incorporate external supports, for example, stakeholders inside and outside the institution such as college alumni and community partners who provide internships, spiritual guidance, and other training opportunities.

The following are specific practice implications for both mentors and mentees:

- Mentors should learn about the ways in which cultural mistrust manifests in mentoring relationships, particularly among college students with disabilities who share multiple marginalized identities. This mistrust may impact mentees' ability to connect with their mentors, seek aid, and offer contributions, in addition to impeding academic progress and educational outcomes for Black students.
- Faculty responsible for the mentorship programs should develop an interdisciplinary team to develop training opportunities and resources to further educate all stakeholders on systems of oppression and other topics that will increase mentor effectiveness in serving BSWDA. The interdisciplinary team should include community members from diverse ethnic and ability backgrounds, disability support services, campus cultural and ethnic organizations, and transition coordinators. Additionally, the interdisciplinary team should facilitate mentees' relationships with other role models, advisers, and mentors on and off campus.
- Recruitment and hiring efforts should focus on attracting program mentors and staff who are diverse, especially in terms of ability, race, ethnicity, and life experiences that mirror those of mentees in the program.
- Program training curricula should include; seminars, brown bag series or town hall events, community-based experiences, mentoring group meetings, and other learning opportunities that highlight elements necessary for effective mentorship including; racial and ethnic identity development; allyship; strategies for resilience and coping; the management of health care transition; cultural socialization; disability legislation, such as the Rehabilitation Act and Americans with Disabilities Act; cultural humility; Strategies to challenge the status quo; internalized privilege; transition planning; self-determination; accommodations in higher education; conscious awareness; and asset-based relationships.
- WHO should implement asset-based program structures that center around youth's gifts and talents instead of designing programs to "fix" youth who are viewed as deficient. The latter reinforces a "savior complex" that is disempowering and recreates a power imbalance.
- WHO should prioritize quality relationships defined by the ethic of caring and allyship, in which mentors function as surrogate family members who advocate for students' holistic well-being, for example,

by addressing mentees' emotional, psychosocial, academic, relational, and professional needs. The mentors should seek to advocate for and meet youth's goals and preferences especially as it relates to the choice of same or cross-ability or race mentoring match. Mentees should be encouraged to assume a leadership role in choosing mentors.

- Program structure should include opportunities for participants to share talents and voice concerns as well as identify biases and prejudices if they occur in the mentoring relationship.
- Mentors should engage in relationality that involves validating mentees' struggles, following through on commitments, and responding to relationship ruptures and distress (Arczynski & Morrow, 2017; Benishek et al., 2004; Chan et al., 2015).

REFERENCES

Abott, A. I., & Martinez, W. F. (2018). Increasing the success of African American males with learning disabilities attending California community colleges. *Journal of Research Initiatives, 3*(2), 1–11.

Alexander, Q. R., & Hermann, M. A. (2016). African-American women's experiences in graduate science, technology, engineering, and mathematics education at a predominantly white university: A qualitative investigation. *Journal of Diversity in Higher Education*, *9*(4), 307–322. https://doi.org/10.1037/a0039705.

Arczynski, A. V., Christensen, M. C., & Hoover, S. M. (2018). Fostering critical feminist multicultural qualitative research mentoring. *The Counseling Psychologist*, *46*(8), 954–978. https://doi.org/10.1177/0011000018823782.

Banks, J. (2019). Are we ready: Faculty perceptions of postsecondary students with learning disabilities at a historically Black university. *Journal of Diversity in Higher Education*, *12*(4), 297–306. https://doi.org/10.1037/dhe0000100.

Banks, M. E. (2015). Whiteness and disability: Double marginalization. *Women & Therapy*, *38*(3–4), 220–231. https://doi.org/10.1080/02703149.2015.1059191.

Banks, J., & Hughes, M. S. (2013). Double consciousness: Postsecondary experiences of African American males with disabilities. *The Journal of Negro Education*, *82*(4), 368–381.

Banks, J. (2017). "These people are never going to stop labeling me": Educational experiences of African American male students labeled with learning disabilities. *Equity & Excellence in Education*, *50*(1), 96–107. https://doi.org/10.1080/10665684.2016.1250235.

Benishek, L. A., Bieschlke, K. J., Park, J., & Slattery, S. M. (2004). A multicultural feminist model of mentoring. *Journal of Multicultural Counseling and Development*, *32*, 428–442.

Beilke, J. R., & Yssel, N. (1999). The chilly climate for students with disabilities in higher education. *College Student Journal*, *33*(3), 364–371.

Bird, K. et al. (eds) (2011) *The Political Representations of Immigrants and Minorities,* Routledge, United States.

Brooms, D. R., Franklin, W., Clark, J. S., & Smith, M. (2021). "It's more than just mentoring": critical mentoring Black and Latino males from college to the community. *Race, Ethnicity and Education, 24*(2), 210–228. https://doi.org/10.1080/1 3613324.2018.1538125.

Brunsma, D. L., Embrick, D.G. & Shin. J. H. (2017). Graduate students of color: Race, racism, and mentoring in the white waters of academia. *Sociology of Race and Ethnicity, 3*(1), 1–13.

Booker, K., & Brevard, E. (2017). Why mentoring matters: African-American students and the transition to college. *The Mentor,* 19, 1–9, 10.26209/MJ1961245.

Booker, K. C., & Brevard, E. (2017). *Why mentoring matters: African American students and the transition to college.* The Mentor: An Academic Advising Journal. https://dus.psu.edu/mentor/2017/01/ why-mentoring-matters-african-american-students-and-the-transition-to-college/.

Byars-Winston, A., & Dahlberg M. L. (2019). Mentoring underrepresented students in STEMM: Why do identities matter? In *The Science of Effective Mentorship in STEMM* (pp. 51–74). National Academies Press.

Burgstahler, S. (2008). Opening doors: Mentoring on the internet. Seattle: University of Washington. Retrieved July 17, 2021, from http://www.washington.edu/doit/ Brochures/Technology/doors.html.

Cartledge, G., Gardner, R., & Tillman L., (1995) "African Americans in higher education special education." *Teacher education and special education, 18*(3), 166–178.

Cameto, R., Levine, P., & Wagner, M. (2004). Transition planning for students with disabilities. A Special Topic Report from the National Longitudinal Transition Study–2 (NLTS-2). Menlo Park, CA: SRI International.

Coles, A. (2011). The Role of Mentoring in College Access and Success. Research to Practice Brief. In *Institute for Higher Education Policy.* Institute for Higher Education Policy.

College Board. (2010). Eight components of college and career readiness counseling. Retrieved from https://secure-media.collegeboard.org/digitalServices/pdf/ nosca/11b_4416_8_Components_WEB_111107.pdf.

DeAngelo, L., Mason, J., & Winters, D. (2016). Faculty engagement in mentoring undergraduate students: How institutional environments regulate and promote extra-role behavior. *Innovative Higher Education, 41*, 317–332. https://doi. org/10.1007/s10755-015-9350-7.

Dolmage, J., & Michigan Publishing publisher. (2017). *Academic ableism: disability and higher education.* University of Michigan Press.

DuBois, D. L., Portillo, N., Rhodes, J. E., Silverthorn, N., & Valentine, J. C. (2011). How effective are mentoring programs for youth? A systematic assessment of the evidence. *Psychological Science in the Public Interest, 12*(2), 57–91. https://doi. org/10.1177 /1529100611414806.

Durodoye, B. A., Combes, B. H., & Bryant, R. M. (2004). Counselor intervention in the post-secondary planning of African-American students with learning disabilities. *Professional School Counseling, 7*, 133–141.

Ehrich, L. C, Hansford, B., & Tennent, L. (2004). Formal mentoring programs in education and other professions: A review of the literature. *Educational Administration Quarterly, 40*(4), 518–540. https://doi.org/10.1177/0013161X04267118.

Erickson, L. D., McDonald, S., & Elder, G. H. (2009). Informal mentors and education: Complementary or compensatory resources? *Sociology of Education, 82*, 344–367.

Fassinger, R. E. (1998). Lesbian, gay, and bisexual identity and student development theory. In R. L. Sanlo (Ed.). *Working with lesbian, gay, bisexual, and transgender college students: A handbook for faculty and administrators* (pp. 13–22). Greenwood Press.

Fassinger, R. E., & Hensler-McGinnis, N. F. (2005). Multicultural feminist mentoring as individual and small-group pedagogy. In C. Z. Enns, & A. L. Sinacore (Eds.), *Teaching and social justice: Integrating multicultural and feminist theories in the classroom* (pp. 143–161). American Psychological Association Books.

Freeman, K. (1999). No services needed? The case for mentoring high-achieving African American students. *Peabody Journal of Education, 74*(2), 15–26.

Geenen, S., Powers, L., Vasquez, A. L., & Bersani, H. (2003). Understanding and promoting the transition of minority adolescents. *Career Development for Exceptional Individuals, 26*(1), 27–46. https://doi.org/10.1177/088572880302600103.

Graham, T. J., & Renee N. J. (2019). School-based mentoring for middle schoolers: The impact on mentees and their pre-service teacher mentors. *Educational Renaissance, 8*, 48–59.

Greene, M. J. (2006). Helping build better lives: Career and life development of gifted and talented students. *Professional School Counseling, 10*, 34–42. https://doi.org/10.1177/2156759X0601001S05.

Grimes S., Scevak J., Southgate E., & Buchanan R. (2017). Non-disclosing students with disabilities or learning challenges: Characteristics and size of a hidden population. *Aust. Educ. Res., 44*, 425–441. https://doi.org/10.1007/s13384-017–0242.

Harper, S. R, & Kuykendall, J. A. (2012). Institutional efforts to improve Black male student achievement: A standards-based approach. *Change (New Rochelle, NY), 44*(2), 23–29. https://doi.org/10.1080/00091383.2012.655234.

Harris, P. C., Mayes, R. D., Vega, D., & Hines, E. M. (2016). Reaching higher: College and career readiness for African American males with learning disabilities. *Journal of African American Males in Education, 7*, 52–69.

Hirt, J, Terrell S, Amelink, C., & Bennett, B. (2006). The nature of student affairs work at historically Black colleges and universities. *Journal of College Student Development, 47*(6), 661–76.

Hurd, N. M., & Sellers, R. M. (2013). Black adolescents' relationship with natural mentors; Associations with academic engagement via social and emotional development. *Cultural Diversity and Ethnic Minority Psychology, 19*(1), 76–86. https://doi.org/10.1037/a0031095.

Johnson-Bailey, J., & Cervero, R. M. (2004). Mentoring in black and white: The intricacies of cross-cultural mentoring. *Mentoring & Tutoring: Partnership in Learning, 12*, 7–21. https://doi.org/10.1080/1361126042000183075.

Johnson, S. L. N. (2019). Culturally responsive teaching and mentoring for African American males attending post-secondary schools: Diversity beyond disability. In *Examining Social Change and Social Responsibility in Higher Education* (pp. 76–93). IGI Global. https://doi.org/10.4018/978-1-7998-2177-9.ch006.

Komarraju, M., Musulkin, S., & Bhattacharya, G. (2010). Role of student-faculty interactions in developing college students' academic self-concept, motivation, and achievement. *Journal of College Student Development, 51*(3), 332–342. https://doi.org/ 10.1353/csd.0.0137.

Lewis, C. W., Ginsberg, R., Davies, T., & Smith, K. (2004). The experiences of African-American PhD students at a predominantly White Carnegie I-research institution. *College Student Journal, 38*(2), 231–245.

Lynn, M., Bacon, J., Totten, T., Bridges III, T., & Jennings, M. (2010). Examining teachers' beliefs about African American male students in a low-performing high school in an African American school district. *Teachers College Record, 112*(1), 289–330.

Mayes, R. D., Hines, E. R., & Bibbs, D. L. (2019). Counselors and psychologists mentoring gifted Black males with disabilities to foster college and career readiness. *Gifted Child Today Magazine, 42*(3), 157–164. https://doi.org/10.1177/1076217519843150.

Mayes, R. D., Hines, E. M., & Moore, J. L., III. (2018). When the rubber meets the road: Educating and supporting twice exceptional African American students. In S. B. Kaufman (Ed.), Supporting and educating bright and creative students with learning difficulties (pp. 290–298). Oxford, UK: Oxford University Press.

Mayes, R. D., & Moore, J. L., III. (2016). Adversity and pitfalls of twice exceptional urban learners. *Journal of Advanced Academics, 27,* 167–189.

McCoy, D. L., Winkle-Wagner, R., & Luedke, C. L. (2015). Colorblind mentoring? Exploring white faculty mentoring of students of color. *Journal of Diversity in Higher Education, 8*, 225–242. https://doi.org/10.1037/a0038676.

McCoy, D. L., Luedke, C. L., & Winkle-Wagner, R. (2017). Encouraged or Weeded Out: Perspectives of Students of Color in the STEM Disciplines on Faculty Interactions. *Journal of College Student Development, 58*(5), 657–673. https://doi.org/10.1353/csd.2017.0052.

Miles, A. L. (2020, April 22). *Disability: What Have Black People Got to Do with It?* Black Perspectives. https://www.aaihs.org/disability-whats-black-people-got-to-do-with-it-angel-love-miles/.

Mullins, L. & Preyde, M. (2013). The lived experience of students with an invisible disability at a Canadian university. *Disability & Society, 28*(2), 147–160. https://doi.org/10.1080/09687599.2012.752127.

Newman, L. (2005). Family Involvement in the Educational Development of Youth with Disabilities. A Special Topic Report of Findings from the National Longitudinal Transition Study-2 (NLTS2). Menlo Park, CA: SRI International. Available at www.nlts2.org/reports/2005_03/nlts2_report_2005_03_complete.pdf.

Noy, S. & Ray, R. (2012). "Graduate students' perceptions of their advisors: Is there systematic disadvantage in mentorship?" *Journal of Higher Education, 83*, 876–914.

Olney, M. F, & Brockelman, K. F. (2003). Out of the disability closet: Strategic use of perception management by select university students with disabilities. *Disability & Society*, *18*(1), 35–50. https://doi.org/10.1080/713662200.

Ortiz-Walters, R. & Gilson, L. L.(2005) "Mentoring in academia: An examination of the experiences of proteges of color." *Journal of Vocational Behavior, 67,* 459–475.

Perry, S, Hilliard, S., C., & Hilliard, A., G. (2003). *Young, gifted, and Black: promoting high achievement among African-American students*. Beacon Press.

Powers, L. E., Turner, A., Westwood, D., Matuszewski, J., Wilson, R., & Phillips, A. (2001). Take charge for the future: A controlled field-test of a model to promote student involvement in transition planning. *Career Development for Exceptional Individuals, 24*, 89–104.

Prasad, S., Sopdie, E., Meya, D., Kalbarczyk, A., & Garcia, P. J. (2019). Conceptual framework of mentoring in low-and middle-income countries to advance global health. *The American Journal of Tropical Medicine and Hygiene*, *100*(1_Suppl), 9–14. https://doi.org/10.4269/ajtmh.18-0557.

Prunuske, A., Wilson, J. J., Walls, M., & Clarke, B. (2013). Experiences of mentors training underrepresented undergraduates in the research laboratory. *CBE—Life Sciences Education, 12*(3), 403–409.

Rueda, R., Monzo, L., Shapiro, J., Gomez, J., & Blacher, J. (2005). Cultural models of transition: Latina mothers of young adults with developmental disabilities.*Exceptional Children*, *71*(4), 401–414. https://doi.org/10.1177/001440290507100402.

Schueths, A., & Carranza, M. (2012). Navigating around educational roadblocks: Mentoring for Pre K to 20+ Latino/a Students. *Latino Studies*, *10*(4), 566–586.

Schlosser, L. Z., & Foley, P. F. (2008). Ethical issues in multicultural student-faculty mentoring relationships in higher education. *Mentoring & Tutoring: Partnership in Learning, 16*(1), 63–75. https://doi.org/10.1080/13611260701801015.

Shawanda, S. (2018). We the minority-of-minorities: A narrative inquiry of Black female academics in the United Kingdom. *British Journal of Sociology of Education*, *39*(7), 1012–1029. https://doi.org/10.1080/01425692.2018.1454297.

Strayhorn, T. L., & Saddler, T. N. (2009). Gender differences in the influence of faculty–student mentoring relationships on satisfaction with college among African Americans. *Journal of African American Studies*, *13*(4), 476–493. https://doi.org/10.1007/s12111-008-9082-1.

Stumbo, N. J., Martin, J. K., Nordstrom, D., Rolfe, T., Burgstahler, S., Whitney, J., Misquez, E. (2011). Evidence-Based Practices in Mentoring Students with Disabilities: Four Case Studies. *Journal of Science Education for Students with Disabilities*, *14*(1), 33–54.

Timmons, J., Mack, M., Sims, A., Hare, R. & Wills, J. (2006). Paving the way to work: A guide to career-focused mentoring for youth with disabilities. Washington, DC: National Collaborative on Workforce and Disability for Youth, Institute for Educational Leadership.

Tovar-Murray, D., Jenifer, E. S., Andrusyk, J., D'Angelo, R., & King, T. (2012). Racism-related stress and ethnic identity as determinants of African American college students' career aspirations. *The Career Development Quarterly, 60,* 254–262.

Trotman, S. M., Mayes, R. D., Griffith, K. G., Garrett, M. T., & Watkins, J. (2015). Effective involvement with urban special education services: What every school counselor should know to support Black male students. In M. Henfield & A. Washington (Eds.), *Black male student success in the 21st century urban schools: School counseling for equity, access, and achievement* (pp. 173–194). Charlotte, NC: Information Age.

U.S. Department of Labor. (2006). Cultivating leadership: Mentoring youth with disabilities. Retrieved July 21, 2021 from www.dol.gov/odep/pubs/fact/cultivate.htm.

Vega, D., Hines, E., Mayes, R., & Harris, P. (2016). Preparing Latino students for life after high school: The important role of school counselors and school psychologists. *National Youth-at-Risk Journal, 2*(1). https://doi.org/10.20429/nyarj.2016.020107.

Weir, C. (2004). Person-centered and collaborative supports for college success. *Education and Training in Developmental Disabilities, 39*(1), 67–73.

Women, minorities, and persons with disabilities in science and engineering: 2013 (Special Report NSF 13–304). Arlington, VA: Author. Retrieved July 22, 2021, from http://www.nsf.gov/statistics/wmpd/.

NOTES

1. Racial and ethnic groups are designated by proper nouns and are capitalized. Therefore, we use of "Black" and "White" instead of black and white (colors) when referring to human racial and ethnic groups.

PART IV

Antiracist Mentoring

Chapter Nine

Black Mentorship Against the Anti-Black Machinery of the University

Timothy J. Lensmire and Brian D. Lozenski

Dear Brian,

I hope you are well.

I am glad that we decided to write this chapter as a dialogue. I think this form will enable us to express not only commitments and concerns that we share, but also to express different perspectives and strengths that we bring to the topic of antiracist mentoring. I am excited to reflect on antiracist mentoring with you, both because I have, in the past, acted as a mentor to you (while you were pursuing your doctorate) and because you have made working with and supporting black[1] youth and students the center of your scholarship and teaching and activism in the community. In other words, I am an old white guy and you are a (relatively) young black man; we have worked and learned together; we are dedicated to antiracism and anticapitalism; and we both think and worry quite a bit about how we are moving among and impacting the people around us.

I thought I would start with two stories that we can then interpret and draw some morals from. The first is maybe less a story and more just a moment. It was fairly early in our relationship and we were walking together to get lunch in Dinkytown, near the University of Minnesota. I remember saying that I could help you with certain critical traditions, but not others. I said that you would need to connect with others on campus—I mentioned Rose Brewer, I think, in our university's African American and African Studies department— to further your grounding in the black intellectual tradition.

The second story takes place later, perhaps in the second year of your program. You had been doing a fair amount of study and writing with two other PhD students, Shannon McManimon and Zac Casey. Being the clever (and old) person that I am, I wrote an email to the three of you and said that you should call yourselves the Mod Squad, after the TV show from the late sixties and early seventies. That show featured three hip undercover police officers solving crimes—and the lame joke I was making was, of course, that the racial and gender identities of those three hip characters matched those of you and Shannon and Zac—a black man, a white woman, and a white man. A less-lame joke was that the three TV characters "represented mainstream society's chief fears involving youth in the 1960s" (Baugess & DeBolt, 2012, p. 629)—so I was also complimenting, if obliquely, the critical and oppositional positions that the three of you were staking out in your work.

Minutes after I sent that email (maybe it was only seconds later), I received an email response from you, Brian, with an attached photo from *The Mod Squad* TV series. Along with the three main characters, that photo featured a fourth character from the series that I had forgotten about—the police captain in charge of the Mod Squad. Your email said something like, "If we're the Mod Squad, then I guess you are that old white police captain."

If I were to draw some morals from these stories, especially for white professors mentoring black students, the first would be that white professors need to have an honest sense of themselves and recognize limits to their own knowledge and networks. I encouraged you to connect with black professors and their knowledges despite the fact that my own work on race in education is grounded in a Du Boisian[2] tradition of theorizing Whiteness and draws on Ralph Ellison's writings on how White racial identities are grounded in scapegoating rituals and on the Reverend Thandeka's psychoanalytic and historical account of how white people learn to be white.

A second moral, drawn from across both stories, would be that we need to challenge the image of mentoring as an isolated and individualistic activity. Too often mentoring is imagined as a private interaction, behind a closed office door, between the knowing mentor and the unknowing mentee (is "mentee" even a real word?). The first story points to my knowing that mentoring would require a larger community of scholars who knew and who had experienced things that I didn't and hadn't. The second story suggests that my mentoring of you would include the ways that I tried to support Shannon, Zac and you in your collective study and writing.

The final moral I will draw, for now, has to do with humor and laughter. Our relationship has, from early on, involved teasing and trying to make each other laugh. In previous scholarship, I have explored the importance of humor for challenging dominant ideas and for creating alternatives (see, for example, Lensmire, 2011). An important part of my mentoring, I think, is that we laugh with each other.

What do you think, Brian?

Peace.

Tim

Dear Tim,

Thank you for starting us off on this project. I'm also excited to write this chapter as a dialogue. It provides a unique and probably more appropriate medium for us to consider the complex terrain of interracial mentorship. As with all things dealing with race, there exists some absurdity that we even need to derive meaning from this notion of "interracial mentorship," as though it is a natural fact of the academy. I guess an initial consideration of which I always have to remind myself of, is that these racialized relationships are still created and maintained for the purpose of social stratification. The premise of this entire book and our chapter, which we cannot lose track of, is that the construction of the white mentor and the mentee of color is based on the accumulation of historical practices, political decisions, attitudes, and the distribution of economic and intellectual resources. If we are not paying attention to the structures that continue to reify these social, political, and economic arrangements, then whatever interpersonal meaning we make from our own experiences together will be moot because the onus will be on individuals or dyads to solve the problems that are much larger than us. Perhaps this does not need to be said, yet, in my experience it is an assumption that I cannot make. So, in our writing I will try to do some shunting from the micro elements of our fun, loving, and supportive mentoring relationship to the macro university context that necessitated our navigation of an institution based in supremacist notions of social hierarchy, erasure, and credentializing, about which you, as a white faculty, were supposed to have some insight.

I prefaced my response to the important stories you retold because I don't want to get caught in the circle of access and opportunity. Success in the academy is not merely a navigational issue. Like Bettina Love (2019) argues in her book *We Want To Do More Than Survive*, we must stop the focus on giving strategies and tactics necessary to merely survive the academy and start eliminating the policies and practices that necessitate these survival tactics. This is one of the presuppositions to mentorship: that the white mentor is already actively working against the anti-Black machinery in the university as an ongoing project. This could be questioning the mechanisms for tenure that discriminate against BIPOCs, critiquing curricula and exposing the gaps that leave out particular traditions and theories, or it could be advocating for additional resources to try to address racialized wealth gaps faced by students, among lots of other examples.

AND, at the same time, there are some very real and practical things that mentors of students of color can do to help them survive the immediate stressors they may face on a daily basis. Certainly, and this may be ironic given my overly long preface, we can't put the weight of social transformation in the academy on the backs of students, although they are most subject to its detrimental impacts. Sometimes just helping people live a somewhat carefree college life is the most immediate need. Reflecting on the two stories you shared can illustrate my point.

I remember talking with you in Dinkytown early in my grad school career. We were just talking about our lives, how we arrived in this place together, and where our interests intersected. I remember discussing my undergraduate experience where I minored in Africana studies, which greatly impacted how I understood my educational endeavors. You immediately recommended I take classes in the African and African American Studies Department, specifically naming Rose Brewer as a "must experience" faculty. To this day, Rose and I are wonderful colleagues, doing educational justice work and trying to expand ethnic studies offerings in Minnesota schools, Pre-K through PhD. Your suggestion that "white professors need to have an honest sense of themselves and recognize limits to their own knowledge and networks" resonates with me. No one can be expected to know ALL of the intellectual traditions, although Whiteness as a construct suggests that white faculty do. Your point that white faculty knowledge is not total critiques this construct. So, yes, white mentors need to interrogate their own traditions, recognizing that they are often steeped in histories of white dominance. Part of being a good mentor is connecting their mentees of color with faculty of color, but more specifically faculty of color situated in critical traditions. It was not the fact of Dr. Brewer's race that was of most importance; rather, it was her capacity to socialize me further into the black radical tradition and black feminism specifically.

Allow me move to a structural critique now. I was lucky that you, as a mentor, were well versed in certain aspects of the black radical tradition. The vast majority of white faculty are not. Having the African American and African Studies Department (AFRO) as part of the University of Minnesota is critical. I'd argue that AFRO is the conscience of the University, reminding it of its imperfection (Brewer, 2019). And yet, AFRO is somewhat ghettoized on campus in terms of its isolation. It is an underresourced department. It is precarious, constantly having to justify its survival. The necessity of you recommending I take classes in AFRO speaks to the absent narratives and erased histories in our home department of Curriculum and Instruction (C&I). Other than in your classes, I was not able to access the black radical tradition in C&I. This illustrates my point that our interracial mentoring relationship also can potentially do the work of masking the broader structural issues on campus.

Before I got to know you as a mentor, I saw how you were operating at the university. You were willing to risk your status and popularity among the faculty and specifically with the deans for racial justice. You were willing to call out certain practices that were detrimental to students like me, and you realized that the curriculum in C&I was lacking. I believe this is why you told me to seek out classes in other departments like AFRO. You were engaged in a serious interrogation of Whiteness in your scholarship and also at the institution. All of this predated our mentoring relationship, and I believe it laid the necessary foundation for it. I knew you were someone who I could trust to approach with issues dealing with race with which I may have ordinarily approached faculty of color. I don't think it's a stretch to say that as a recommendation any white faculty who is interested in mentoring black students must be a critical Whiteness scholar, even if that is not the focus of their scholarship. If white faculty don't have a sense of how they became *white faculty*, then they will most likely be offering survival tactics as the end game and not as a means to a racial abolitionist end.

My sense is that the interrogation of Whiteness and knowing one's limitations as a white mentor is directly connected to the second story you shared. The Mod Squad label stuck with Shannon, Zac, and me throughout our doctoral tenure. I remember finding it hilarious the first time you mentioned it because it was so ridiculous that our independent study on Marxism was being paralleled with a group of undercover police (I'm still chuckling as I write this). I've always appreciated your Bahktinian (see Lensmire, 1994, 2011) analysis of education. Perhaps you can elaborate more on the meat of your analysis, but on a psychological level it allowed us (the Mod Squad) to engage with our material in a space of silliness and mockery. Although we were reading the Frankfurt School, Bourdieu, and Althusser, we were having fun with the theorizing. It seems to me that this play is an undertheorized aspect of intentional, serious study. This play allowed us to strip down the airs the academy puts on, making these complex texts more accessible.

I also wonder how I would have responded to other faculty, who were not doing the work of interrogating Whiteness, referring to us as the Mod Squad. I remember that the name even evoked some eye rolls from other faculty who got the joke, but missed the direction of the mockery. I don't think I would have taken the racial reference to the Mod Squad well from a mentor who was not interrogating their Whiteness and trying to get smarter about race. It's not a far jump, then, to suggest that if white faculty are getting smarter about their racialization then they can also help black students get smarter about their racialization. I think this connects to your point about laughter. The idea of race is so absurd that sometimes you need to laugh to keep from crying about it. When we venerate race and place it on a pedestal it becomes this overwhelming concept. You somehow found a way to mock race in a way of which it's deserving. But this mockery came with a deep understanding of racialism and white supremacy. It all goes together. There are white mentors who don't want to talk about race because they are afraid of their black mentees and making a mistake. Fear cannot be part of a healthy mentoring relationship. The fact is that black people still need to interrogate race. Living as a negatively racialized person is not sufficient to understand race. You can know race as a BIPOC and not understand it. The interracial mentoring relationship provides a unique instance for two people to work through the tensions of race and the depths of racism.

Another story that comes to mind is from a conversation we had in your office. I remember that I was struggling with the nature of my dissertation and feeling pressure to move away from the marginalized methodology of participatory action research. You asked me questions about why I was feeling pressure and pushed me to think about my larger purpose in the academy. I remember leaving your office feeling empowered to make my dissertation what I wanted it to be. I think the word "permission" is problematic in this context, but I do feel as though you gave me permission, or perhaps just support, in doing a study that was a bit different. Connecting back to the idea of laughter and mockery, I feel like there was also a permission given to engage with the academy in ways that were less formal. Again, this is a critique of Whiteness, where the performance of formality is based in a subjectivity of hierarchy and normality. I'm wondering what you think about this idea of permission; not in its restrictive sense of needing to ask to be able to do something, but in a more freeing sense of breaking the norms of formality and power that often mediate mentorship.

In solidarity,

Brian

Dear Brian,

As usual, I am blown away by your intellectual, moral, and political clarity. Your reminders and explanations of how, when discussing our experiences with mentoring, we cannot forget about the "structures that continue to reify these social, political, and economic arrangements," are crucial for this chapter. They are crucial, especially, if we reject the idea that access and survival exhaust our goals for mentoring relationships. Instead, as you make plain, these relationships are part of and need to be pursued, with intention, in relation to the larger ongoing project of "actively working against the anti-Black machinery" that characterizes our colleges and universities.

Your brilliance performs another crucial point about mentoring that I hope potential mentors will find reassuring: that good things can happen even in situations, as in ours, where the *mentee* is clearly more intelligent and talented than the *mentor*. (I know that "mentee" is a real, actual word, and I promise, in the rest of the chapter, not to comment on this again—but I must say that I dislike the word "mentee" and wish it were not so convenient to use with "mentor." Unfortunately, my dislike of the word is not grounded in anything profound. Rather, the sound of "mentee" conjures "manatee" for me, and this is simply not helpful when trying to think deeply about antiracist mentoring.)

In order to discuss your questions about permission-giving in relation to your dissertation research, I need to first attend to something you said earlier, about trust. Often, trust is imagined as developing, as being created, within the space and time of a relationship. But you pointed to something different, to knowing ahead of time, before we got to know each other, that you could talk with me about things racist and racial; and that you knew this because you had been watching how I was "operating at the university." Similar to how we've argued that mentoring should not be conceptualized without reference to larger structures and to other people, here you are expanding the mentoring relationship to include what happens before that relationship even begins. In this case, what this means is that our mentoring relationship might never have happened or been successful if I had not already, before we met, been fighting the anti-Black machinery of our university. This suggests a different sort of test or criterion than is usually applied for determining the fitness of a white professor for mentoring black students.

It also raises the question of why or how I came to be "operating" the way that I was. You noted that I was "well versed in certain aspects of the black radical tradition" and that I was "engaged in a serious interrogation of Whiteness" in my scholarship and at our institution. I have tried, in previous writing and in various ways, to make sense of how I came to be living the particular life I am living as a scholar and professor. For the purposes of this chapter, I will point to three aspects of my past that contributed significantly to how I was "operating" when you came to study in our C&I department.

The first is that, from kindergarten on, I hated school (yes, my children and other loved ones tease me regularly about how silly I am, to hate school and then decide to work in schools for the rest of my life). The immediate occasion of my hatred was the tight control schools attempted to exert over my body and its movements. Later, as I studied education and varied critical traditions, and as I reflected on and tried to make sense of this hatred, I came to interpret it as grounded in the fact of my working-class upbringing in rural Wisconsin. In an early, autoethnographic chapter of my most recent book, I described,

> The struggle that has defined my life in school, all the way from elementary through graduate school, and on into my life as a professor. I was struggling

with the offer, made by school, to join the middle class. I was struggling with
its demand that I remake (or at least hide) my working-class insides. (Lensmire,
2017, p. 17)

An experience (actually, a series of experiences) I had when I was an assistant
professor at Washington University in St. Louis is a second crucial contribu-
tor to how I have come to orient myself toward and move within the university. During my third year there, in the early 1990s, my friend and colleague,
Lauren Sosniak, brought a gender discrimination case against the university
after it denied her tenure. There was no question Lauren deserved tenure (her
case was ridiculously strong) and I was persuaded that gender discrimination
was at play. Soon enough, I found myself preparing to testify against the (all
male) tenured faculty in our small education department—men who would be
considering and voting on my own tenure case in a few years.

The third and final circumstance that I will point to also occurred while I
lived in St. Louis. I had black mentors. The most important were Emmanuel
Harris II ("Manny" to his family and friends) and Garrett Duncan. Manny
and Garrett were not official, institutional mentors—Manny was pursuing
his PhD in Hispanic Languages and Literatures and Garrett joined the education department as an assistant professor a few years after me. They were
friends. But they were also mentors. Both engaged me in long conversations
about how race and racism worked in the United States. Both gave me books
(and then more books) to read. With Manny, I also played basketball three
or four or five times a week, and when we played on the outdoor courts in
St. Louis, I was usually the only white person around. So that meant I was
learning about what it meant to be a white man among black men, as I tried
to coordinate the movements of my white body in close relation to black bodies. Garrett is, among other things, a Freirean[3] scholar, so he tutored me in
Freire's work and helped me connect it to the black radical tradition in which
he was also grounded.

I will draw two conclusions from these narrations of my past. First, I was
never comfortable (and remain uncomfortable) in schools, including the university. Much of this discomfort springs from the control these institutions
have attempted to wield, not just of my body's behaviors and movements, but
also of my insides—my head, my heart. Second, I do not trust these institutions. I know that—sometimes dramatically, sometimes quietly, but always
continuously—bad things happen in our places of work. For the last two
decades or so, I have focused my scholarship and action on understanding
and opposing how race and racism play out in classrooms and schools and
universities, with particular attention to Whiteness and white racial identity.

My response to the discomfort and lack of trust inspired in me by the
university—my way of "operating" there—has included not only criticism and

opposition, but also play and laughter. I learned to laugh in rural Wisconsin, from my dad, John Lensmire, who laughs loudly. My dad is also often heard singing tunes from the Great American Songbook, except that he makes up his own lyrics (which are, sometimes, just a wee bit off-color). I do this, too, so naturally, at the small gathering we held for Lauren after the university admitted its wrong-doing and gave her a lot (a lot) of money—they wouldn't, of course, agree to the one and only thing she actually wanted, which was to be a tenured professor at Washington University in St. Louis—so, naturally, for this small gathering, I wrote and then sang my own version of Nat King Cole's "Unforgettable." My version started like this:

> Untenurable
> That's what you are
> Untenurable
> You're no rising star . . .

Bakhtin (1984) explored medieval folk humor and popular festivals because he saw in them lessons for how to oppose an oppressive social order and official ideology. Bakhtin thought that official truth was held in place, was secured, by fear. Thus, he was interested in how that fear might be weakened or countered. He thought that sitting with friends and eating, drinking, and laughing together might provide for moments of fearlessness—and in these moments of fearlessness, countertruths might be perceived and expressed.

When you came to my office to discuss your dissertation research and shared that you were feeling various pressures to pursue research that was somehow more conventional or "official," the danger was what Bakhtin (1984) called *false seriousness*. False seriousness results from fear and reproduces things as they are, because everything seems heavy and already-determined and unavoidable. Bakhtin helps us understand that this wrong kind of seriousness actually undermines the pursuit of truths; he helps us understand that laughter and play might be required in order to do serious work, to criticize and rei-magine ourselves and the world in powerful ways. Our scholarship, teaching, and mentorship must, as Bakhtin (1984) put it, engage in a "gay and free play with objects and concepts, but it is a play that pursues a distant, prophetic goal: to dispel the atmosphere of gloomy and false seriousness enveloping the world and all its phenomenon" (p. 380).

What I needed to do that day with you, in my office, was to help you to continue being fearless. I admired you and the rest of the Mod Squad, in part, because you had been practicing Bakhtin's laughing fearlessness for some time already—when, for example, the three of you published that article tracing current classroom management techniques back through history to their origins in the control of black bodies during slavery (Casey, Lozenski,

& McManimon, 2013). I remember almost barking with laughter when the three of you told me about that piece, because what was playing out in my mind were scenes of all these panicked, wide-eyed, fearful teacher educators reading your piece and wondering what in the world they were going to teach their future teachers now.

So you are right that "giving permission" doesn't exactly capture what was happening that day. It was more just that I needed to remind you of who you were and how you wanted to move in the world.

Any final words, Brian?

Peace.

Tim

Dear Tim,

As always you are able to bring me to a place of audible laughter (the academic equivalent of LOL). (I cannot believe that you have me searching "manatee" on Wikipedia. But it turns out that manatees live largely solitary lives, which speaks to the isolation of the academy; and like the ocean our academic institutions are quite polluted. So, whether you knew it or not, you were on to something there.)

You provide so much to chew on in your above passage. Certainly the *construction of trust, the challenge to individualistic notions of mentorship, and the intersectional work of antioppressive action* are all deeply important to how we might continue this dialogue. The biographical tracing of how you became a particular kind of actor in the academy is fascinating. This kind of self-interrogation is another component of deep transformational mentorship. Unlike you, I kind of enjoyed school. I found it somewhat easy, and I learned early on that I liked the external affirmations that came with good grades and being told I was smart, although it came with plenty of the bodily disciplining that you experienced. I received messages when compared to my friends, who were mostly African American, that I was "different" and somehow "special." It was not until I was an adult and a teacher myself in Philadelphia that I recognized the educational social capital that, unlike you, was part of my family. Both of my parents were teachers in the School District of Philadelphia. A moment that sticks out to me, upon reflection, that has utterly reframed my positive memories of my schooling happened when I was going into seventh grade. In the school I attended, seventh grade was when another, more rigid layer, of "ability" tracking kicked in. My class was separated into five sections that ranged from advanced to remedial across the entire curriculum. So if a student was placed into an advanced section, they would take advanced Algebra, English, Social Studies, and Physical Science. Over the summer I was placed into a middle track—the grade level track—along with most of my friends. My parents were upset. They thought I should be advanced; at least that's what I believed. In reality, they knew that I would be relegated to that middle track for the rest of my academic career. I'm sure they believed I was capable of "advanced" work, but their concern was more material than academic. Working in schools for their entire adult lives, they knew that school wasn't just school. It was scalar. There are schools within schools, and they needed me to be in the best school so that I could continue to be in the best schools.

I remember them taking me to a meeting with the principal to demand that I be placed in section 7–3. This was the advanced section, but the school thought they would outsmart everyone by mixing up the numbers one through five. Thinking back, I remember the pretense of sitting in Ms. Felix's (the principal) office. The only time I had ever spoken to her before then was in regard to my behavior. She stared at me and asked if I thought I could do advanced work, to which I responded that I could. It was a pretense because all of us knew that my mother, Gail Lozenski, would not be leaving that office without me being placed into 7–3, and so it was done. Ironically, although I liked the elite status of section 7–3, I was hurt by not being with my friends. I became racially isolated in that section, where I was the only person of African descent except for a girl who was a second-generation immigrant from Zimbabwe, I think. It was there where I learned to be a racial chameleon so that I could get along with my white peers, with whom I spent 90 percent of my day. Like you, after school playing basketball was where I was able to connect back with my friends, my social group; some of whom would face-tiously tease me that I was "too smart" to hang with them. We all knew it was bullshit. This was my story of coming to not trust these institutions. School literally took my friends away as it was molding me to fit neatly into the kind of student of color who could be in a doctoral program. Similar to Dumas's (2014) exceptional metaphor of schooling for black children being like losing an arm, I learned that the very process that would eventually lead me to graduate school was simultaneously taking something precious from me. Yes, I succeeded, but at what expense?

Dumas writes, "Informed by a theory of suffering, our analysis moves beyond simply acknowledging racism, or bemoaning racially imbalanced outcomes, to deeper social explanation of how racialized subjects make meaning of the confluence of school malaise and racial melancholia" (p. 4). It seems that our mentoring relationship was fruitful not only because of the trust we were able to place in each other, but also because of our distrust of the institution. Perhaps a generative interracial mentoring relationship must ultimately be distrustful of institutions and cognizant of black suffering. How do we begin to construct and theorize mentorship that does the work of moving beyond the acknowledgment of racism? I feel like this is what we have been speaking to in our exchange. Mentorship that seeks to be agentic and offensive to racialization must explicate the mechanisms of racialization. Ultimately our mentorship was not between you and me, it was between you, me, Manny, Garrett, my parents, Rose, your dad, the Mod Squad, and so many others we did not name here. I think it is appropriate to name this mentorship network (maybe even as a recommendation) because we are dealing with institutions created to dispossess and isolate black people.[4]

In my earlier writing I began referring to you as the "white mentor," I guess making me the "black mentee." I'm beginning to rethink these labels now because what I think we are talking about is not interracial mentorship, but *black mentorship*. Black mentorship must be framed as antithetical to the white institution. It must take as its starting point Dumas's notion of black suffering. Cornel West (see Taylor, 2008) suggests that this suffering, or what he calls "catastrophe," is a space of truth in the Adornoian (2003) sense that "the need to let suffering speak is a condition of all truth" (p. 17). If we construct the *mentorship of black students as a space for truth-telling coming out of social suffering mediated by schooling*, it illustrates some of your earlier ideas.

For instance, black mentorship would need to emerge from a mentoring fabric made up of caring people who can see through the guise of the institution—who literally distrust the university. As opposed to white mentorship, which would be connected to an atomized set of credentializing criteria (i.e., "did you follow the dissertation proposal format correctly?"), black mentorship would engage in a Bahktinian mocking of the social order and "oppose an oppressive social order and official ideology" (i.e., "You should know that the dissertation proposal format reproduces supremacist constructs of official knowledge. Now let's figure out what you actually want to do."). Black mentorship would recognize the notions of "untenurability." Here, in addition to your story of Lauren at Washington University in St. Louis, I am thinking of all the black academics, especially black women academics, who did not receive a PhD or tenure because they were denied access or could not formulate a committee that could evaluate or even comment on their research in the black intellectual tradition. If white mentorship is about tradition, deference to authority, and false seriousness, then black mentorship is about expression through laughter and tears, recognition of eldership, and the pursuit of truth, no matter who it offends.

As I write, I can already feel the white gaze (Esposito, 2011) on me asking if I truly care if we increase scholars of color in the academy, or if I am being too radical in terms of what I am suggesting. To be clear, I am suggesting the eradication of the "white mentor" in the ways that mentorship reifies the structures of Whiteness. Obviously, I want to see diversity in academia. I am a professor at a selective private liberal arts college. I am part of the academy. I also come from the black radical tradition, and thus, my defining purpose in the academy is one of insurgence. Through this framing, the purpose of credentializing more scholars of color must be to create a polar shift in society. The academy does not need more scholars of color who are wedded to the white institution. It needs more scholars of color who know and can articulate their asymmetry to a structure built on the social hierarchy that demands their marginalization. I have been theorizing and writing about this understanding:

> As scholars of color, we are often born into and shaped by communities that have been historically marginalized by postsecondary institutions. Our native communities nurture us with the knowledges of survivance, cultural pride, and ingenuity amidst a dearth of access to material wealth. As children, we are sent into schooling systems that seek to strip much of this knowledge from us and repackage us in the model of our colonizers, replete with colonial thinking. Many of us resist this repackaging, yet our success in these schooling systems is contingent on our ability to either disguise our resistance or acquiesce to the colonial desires and bury our cultural heritage in the depths of our subconscious. The few of us who "succeed" in these structures, then, are positioned as leaders of our native communities and used to rationalize the entire process of cultural stripping. (Lozenski, 2020)

Here, I am working through a metaphor of faculty of color being the trains that are used to carry the extracted wealth from communities (knowledge systems) to the universities for their benefit as hoarders of knowledge. Black mentorship must first name, and then resist this project.

If black mentorship is what I am suggesting as the goal of mentorship, then a simple question that may be asked is: "Who can participate in black mentorship?" I would suggest that black and white mentorship are not simply about individual racial identity, but more so about the goals of mentorship. A text that has really pushed my thinking regarding racial configurations and the academy is la paperson's (2017) *A Third University is Possible*. la paperson writes,

> Regardless of its colonial structure, because school is an assemblage of machines and not a monolithic institution, its machinery is always being subverted toward decolonizing purposes. The bits of machinery that make up a decolonizing university are driven by decolonial desires, with decolonizing dreamers who are subversively part of the machinery and part machine themselves. These subversive beings wreck, scavenge, retool, and reassemble the colonizing university into decolonizing contraptions. (p. xiii)

la paperson is interested in how we can craft a decolonial (third university) space from the very parts of what they call "first and second" universities. These are the universities that you and I inhabit, Tim. The first being the research-based institution and the second being the progressive liberal arts institution. Mentorship can be seen as a technology of the institution that perpetuates its desires for disciplining and manufacturing scholars of any racial or ethnic background to continue the work of maintaining social hierarchy. Yet, as a technology, mentorship *can be used to disrupt this colonial desire if the person(s) wielding it as a tool have a different desire.* As such, the racial identities of the people involved in the mentorship become less important, although they still matter. What matters more are the aims and goals of those engaging in mentorship.

If mentorship is simply about credentials, then it is doing the work of the institution, and thus it is not to be trusted. If mentorship is about solidarity and the breaking of the traditions of the institution, then it is doing the work of truth-telling. I don't know if we can boil any of this down to a recommendation, but it seems that we are describing a set of relationships: interpersonal mentoring relationships situated within institutional relationships. It is not possible for the interpersonal relationship to supersede the institution, however the interpersonal mentoring relationship can greatly impact how scholars, and particularly scholars of color, develop their ongoing relationship to the academy.

In solidarity,

Brian

RECOMMENDATIONS FOR CULTURALLY RESPONSIVE MENTORING

Our framing of mentorship, and specifically black mentorship, as a tool to dismantle the anti-Black machinery of the academy requires actions that go beyond talking and listening. As historian and Black Studies scholar Robin D. G. Kelley (2018) identifies in his essay "Black Study, Black Struggle," this work necessitates a symbiotic praxis blending continued self-education and dogged persistence. We explored several recommendations for white faculty who want to engage in black mentorship throughout our above discourse, including interrogating their relationship to the university and schooling in general, and remembering that laughter and joy can be disruptive and acts of resistance. Below are additional suggestions for white faculty who are serious about black mentoring and becoming a wrench in the anti-Black machinery of the university:

1. Take an action within your university that opposes its anti-Black machinery. The action could be a small one, but should be big enough to disturb or anger someone above you in the university's hierarchy.

2. In making sense of what happened after you took action (see #1), explore your own relationship to Whiteness by reading:
   - Chapter 12 of W. E. B. Du Bois's *Black Reconstruction in America, 1860–1880*
   - Toni Morrison's *Playing in the dark*
   - Thandeka's *Learning to be white*
   - David Roediger's *Wages of whiteness*
   - and 50 additional books and articles on the topic
3. In making sense of what happened after you took action (see #1), explore your university's anti-Black machinery by reading:
   - Craig Wilder's *Ebony and ivy*
   - la paperson's *A third university is possible*
   - Cedric Robinson's *Black Marxism*
   - Fred Moten & Stefano Harney's *The undercommons*
   - and 50 additional books and articles on the topic
4. Form or join a collective of people working to dismantle the anti-Black machinery of your university and continue taking action.
5. As you begin an actual interpersonal mentoring relationship, take time to map out networks of influences and knowledges, together, in order to situate your work in historical and contemporary contexts.

REFERENCES

Adorno, T. (2003). *Negative dialectics*. Routledge.

Bakhtin, M. M. (1984). *Rabelais and his world*. H. Iswolsky, Trans.). Indiana University.

Baugess, J., & DeBolt, A. (2012). *Encyclopedia of the sixties: A decade of culture and counterculture.* Greenwood.

Brewer, R. (2019, April 19). Demanding relevance: 50 years of Black Studies and protest. *Free Minds, Free People.* https://fmfp.org/2019/04/afro-50-black-studies-and-protest-at-the-university-of-minnesota/.

Casey, Z., Lozenski, B., & McManimon, S. (2013). From neoliberal policy to neoliberal pedagogy: Racializing and historicizing classroom management. *Journal of Pedagogy, 4*(1), 36–58. https://doi.org/10.2478/jped-2013-0003.

Du Bois, W. E. B. (1992). *Black reconstruction in America*. New York: The Free Press. (Original work published 1935).

Dumas, M. J. (2014). "Losing an arm": Schooling as a site of black suffering. *Race Ethnicity and Education, 17*(1), 1–29. https://doi.org/10.1080/13613324.2013.850 412.

Ellison, R. (1995). *Shadow and act*. New York: Vintage International. (Original work published 1953).

Esposito, J. (2011). Negotiating the gaze and learning the hidden curriculum: A critical race analysis of the embodiment of female students of color at a Predominantly White Institution. *Journal for Critical Education Policy Studies*, 9(2), 143–164.

Kelley, R. D. (2018). Black study, black struggle. *Ufahamu: A Journal of African Studies*, *40*(2).

la paperson (2017). *A third university is possible.* University of Minnesota Press.

Lensmire, T. (1994). Writing workshop as carnival: Reflections on an alternative learning environment. *Harvard Educational Review*, *64*(4), 371–391.

Lensmire, T. (2011). Too serious: Learning, schools, and Bakhtin's carnival. In E. J. White & M. Peters (Eds.), *Bakhtinian pedagogy: Opportunities and challenges for research, policy and practice in education across the globe* (pp. 117–128). Peter Lang.

Lensmire, T. (2017). *White folks: Race and identity in rural America.* Routledge.

Love, B. L. (2019). *We want to do more than survive: Abolitionist teaching and the pursuit of educational freedom.* Beacon Press.

Lozenski, B. D. (2020). From consumption to refusal: A four-part exploration of the dilemmas of black academics and radical knowledge. In R. Endo (Ed.), *Experiences of Racialization in Predominantly White Institutions: Critical Reflections on Inclusion in US Colleges and Schools of Education.* New York: Routledge.

Roediger, D. (1991). *The wages of whiteness.* Verso.

Taylor, A. (Director). (2008). *Examined Life* [Motion Picture]. Zeitgeist Films.

Thandeka. (2001). *Learning to be white: Money, race, and God in America.* New York: Continuum.

NOTES

1. We follow the convention that when used as an adjective "black" and "white" will be lowercase, and when used as a noun, designating a group of people, "Black" and "White" will be capitalized.

2. David Roediger's (1991) *Wages of whiteness* is often credited with initiating the modern study of Whiteness. Roediger himself points, instead, to Du Bois's (1935/1992) *Black Reconstruction in America, 1860–1880*—and especially Du Bois's notion of a "psychological wage" paid to white workers, so they aligned themselves with white elites rather than their black sisters and brothers—as a more suitable place to start the story. See Ellison's essays in *Shadow and Act* (1953/1995) for his account of stereotypes and scapegoating rituals; and Thandeka's *Learning to be white* (2001) for her account of how white racial identity originates in the abuse of prewhite youth by their own white community.

3. The Brazilian educator, Paulo Freire, is a central figure within the tradition known as critical pedagogy. His most widely celebrated text is *Pedagogy of the Oppressed* (1970).

4. Like manatees.

Chapter Ten

"I Just Really Wanted Them To See Me"

Mentoring Black Students on Days after Injustice

Alyssa Hadley Dunn

Scene 1: *It is November 8, 2016. DJ, a Black college student, is voting for the first time in the presidential election. He wakes up and says to himself, "'I can't believe we are about to have the opportunity to vote for a woman to become the Commander-in-Chief. I can't believe that tonight we might shatter a national glass ceiling.'" He puts on "blue pants. I wore a blue, red, and white Tommy Hilfiger sweater. I had never been so patriotic in my life; not any Fourth of July I've ever experienced was as patriotic as November 8th, 2016!" He surprises himself with how emotional he gets: "I wasn't in tears or anything, but I was definitely kind of nostalgic. At that point, you had to take a stance, no matter who you were supporting from the beginning, whether your candidate made it or not, you were going to have to take a stance. . . . You were going to vote for a candidate who had potentially promised to uplift all people of color, of all genders, of all sexual orientations and who was going to overall, supposedly, support all Americans. And then on the other side, you had the opportunity to support someone who had discriminated against so many people, who has made some very foul and potent comments." He heads to the voting booth. "[I] knew that I could not support Donald Trump . . . to apparently make it great again. That slogan was also something that I couldn't agree with because, if I think about who I am and I look at my ancestors, I can't think of a time where it was great for them. . . . It* *brings up a lot more than something that looks great on t-shirts and hats. It was a very philosophical thing, you know." Casting his vote makes DJ feel "proud to be an American. It was a good day."*

Scene 2: *Three days later, the sidewalk chalking was still clearly visible:* Trump 2016. Make America Great Again. *It was right in front of the campus library, bright blue writing with pink stars adorning the top and bottom of the message. Some students quietly step over it, and two students look down, notice it, and then walk around it. Another stops and takes a photo with her cell phone. DJ sees it, too, and wonders when it will rain, so it can finally be washed away.*

Scene 3: *It has been a week, and still none of his professors have mentioned the election. He goes to class almost robotically now, wondering if all of his white peers around him voted for Trump. He had wondered who they sup-ported leading up the election; but he really wonders now. And what about his professors? Is that why they're not mentioning it? Are they happy, too? "Here's the thing," he notes, "I just really wanted them to see me. I want them to see me enough to know to talk about it. But it's clear they didn't see me at all."*

In the days after the 2016 presidential election, the students remember, it was eerily quiet. Not just in their classes, but among their multiracial friend groups, at work, and sometimes in their own families. Even walking around campus felt different, they recall. The sense of hope and possibility that they'd felt just days prior—and the sense of energy that pulsed around campus because of it—was conspicuously absent. At least it wasn't like the middle school a few miles away, where white[1] children had chanted "Build that wall" at their immigrant peers in the cafeteria. But the silence was still noticeable, still palpable and still, ultimately, a daily reminder that they were in a place where they did not always feel like they belonged.

This is how students responded when, two weeks after the Presidential Inauguration in 2017, I began interviewing Black college students about their experiences on election day in 2016 and in the days after. I wanted to know what it meant for them to experience the election as Black students at a Predominantly White Institution (PWI), on a college campus of nearly 50,000 students. Nationwide, results from the election showed that the majority of young adults, mostly "millennials," voted for Clinton, but the percentage voting for Trump (37 percent) was anything but negligible (CIRCLE, 2016). Black millennials (the age group of which they were a part) had nearly uni-versally voted for Clinton, while the percentage of white millennials voting for Trump had shocked many people who believed that Trump's politics were generational.

Similarly, I wondered how higher education faculty were responding and, given my particular role as a faculty member in education, how other teacher educators were responding. Did they address the election outcome and, if so, how? I was simultaneously working with colleagues on research about how, if at all, PK-12 teachers changed their pedagogy postelection (Baggett et al., 2020; Dunn et al., 2019; Sondel et al., 2018). So many teachers were feeling traumatized and echoing that their students felt the same; yet, many felt limited in what they could do and say because of the sociopolitical contexts of teaching in public schools. Despite this, teachers around the country enacted what we came to call a "pedagogy of political trauma" that "serves the democratic and emancipatory purposes of education while simultaneously alleviating and/or mediating trauma caused by events in the political sphere" (Dunn et al., 2019, p. 179). This pedagogy included "Tending to students' socioemotional well-being; Cultivating students' civic knowledge and capacities; Teaching toward critical consciousness, activism, and resistance" (p. 179). Would the same be true of higher education, where faculty might have more academic freedom but also be concerned because of increasing critiques of faculty who discuss politics in the classroom (American Association of University Professors, 2017)? Where faculty may be less pressured to cover certain "content" in their courses because of external standards regulated by the state, but also, by and large, have much less pedagogical preparation and a set of pedagogical tools to pull from?

The days after the 2016 election are but one example of "days after." In my work on teaching for justice on days after (Dunn, 2021), I conceptualize *days after pedagogy* as that which pushes against tropes of neutrality by teaching explicitly about the equity-related issues that happen at the international, national, state, and local levels. They are not days to avoid what is happening outside the classroom, but rather days to bring those ideas into the space in ways that best support what students need. At the level of higher education, this is deeply important as our students grapple with learning how to make sense of the world around them as young adults, new voters, activists, and more. This is especially true for white faculty at PWIs who are looking to support and sustain Black students. In my field of teacher education and beyond, we must "actively aim to transgress the practices of whiteness that render millennial teachers of color (MTOC), along with their knowledge, experiences, and perspectives, as invisible" (Brown & Ward, 2018, p. 103). Especially on days after incidents of racial violence or trauma, we cannot ignore the present moment in favor of a supposed commitment to "content" and/or "neutrality."

While we don't know what "days after" will come next, we know that these days will continue to happen. As I write in January of 2021, we are in the midst of what feels like an ongoing day after: the COVID-19 pandemic. We have just concluded another divisive and dehumanizing election season, though with a different result than 2016. We are mere weeks beyond an attack on the U.S. Capitol, replete with white supremacist and anti-Semitic violence. We spent the summer amidst a social revolution, precipitated by ongoing police brutality and racial violence. And through it all, our students had to make sense of what this all meant for them and what their institutions would do (or not do) in the wake of these events. In the summer of 2020, many institutions issued statements that proclaimed "Black Lives Matter" for the first time, but little has changed in the day-to-day campus climate for Black students. In recent conversations with students, Black students still reported that their faculty did not mention any of these moments or they seemed reticent to discuss them in substantive ways. One student told me that their professor said, when asked, "That's too political for us to talk about here. This is a history class, not a political science one."

We have extensive research illustrating that "we teach who we are" (Palmer, 1998, p. 2) and that it is impossible to keep one's politics out of the classroom (Freire, 1993), no matter what the subject. By politics here, I do not just mean one's political affiliation and one's tendency (or not) to disclose this to students. Rather, "politics" can manifest in many ways, not merely political disclosure. It is also how teachers interact with each other and with students, and what choices they make for curricular inclusion and pedagogy (Apple, 2001; Au, 2006; Kumashiro, 2011). Thus, it is important to know how Black college students experience and respond to critical political moments. Knowing this can help us better understand the ongoing challenges and possibilities for sustaining Black college students in general, as well as in instances of significant political and social change (Brown, 2014). In today's climate—both at the K-12 and higher education levels—it is more important than ever that educators understand the relationship between politics, policies, and teaching (Kelchtermans, 2005).

I come to this work as a former high school teacher and current teacher educator, deeply invested in racial justice and in preparing the next generation of teachers as change agents (Freire, 1993). I am also committed to dismantling whiteness and white supremacy in schools and society, including the institutions in which I work. Yet, I also recognize the interest convergence (Delgado & Stefancic, 2017) at work here, that I benefit from writing about the experiences of people of color and that my whiteness affords me the privilege to call out institutions for their implicit and explicit attention to and perpetuation of dominant white norms. The only reason I am writing this chapter is because of the grace, generosity, and care of my Black colleagues and students. After all, who am I, as a white scholar, to say what it means to mentor and sustain Black students? The only reason I know anything about this is because my Black students and colleagues have taught me, implicitly and explicitly, through modeling and dialogue. It is for them and with them that I continue to strive to do this work, continually learning and improving my praxis in order to sustain the lives of Black students.

In the sections that follow, I explain a study I conducted with Black college students, specifically Black pre-service teachers (PSTs) at a PWI in the wake of the 2016 election. Though this research happened several years prior to writing, their experiences are important for helping faculty understand what it means to mentor and sustain Black college students more broadly on days after injustices, when too often our universities ignore what is happening. On these days, it is up to us as faculty to ensure that our Black students do not feel even more hurt and silenced in the wake of yet another incident of racism or white supremacy. I see the 2016 election of a white supremacist president as an example of such a day after. In particular, I asked the following research questions: (1) How did Black college students in a teacher preparation program at a PWI experience the U.S. 2016 presidential election? In the days after the election, (2) how did they respond, and (3) how did they perceive how faculty responded?

BLACK PSTS AS MILLENNIAL TEACHERS OF COLOR

While the other texts in this collection contextualize the experiences of Black college students writ large, here I share a bit more about a specific group: Black PSTs. Given the age of the participants in this study, their experiences are similar to those of MTOC, and below I review some literature on the experiences of MTOC from the field of teacher education.

As future PK-12 educators, MTOC, including Black PSTs, are entering the profession "during a time of rapidly changing social, political, economic, and educational landscapes" (Freeman, 2018, p. 63). MTOC are coming of age in institutions and preparation programs "where their knowledge and cultural experiences are often disregarded" (Dilworth, 2018, p. 3). Extensive research with preservice teachers of color (both those classified as millennials and those from previous generations) illustrate that their experiences are often filled with hostility and/or invisibility, as their perspectives remain unacknowledged even as their "diversity" is celebrated. Treated as commodities in their preparation programs and later jobs (Kohli, 2018), they do not often learn about race or culturally relevant and responsive pedagogies (Brown, 2014; Brown & Ward, 2018; Jackson, 2015; Kohli, 2009). Even in programs with an explicit focus on social justice, like the one studied here, "there is often a stark contrast between the espoused and the enacted equity and inclusivity of postsecondary college campuses" (Herrera & Morales, 2018, p. 46). They are tasked with learning "within the purportedly welcoming environments marketed in the promotional literature and messages generated by recruiting colleges and universities" (Abrica & Morales, 2017, as cited in Herrera & Morales, 2018).

Amidst these challenging conditions, MTOC must often advocate for political and social recognition for themselves and their future students. In contrast to descriptions of millennials as apolitical, research on MTOC, including Black preservice teachers, shows just the opposite. Indeed, for them, "as for many teachers from previous generations, the project of public education, then, is often deeply personal as well as political" (Catone & Tahbildar, 2018, p. 73). Magaldi et al. and Trub (2016) argue that MTOC "demonstrate a stronger sense of responsibility not only to take up issues of diversity in their teaching and professional practice but also to serve as potential agents of social change in addressing inequities in education" (p. 2). In the words of MTOC Genesis A. Chavez, "The biggest shock was when I stepped into my school and not only felt isolated, but also recognized that no one around me shared the same sense of urgency about the racial and socioeconomic disparities that our students experience" (Ishmael et al., 2018, p. 17). She continues, "Although I don't hide my realities, there certainly is no place for them" (p. 18). A particularly powerful finding comes from Herrera and Morales's (2018) study of culturally and linguistically diverse millennial teachers:

> Their persistence and agency for doing what is right is anchored in their need to give to others, to ensure that those like them do not experience and suffer from the same type of discrimination and marginalization that they have endured. Their commitment is grounded in the learner, the family, and the community. With the mission to work hard to dismantle the racism, prejudice, and symbolic violence they witness in schools every day, these participants stand in complete contrast to what the literature describes as the characteristics and dispositions of millennials. (pp. 60–1)

As the authors contend, MOTC are poised to deeply contribute to justice and equity in their future workplaces, if only those workplaces would be better structured to support them.

METHODS

The participants in this study were twelve Black PSTs enrolled in a nationally ranked teacher preparation program at a major research university in the Midwestern United States. They were over eighteen years of age and all voted in the U.S. presidential election for the first time in 2016. Participants were part of an urban-focused track within their certification program; this track served a greater proportion of Black students than the larger program. I purposefully sought participants from a variety of years in school, sex, and grade level/content major in an attempt to have different experiences represented (see table 10.1 below). That is, I was curious if and how both the students and their faculty responded differently depending on where students were in the program. Ultimately, there was no discernible difference across years, grade level, or content areas.

Two weeks after the Presidential Inauguration in January 2017, participants shared their experiences in 60–90 minute semistructured audio recorded interviews with myself and/or one of two undergraduate research assistants, both of whom identified as students of color. Sample interview questions included: *How did you feel about the 2016 election? How did you feel about the results of the election? What was your day like on November 9th? How did you feel when your professors did/did not address the election results?*

A total of fifteen interviews were conducted and later transcribed; twelve Black students' interviews are included here. In addition to interviews, participants were also invited to share any related documents. Primarily, they shared social media posts from during the presidential campaign and the election aftermath. While the interview data is highlighted here, other sources were consulted when developing the discussion below.

In my analysis of the data, I used memoing to "capture [my] analytic thinking about [the] data, but also facilitate such thinking, stimulating analytic

Table 10.1 Participants

Note.(**) Participants were offered the opportunity to select their own pseudonyms. Two participants chose Jasmine as their first name, so I have distinguished between the two with a last initial.

Pseudonym	Year in Program	Grade Level & Content Area	Sex
Jasmine S. **	Freshman	Secondary social studies	F
Aeriyelle	Freshman	Elementary (language arts focus)	M
Conner	Sophomore	Elementary (all subjects)	M
DJ	Sophomore	Secondary social studies	M
Keisha	Sophomore	Secondary mathematics	F
Jasmine I. **	Sophomore	Elementary (all subjects)	F
Kendra	Sophomore	Secondary English and English as a Second Language	F
John	Sophomore	Secondary English	M
Jackson	Junior	Secondary social studies	M
Samuel	Junior	Secondary social studies	M
Maria	Junior	Elementary (language arts focus)	F
Shelly	Senior	Elementary (social studies focus)	F

insights" (Maxwell, 2005, p. 96). I also made use of open coding techniques through three rounds of hand coding (Strauss & Corbin 1998). First, I collected relevant excerpts from transcriptions, as they related to my three research questions. I coded these for any elements that stood out as especially related to the participants' lived experiences. Then, in a second round, I coded across participants, condensing and narrowing down codes. In a third round, I coded related documents and finalized the list of codes. Finally, I condensed the codes once again into the themes presented below (Creswell, 1998).

FINDINGS

Findings from this study revealed that Black PSTs were heavily invested in the election and its outcome, and that they had strong perspectives on the responses of their faculty. Overall, they saw it as a critical and significant moment in their development as political beings and as future educators, but were disappointed with and troubled by the outcome of the election and the environment on campus. Their disappointment was exacerbated by the silence of higher education faculty in the wake of what they saw as a traumatic election outcome. Below, I highlight participants' voices to preserve as much of their lived experience as possible.

HOW BLACK PSTS EXPERIENCED THE ELECTION

With the exception of one person, all other participants voted in the election, and all voted for Clinton. This trend is despite the fact that some participants did not like Clinton or saw the choice as a "lesser of two evils." Others saw the result as a foregone conclusion and assumed Clinton would win, no matter who they voted for. Across participants, findings emerged that they experienced the election as a historic moment, an issue of divisiveness, and as more personal than political.

A Historic Moment

Participants were all just over 18 years old, marking this as the first time any of them had voted in a Presidential election. To describe the "major moment" of voting for the first time, participants used adjectives like "empowered," "good," "excited," "really cool," and "hopeful." They agreed that voting "felt like I was making a difference" (Shelly), "kinda like you're making a change, a little bit" (Aeriyelle), or "like me doing my small part" (Samuel). Kendra, too, remembered that "it felt exhilarating" when she saw how "extremely long" the voting lines were on campus. She waited "for at least a hour, but I wanted to say I voted, and I wanted to exercise my right."

Some participants also discussed the historical significance of voting, as when Conner noted that "I felt good and thankful to my ancestors for fighting so hard for my right to vote." In addition to feeling thankful for "how much people went through just to allow people the right to vote, after so much racism and discrimination" (DJ), participants also said they "felt like I was obligated. There was no question I was going to vote" (John) because of the historical legacy of their ancestors' fight for civil rights. Similarly, commenting on how she felt in the moment of voting, Keisha reflected:

> It felt good . . . and I think a lot of people need to utilize this power because some of our ancestors never had this power to vote. It felt like, you know, my voice could be heard. In the end, the result wasn't, you know, as I wanted, so that was kind of like, you know, discouraging. But during the process of voting, it felt powerful. And it felt like, "Wow, like, people fought for me to do this," and I just really appreciated that I had that right to vote because years ago, I wouldn't have had that right.

An Issue of Divisiveness

All of the participants commented on the "inflammatory," "degrading," and "derogatory" nature of Trump's discourse as a key component of how they experienced this election. DJ stated, "I was glad to cast my vote *for* someone, but just as much, I was glad to cast my vote *against* someone to stand up for equality for all people." Participants noted the stark divide between Democratic and Republican views, and what it was like to be on a campus that they had heard included many Republican students and potential Trump supporters. They recalled that it was hard to hear from other students that they supported Trump because they saw a vote for Clinton as more "moral." "I just don't see how someone could vote for Trump with the things he said about multiple cultures, groups, races and all the above," recalled Conner. Aerieylle agreed that Trump's rhetoric was "extremely wild, like just some of the stuff he says, I find extremely offensive and he offends pretty much all. Everybody." Keisha remarked that even though she thought "this presidential election was really just choosing the lesser of two evils," she chose to vote for Clinton because of the divisive traits exhibited by Trump: "It's just that Donald Trump, he is just someone who represent things so negatively—racist, misogynistic. Just all different traits that I just did not want this country to have a president or a leader like this."

They also commented on how the campaign made clear the racist underpinnings of both Trump's views and in society as a whole. Participants recalled that discussions about the election often revealed that some of their peers—and even their friends—were racist. Jasmine called this one of the "dark little secrets that are slowly popping out with each passing day." Samuel remarked that life on campus was more difficult as a Black student because "I just saw more people being more outright about their racism. Like 'okay the presidential candidate is doing it, it must be okay.' And that's what he wants." Jackson, who said he would not "consider myself a Democrat or a Republican" and that his friends consider him a conservative "because I don't hold too many liberal views," spoke at length about the division that the election had created within his friend group:

> My Republican friends who I do know voted for Trump, you know, it's really interesting [*sighs*]. It is interesting to find out, you know, like how [they could do that]. [*pauses, sighs*] Cause I have white friends who voted for him, and you know, I'm like, "so how do you think that makes me feel. Or how do you think that's going to affect just me as a person or others that you see on campus who would be affected by his plans." [*sighs*]

Multiple students had similar experiences of trying to make sense of those they called "friends" voting for a candidate whose rhetoric and policies directly threatened them as Black students.

A Personal versus Political Issue

Experiencing the election as a divisive issue and racist situation also related to how Black students experienced it as a deeply personal issue. While some of their white friends may have argued that "it's not personal, it's political," the participants in this study experienced the political *as* personal. In addition to strained friendships and feelings of empowerment and excitement, they also worked to balance their personal school commitments and political engagement. They talked about how they voted in between classes, or how they studied as they were watching the results come in. Some mentioned not being able to go home to vote because of their class schedules, which almost resulted in not being able to vote for at least two participants. Some participants also joined in canvassing efforts through political or campus organizations. Jasmine I. spoke about visiting people in her dorm to remind everyone to vote. Participants took on this extra civic commitment because, Jasmine I. said, "as Black people, it's just something we have to do, to make sure everyone knows to vote and doesn't forget, because it really matters for us."

HOW BLACK PSTS RESPONDED TO THE ELECTION

None of the participants were pleased with the result of the election. They all initially responded with upset emotions: anger, fear, and hopelessness. A statement from Jasmine S. sums up the general attitude of these first time college voters: "I was just disappointed in the whole process, like I just felt like 'wow, did my vote even matter?'" Later, however, some participants spoke of the resolve and renewed commitment they felt.

Initial Upset

The participants in this research were divided on whether or not the outcome was a surprise. While some said they were shocked by the outcome, others stated that even if they had hoped differently, they were "accustomed" or "used to" things working out in this way. For John, the outcome simply reinforced that "America is just a joke" when it comes to "equality and justice."

They felt the election of Trump gave license for racist, sexist, ableist, and xenophobic acts and discourse to continue, both on campus and in society as a whole. For example, Jasmine S. commented at length about what it felt like, as a Black woman, to leave her dorm room on the morning after the election:

> I just felt like, are we going to be under attack now? I know the majority of this campus is majority Republican probably. So I was just thinking, if I walk outside . . . the white population, do they feel like they can do whatever now? Because some of the things that Donald Trump said were very gruesome and people followed after that. . . . Do they think that they can talk to us any type of way now? How do they feel about it? Because I don't know. When I just stepped outside, campus was just so shallow. Like nobody was saying anything, like everyone was just basically silent. . . . What does this mean for people? What does this mean for me as a Black person? What does this mean for me as a woman?

Whether the student population was, in fact, "majority Republican," did not matter for Jasmine S. on that day, or any day. She experienced the campus as a hostile environment, which she attributed, in part, to political alignments. Shelly responded that she and her peers decided ahead of time that, in their classes, "if one person talk[s] about Donald Trump winning and is happy about it, we're going off." In particular, she said this decision was because there are only "two or three Black people" in each of her classes. On the morning after the election, "I walked in late, like I did not care. [The white students] were just like, 'Aww.' [*indicates that students were mocking her for being upset*] I kind of felt it, but I didn't care, cause it's, like, you know who I voted for, and you know I'm upset. The whole day . . . it was just horrible."

Future Resolve

Participants also responded to the election, after initial hopelessness, with resolve. Some stated that the election had laid bare that there was much work to do, and they rested in the hopes that the surprising outcome would shake other liberals (especially white students) out of their "bubble" and inspire more political engagement and justice-related action. That is, while they were not happy with the election result, they still saw a reason for hope and viewed the election as disequilibrium. It had the potential to be a transformative event. Maria said she was "finished" thinking about the election because "we need to figure out what now," and that her father assured her everything was going to be okay. She hoped that the "shock" that white people felt would motivate them to do something because, as a Black person, she was "amazed that people were surprised." Jasmine S. described trying to move forward by thinking: "What is the next move? What is the next step?"

Keisha's description of her feelings on November 9th highlights several of these day-after responses:

> Honestly, I was hurt. I was surprised. I cried. I was afraid. I was afraid to walk on this campus. [There is] a lot of racism on the campus that I walk on. . . . But I had to . . . go and keep going. [The election results] really motivated and pushed me to. I had to go further. I have to really get this degree because when I get this degree, that's gonna hurt them, really.

Overall, as Keisha explained, participants did their best to use the disappointing experience of the election to motivate them toward the future, be it graduating, becoming a teacher, or engaging in more civic action.

HOW BLACK PSTS PERCEIVED FACULTY RESPONSES TO ELECTION

All of the participants had class on the day or two following the election. Only one participant stated that she skipped class on November 9 because she was too upset. Additionally, all of the participants had both teacher education and courses in other departments on those days, so they were able to discuss if and how professors in different fields responded differently.

Within Teacher Education: Silence

The majority of participants stated that their teacher education instructors did not say anything about the election results. Jasmine S. recalled how, "none of my professors wanted to say anything about it. They didn't have nothing to say." She was conflicted about this and considered that maybe it was better to be silent: "To be honest, I would rather them not talk to me about it because what if, what if my professor voted for Donald Trump, you know? It was something I wouldn't agree with, and it would honestly probably piss me off, and I probably won't want to go to class." Other than Jasmine S., the other participants stated that it was disappointing and discouraging that their education instructors did not address it. In their interviews, students wondered aloud about why the faculty might not have responded. They pondered, for example: Was it that the instructors did not care? Was it that they voted for Trump? Was it that the faculty did not know how to respond or how to address the result when the class may have had voters from both sides? Might it have been that the faculty thought there wasn't time in the schedule to have a discussion, or that it didn't relate to the subject matter (though clearly the students thought it did)?

Beyond Teacher Education

Several participants commented on what professors in other courses did, even if their teacher education faculty did not address it. In a history course, Aeiryelle noted that the professor "said it felt like the sixties to him, with Donald Trump becoming president and all this racial tension and it reminds him of a similar time," but the instructor did not expand on how students might be responding or what they might need. Conner said that "some of my professors were sympathetic in saying how people might not come to class because of the election and they realized that people were saddened by it, but that was it." This took "maybe 20 seconds" of class time, and then it was "back to a lecture." Only one student remembered substantive commentary or discussion from her instructor. Kendra recalled how her English professor, after the class "debriefed" on what it meant to "have a president who stands for . . . racism, classism, and sexism," sent students home from class early: "Like it was that deep, he literally was like, 'I just can't have class today, I have to honestly really think about it; he's really our president.' So it got to being that serious."

Identities in the Classroom

Part of what made the day after so horrible, as they described it, was that their faculty did not talk about what happened, with the exception of Kendra's English professor above. And, it should be noted (likely to the surprise of no one), that Kendra's professor was Black. The other faculty that participants encountered in the days after were all white. Does this mean that, had they had a more racially diverse faculty, that it would have come up in the classroom? Not necessarily. Does this mean that other white faculty who were not participants' instructors also did not address the election results? Not necessarily that either. What is meant is that twelve Black students had approximately fifty-five different faculty members in the days after the election and all but three remained silent. Only one from those fifty-five opened space in their classroom to discuss and process in any kind of substantive way. What it meant is that, in a national context of anti-Blackness, twelve Black students experienced their campus in the same way. That is twelve students too many.

WHAT THIS MEANS FOR MENTORING
BLACK STUDENTS ON DAYS AFTER

Lisa Delpit (2018) states that, "learning about how millennial teachers of color approach the world can expand our own awareness of how to meet the challenges of our collective futures in this great, but often flawed country—in ways we might never have imagined" (p. xv). Thus, what does it mean that some of the Black PSTs whose experiences were shared above went from feeling excited and empowered to feeling disenchanted and disempowered, like their voices do not matter? In teacher education programs and higher education more broadly, how do we show them to stay strong and involved, as they indicated they hoped for, while recognizing the intersectional identities that individual students inhabit? For example, take this excerpt from an interview with Samuel, where he reflects upon the changes in his emotions before and after the election and where he is struggling to articulate a feeling of disillusionment:

> *Samuel*: I remember thinking we had progressed. We had moved forward. And then the day after the election, I just felt like we took a step back and now what I see has been going on . . . I feel like stuff is getting taken away. I lost a good amount of hope that day. Like, the idea that we would, that like, just . . . I don't know how to explain it. When he [Trump] was elected, he . . . I don't know how to explain it. He just . . . [*sighs and pauses*]
>
> *Interviewer:* How does it make you feel to talk about this topic?

Samuel: I mean, it . . . it sucks with just him being in that position. Just [*sighs*] like anytime I think about it, I get, I get upset. [*long pause*] I get sad.

Some Black college students reported that they experienced the election as disequilibrium, that they saw it as an inciting incident or transformative moment. For some Black PSTs, the election galvanized them, and higher education should nurture this attitude toward an increased commitment to justice. Such commitments are harder to sustain, however, in institutions that continue to marginalize and silence Black students. As Catone and Thilbidar (2018) write, "almost by definition, we are asking that they [MTOC] become teachers inside institutions that have not caught up to these [activist] beliefs in their systemic organization, policies, and practices. This gap between 'wokeness' and institutional practice makes it more difficult to help millennial teachers of color connect their understanding of power and their roles as change agents to their teaching practice" (p. 85).

Further, a huge challenge is the commitment (intentional or not) to silence in the face of injustice. Faculty clearly wrestle with what Hess (2005) terms "the disclosure dilemma," where educators remain unsure and uneasy about whether or not to disclose their voting habits and political leanings, especially at a time when academics are under attack from various groups that seek to publicly shame and harass scholars for their "liberal" or "indoctrinating" views (AAUP, 2017). Yet, within this political context, how do we make sure we are modeling for our PSTs the need to address current and controversial events in their future classrooms? This question is not to discount the very real fear and concern that many academics feel about addressing politics in the classroom, but research continues to show that such claims at neutrality are unrealistic. As Journell (2016) writes, "teachers cannot realistically remain politically neutral because teachers are political beings . . . It is unrealistic to expect [them] to be able to remove themselves from their political personas once they walk into a classroom" (p. 102). It is imperative that teacher educators understand this and structure curricula that allow for these discussions.

One would hope that, if the election were to be addressed and discussed anywhere, it might be in a College of Education with a commitment to inquiry and justice. Yet, many of their faculty did not address it, nor did the College as a whole issue any statement in support of students who might be struggling. I argue that this is more evidence of the "overwhelming presence of Whiteness" in teacher education (Sleeter, 2001, p. 94). As Sleeter (2017) argues, "processes and structures of teacher education that purport to be color blind in fact serve to perpetuate Whiteness in teacher education" (p. 8). When we have Black PSTs like Keisha saying that there is "a lot of racism on the campus that I walk on," we perpetuate this racism by not addressing her lived experiences as a Black student at a PWI in the wake of a traumatic election.

When students like Jasmine S. are saying that she experienced campus as "so shallow" where "everyone was just basically silent," it is akin to educational malpractice to ignore what she is experiencing under the guise of neutrality. Claims of neutrality, in this instance, do more harm than good, both in the present moment and for their future.

Just as the English professor referenced above did for Kendra's class, faculty can model for PSTs what it looks like to push back against neutrality and how to deal with controversial events in the classroom, as well as how to move between hopelessness and galvanization. One way to do this is for more teacher educators to learn about and enact methods of caring that are focused on supporting Black students and other students of color. One form is *culturally relevant critical care* (Roberts, 2010), a method of caring for students of color in which teachers "emphasized a concern for the futures of their students and strove to provide political clarity as it relates to race" (Watson et al., 2016). This theory of care, like Parsons' (2005) concept of *culturally relevant care*, emphasizes the intersections of traditional notions of care (see Noddings) with justice-oriented commitments to maintaining and furthering students' rights and perspectives. Similarly, educators who enact *culturally relevant critical teacher care* "prepare their students with the dispositions, knowledge, and skills to construct what Carl Grant has called 'flourishing lives'" (Hambacher & Bondy, 2016, p. 327).

This praxis requires, however, constant attention to the ways that individuals and institutions have been built—and continue to be maintained—as places that are hostile to Black students and faculty, and a clear, conscious, and continuous commitment to dismantling these systems in favor of more liberatory, caring ones. That is, as Catone and Thilbidar (2018) call on teacher educators to do: "We must answer the paradoxical call that activist millennials of color are making to all of us: Dream big and stay woke" (p. 85).

RECOMMENDATIONS FOR CULTURALLY RESPONSIVE MENTORING

The findings above, and more importantly, the lived experiences of the Black college students within and beyond this research illustrate how vital it is that higher education faculty commit to teaching for justice and equity on days after. The 2016 election is but one example of days after and, indeed, there are many more in the past and to come in the future. The recommendations below—adapted from Dunn (2021)—offer higher education faculty suggestions for how to teach for justice and equity on days after, which certainly support their Black students, but are also best practice for supporting *all* students in these critical moments. The foundation for these recommendations is an understanding of and practice toward culturally relevant critical teacher care.

Be Prepared and Proactive. Remember that we do not have to know *which* event will occur in order to be prepared for "a days after" discussion. It is less about the particularities of the event and the ensuing discussion than about an overall disposition and commitment to educating for equity and justice. We should commit to being flexible in our practice, to learning strategies for days after pedagogy (Dunn, 2021), and to engaging with Black students, colleagues, and communities in ways that enable our actions to be authentic rather than reactionary. To be proactive, we can practice what we will say and how we will say it and move beyond the concern that talking about politics or injustice should be left out of the classroom. We have nothing to defend when we teach about these moments; we do not have to ask for either permission or forgiveness. We are not indoctrinating students; we are not politicking. We are teaching *for* justice and equity. We are not teaching to be partisan; we are teaching to address human rights.

Develop and Sustain Community Norms that Support Black Students. At the beginning of each semester, I have my students—from first-semester freshmen to advanced doctoral students—create class dialogue norms as a collective. They can come up with expectations for them themselves, for their peers, and for me as an instructor. For example, one that we consistently discuss is that intent does not mitigate impact. That is, we discuss why it does not necessarily matter what you intend to do or say; if the impact is harmful, you have still caused harm. I also share with them an extended quotation from writer Tayari Jones' *Time* magazine (2018) essay "There's nothing virtuous about finding common ground," in response to the constant public refrain that we should be teaching two sides or both sides:

> The middle is a point equidistant from two poles. That's it. There is nothing inherently virtuous about being neither here nor there. Buried in this is a false equivalency of ideas, what you might call the "good people on both sides" phenomenon. When we revisit our shameful past, ask yourself, Where was the middle? Rather than chattel slavery, perhaps we could agree on a nice program of indentured servitude? Instead of subjecting Japanese-American citizens to indefinite detention during WWII, what if we had agreed to give them actual sentences and perhaps provided a receipt for them to reclaim their things when they were released? What is halfway between moral and immoral?

Finally, I have students read Ozlem and Sensoy's (2012, 2014) article on how to engage in classes with social justice content. Though the authors' intended

audience is preservice teachers, the engagement norms they outline are relevant for all fields. Some examples of the norms they suggest include:

> Recognize the difference between opinions and informed knowledge; Recognize
> how your own social positionality (such as your race, class, gender, sexuality,
> ability-status) informs your perspectives and reactions to your instructor and
> those whose work you study in the course; Differentiate between safety and
> comfort; Accept discomfort as necessary for social justice growth; Identify
> where your learning edge is and push it. For example, whenever you think,
> *I already know this,* ask yourself, *How can I take this deeper?* Or, *How am I
> applying in practice what I already know.*

While I appreciate very much these suggestions for how students can be
pushed to engage in discussions of justice and equity, they also seem to be
normatively written for a white audience. Not all of those norms apply to all
people in the same way. For example, in discussions about racism and white
supremacy, white students' discomfort is very different from Black students'
discomfort. Thus, I also start each semester with a list of additional communication norms that focus on the things we will *not* call upon marginalized
groups, including Black students, to do in our course. We will not ask them to:

- Be "nice," "civil," or "calm" in the face of dehumanization or discus-
  sions about this oppression;
- Educate others about their experiences;
- Speak for their particular marginalized group(s);
- "Debate" or prove the existence of oppression or marginalization;
- Make others feel comfortable;
- Give others' "opinions" equal weight to their experiences.

To expect our Black students to do any of these things in our classes, whether
on days after or not, is to engage in continued oppression and dehumanization.

Resist Silence and Neutrality. Claiming neutrality in the wake of injustice actually perpetuates the injustice itself, especially for the marginalized
groups who are most impacted by injustice. In the case of the 2016 election,
the Black college students I interviewed were devastated by the outcome, but
equally so that their faculty did not address what happened. To be silent in
the face of our Black students' pain and trauma means that we are contribut-
ing to their pain and trauma. To not talk about these events on days after is
perpetuating more racial violence and is a form of anti-Blackness, especially
at PWIs, especially by white faculty.

Focus on Harm Reduction. I'm not personally a fan of the "safe space"
language when it comes to classroom community. First, we can never

guarantee a completely "safe" space in our classrooms because we do not know what students are going to say to and about each other and each other's communities and contexts. Further, I don't actually think the classroom *should* be safe for all viewpoints. I am not going to debate another person's right to exist. I am not going to debate another person's humanity. And even if I could guarantee what happens in my small classroom space, we are working in, as bell hooks says, an "imperialist, capitalist, white supremacist, cis hetero patriarchy." I am working at a supposedly "land-grant" institution that exists on stolen land. I can absolutely do my best to ensure, for example, that no one makes explicit racist, homophobic, sexist, transphobic, xenophobic, or otherwise discriminatory statements. But truly the most I can do is engage in what scholars call "harm reduction": address it when it happens and be swift and decisive and clear in how I do so. I cannot do *no* harm, but I can work to do *less* harm.

White Faculty: Do Not Let Your Colleagues of Color be the Only Ones to Address This. Our positionality matters greatly here. If we identify as white, we cannot rely on our colleagues of color to be the only ones teaching about these issues and moments as they happen. Black faculty cannot be the only ones who directly address the ongoing instances of racial violence and white supremacy. It is an act of white privilege, fragility, and protectionism to (pretend to) be surprised when another "day after" arises. Now, a fairly large caution here: We should not engage in these discussions if we do not know how to do it in a caring, thoughtful, and critical way. That risks more harm. But we also cannot use the excuse of not knowing how as a reason to continue not to do it. It's past time to learn how. This book is one place to start.

REFERENCES

Abrica, E. J. & Morales, A. R. (2017). *Conceptualizing Latino experiences and outcomes in post-secondary institutions: Deficiencies, assets, and a post-racial contract*. Paper presented at the Childhoods in Motion: Children, Youth, Migration, and Education Conference, Los Angeles, CA.

Achinstein, B., & Aguirre, J. (2008). Cultural match or culturally suspect: How new teachers of color negotiate sociocultural challenges in the classroom. *Teachers College Record, 110*(8), 1505–1540.

Allcott, H., & Gentzkow, M. (2017). *Social media and fake news in the 2016 election* (No. w23089). National Bureau of Economic Research.

American Association of University Professors. (2017). *Academic freedom of students and professors, and political discrimination*. http://www.aaup.org.

Apollon, D. (2011). *Don't call them 'post-racial': Millennials' attitudes on race, racism, and key systems in our society*. Applied Research Center.

Ayers, R., & Ayers, W. (2014). *Teaching the taboo: Courage and imagination in the classroom*. Teachers College Press.

Brown, K. D. (2014). Teaching in color: A critical race theory in education analysis of the literature on preservice teachers of color and teacher education in the US. *Race, Ethnicity, and Education, 17*(3), 326–345. https://doi.org/10.1080/1361332 4.2013.832921.

Brown, K. D. & Ward, A. M. (2018). Black preservice teachers on race and racism in the millennial era: Considerations for teacher education. In M. E. Dilworth (Ed.), *Black PSTs* (pp. 89–104). Harvard Education Press.

Castillo, W. & Schramm, M. (2016, November 9). *How we voted: by age, education, race, and sexual orientation*. USA Today. http://college.usatoday.com.

Catone, K. C. & Tahbildar, D. (2018). Ushering in a new era of teacher activism: Beyond Hashtags, building hope. In M. E. Dilworth (Ed.), *Millennial teachers of color* (pp. 73–88). Harvard Education Press.

The Center for Information and Research on Civic Learning and Engagement (CIRCLE). (2008). *Trends by race, ethnicity and gender*. http://civicyouth.org.

The Center for Information and Research on Civic Learning and Engagement. (2016). *The 2016 Youth Vote*. http://civicyouth.org.

Creswell, J. W., & Poth, C. N. (2017). *Qualitative inquiry and research design: Choosing among five approaches*. Sage.

Delpit, L. (2018). Foreword. In M.E. Dilworth (Ed.), *Millennial teachers of color* (pp. xiii–xv). Harvard Education Press.

Dilworth, M. E. (2018). *Millennial teachers of color*. Harvard Education Press.

Einfeld, A., & Collins, D. (2008). The relationships between service-learning, social justice, multicultural competence, and civic engagement. *Journal of College Student Development, 49*(2), 95–109. https://doi.org/10.1353/csd.2008.0017.

Evans, R. W., Avery, P. G., & Pederson, P. V. (2000). Taboo topics: Cultural restraint on teaching social issues. *The Clearing House, 73*(5), 295–302. https://doi.org/10.1080/00098650009600973.

Flanagan. C. & Levine, P. (2010). Civic engagement and the transition to adulthood. *The Future of Children, 20*(1), 159–179. https://doi.org/10.1353/foc.0.0043.

Freeman, H. R. (2018). Millennial teachers of color and their quest for community. In M.E. Dilworth (Ed.), *Millennial teachers of color* (pp. 25–38). Harvard Education Press.

Hambacher, E., & Bondy, E. (2016). Creating communities of culturally relevant critical teacher care. *Action in Teacher Education, 38*(4), 327–343. https://doi.org/10.1080/01626620.2016.1226206.

Herrera, S. G., & Morales, A. R. (2018). Understanding "me" within "Generation Me: The meaning perspectives held toward and by millennial culturally and linguistically diverse teachers. In M. E. Dilworth (Ed.), *Millennial teachers of color*. Harvard Education Press.

Hess, D. E. (2005). How do teachers' political views influence teaching about controversial issues? *Social Education, 69*(1), 47–49.

Hess, D. E. (2010). Teaching student teachers to examine how their political views in their teaching. In E. E., Heilman, R. F. Amthor, & M. T. Missias (Eds.), *Social studies and diversity education: What we do and why we do it* (pp. 226–229). Routledge.

Higher Education Research Institute. (2010). *Voting behavior among college students.* https://heri.ucla.edu/PDFs/pubs/briefs/HERI_ResearchBrief_Politics_Oct_2010. pdf.

Higher Education Research Institute. (2015). *The American freshman: National norms Fall 2015.* https://www.heri.ucla.edu/monographs/TheAmericanFreshman2015. pdf.

Hope, E. C., Keels, M., & Durkee, M. I. (2016). Participation in Black Lives Matter and deferred action for childhood arrivals: Modern activism among Black and Latino college students. *Journal of Diversity in Higher Education*, *9*(3), 203. https://doi.org/10.1037/dhe0000032.

Ishmael, S., Kuranishi, A. T., Chavez, G. A., & Miller, L. A. (2018). Stagger Lee: Millennial teachers' perspectives, politics, and prose. In M. E. Dilworth (Ed.), *Millennial teachers of color* (pp. 11–24). Harvard Education Press.

Jackson, T. O. (2015). Perspectives and insights from preservice teachers of color on developing culturally responsive pedagogy at predominantly white institutions. *Action in Teacher Education*, *37*(3), 223–237. https://doi.org/10.1080/01626620.2 015.1048007.

James, J. H. (2009). Reframing the disclosure debate: Confronting issues of transparency in teaching controversial content. *Social Studies Research & Practice*, *4*(1).

Journell, W. (2011). Teachers' controversial issue decisions related to race, gender, and religion during the 2008 Presidential Election. *Theory & Research in Social Education*, *39*(3), 348–392. https://doi.org/10.1080/00933104.2011.10473459.

Journell, W. (2016). Making a case for teacher political disclosure. *JCT (Online)*, *31*(1), 100.

Kelchtermans, G. (2005). Teachers' emotions in educational reforms: Self-understanding, vulnerable commitment and micropolitical literacy. *Teaching and teacher education*, *21*(8), 995–1006. https://doi.org/10.1016/j.tate.2005.06.009.

Kohli, R. (2009). Critical race reflections: Valuing the experiences of teachers of color in teacher education. *Race, Ethnicity, and Education*, *12*(2), 235–251. https://doi.org/10.1080/13613320902995491.

Kohli, R. (2018). Behind school doors: The impact of hostile racial climates on urban teachers of color. *Urban Education*, *53*(3), 307–333. https://doi.org/10.1177/0042085916636653.

Magaldi, D., Conway, T., & Trub, L. (2018). "I am here for a reason": Minority teachers bridging many divides in urban education. *Race, Ethnicity, and Education*, *21*(3), 306–318. https://doi.org/10.1080/13613324.2016.1248822.

Maxwell, J. A. (2012). *Qualitative research design: An interactive approach* (Vol. 41). Sage.

Myers, J. P. (2009). Learning in politics: Teachers' political experiences as a pedagogical resource. *International Journal of Educational Research*, *48*(1), 30–39. https://doi.org /10.1016/j.ijer.2009.03.001.

Palmer, P. J. (1998). *The courage to teach: Exploring the inner landscape of a teacher's life*. John Wiley & Sons.

Parsons, E. C. (2005). From caring as a relation to culturally relevant caring: A white teacher's bridge to Black students. *Equity and Excellence in Education, 38*(1), 25–34. https://doi.org/10.1080/10665680390907884.

Richmond, E. (2017, January 10). *What is the future of public education?* The Atlantic. https://www.theatlantic.com.

Roberts, M. A. 2010. Toward a theory of Culturally Relevant Critical Teacher Care: African American teachers' definitions and perceptions of care for African-American Students. *Journal of Moral Education, 39*(4), 449–467. https://doi.org/10.1080/03057241003754922.

Sleeter, C. E. (2017). Critical Race Theory and the Whiteness of teacher education. *Urban Education, 52*(2), 155–169. https://doi.org/10.1177/0042085916668957.

Strauss, A., & Corbin, J. (1998). *Basics of qualitative research techniques*. Sage.

Taylor, P. (2016). *The next America: Boomers, millennials, and the looming generational showdown*. Hachette.

Watson, W., Sealey-Ruiz, Y., & Jackson, I., (2016). Daring to care: the role of culturally relevant care in mentoring Black and Latino male high school students. *Race, Ethnicity, and Education, 19*(5), 980–1002. https://doi.org/10.1080/13613324.2014.911169.

NOTE

1. While APA guidelines recommend that all racial identities be capitalized, this chapter has intentionally chosen to lowercase white as a way to dismantle anti-Blackness in academia.

PART V

Mentoring and Social Media

Chapter Eleven

Mentoring and Social Media

Lessons Learned from R.A.C.E. Mentoring

Jemimah L. Young,
Erinn F. Floyd, and Donna Y. Ford

INTRODUCTION

Graduate student access to African American faculty mentors is often limited due to the underrepresentation of African American faculty across the nation. According to the most recent data from the U.S. Department of Education, the National Center for Education Statistics, 9.5 percent of all full-time faculty members were African American compared to 65.5 percent of full-time faculty who were White[1] (Snyder, de Brey, & Dillow, 2019). Although there has been a minor increase in the representation of African American faculty members within higher education, the progression has been measured. Since African American faculty are spread across multiple colleges and universities across the nation, it is feasible to conclude that many African American graduate students lack direct access to African American faculty within their respective colleges and universities.

Historically, most African American students have utilized informal networks to gain access to the rules and procedures of academic spaces hidden from people of color. Thus, as African American students graduate, they shared their information with peers and students from different institutions while attending conferences or over lengthy phone conversations. This mentoring process, though effective, was inefficient and limited in scope. Because mentorship in previous models was built on one's access to networks of scholars of color maintained through invitation, it is not surprising that these networks were unable to meet the field's demand. However, social media mentoring networks have emerged as a viable and effective means to address this enduring challenge.

Social media offers numerous affordances with minimal constraints to support broader networking and mentorship opportunities for African American graduate students. Social media outlets represent the fastest-growing news and information media resources globally (Lenhart, 2015). Social media has become a viable resource for disseminating research and policy-related information within K-12 and higher education settings. Thus, Twitter, Facebook, and Instagram are often the first choice of teachers, policymakers, and educational researchers for education-related information. Likewise, young professionals across urbanicity (e.g., urban, suburban, and rural environments) tend to interact on multiple social media outlets throughout the day. These social media utilization trends indicate that social media outlets are accessible and effective means of global communication that can be leveraged to support effective mentoring networks for African American students. Thus, the purpose of this chapter is to explore the affordances of social media mentoring for African American graduate students with an acute emphasis on lessons learned from the R.A.C.E. (Research, Advocacy, Collaboration, Empowerment) Mentoring social media network.

In the sections that follow, we first provide a background for the chapter through a brief overview of the importance of ethnically matched mentoring for the success of African American students and the enduring challenges. Second, we elaborate on the benefits and challenges of mentoring for African American scholars. This section elucidates the need for nontraditional mechanisms to facilitate access to high-quality mentorship for African American scholars. Finally, we outline the affordances and constraints of social media as a mechanism to connect African American scholars through closed mentoring networks unsanctioned and controlled by an institution or other entity. Finally, we highlight the R.A.C.E Mentoring social media network as an exemplar by presenting some examples of the network's structure and documented success.

BACKGROUND

The need for ethnically matched mentoring was present throughout the history of African American people in the United States as a means to ensure the survival and success of future generations. This tradition remains today throughout society and is commonplace within the structure and culture of colleges and universities. The concept of mentoring dates back to thirteenth-century West African culture in the role of griots, or traveling poets, musicians, and storytellers. Griots served as leaders and preserved the oral history of the empire (Freeman, 2004). This early model of empowerment through ethnically matched mentorship within African society survived the Atlantic Slave Trade and stringent laws, which prohibited communication, social gathering, and the cultivation of heritage and tradition among slaves to become a staple in the lives of African Americans in the Deep South and beyond.

The early and enduring experiences of African Americans in the United States necessitate the need for a sustained emphasis on the ethnically matched mentorship of African Americans. Specifically, as African American students matriculate to the highest academic levels new challenges arise that transcend issues of assimilation and acculturation (Green & Scott, 2003). Navigating the academic policies and politics of higher education requires insider knowledge from trusted and experienced advisors with shared cultural and ethnic backgrounds. Therefore, ethnically matched academic mentoring is historically and practically relevant to the development and sustainability of a critical mass of African American scholars.

ETHNICALLY MATCHED MENTORSHIP

Mentorship is recognized across professions and society as an important tool to support success and upward mobility. Given the underrepresentation of African Americans within the professoriate, it is essential that African American graduate students receive ethnically matched mentorship because mentors' racial/ethnic backgrounds influence mentoring practices (Steele & Korn, 2014). Mentorship is a relationship between two people where the individual with more experience, knowledge, and connections is able to pass along what they have learned to a more junior individual within a certain field (Oshinkale, 2019). The key elements of this definition are the experience, knowledge, and connections the mentor can provide the mentee. Although African American and White faculty members exist in the same educational spaces, their experiences, knowledge, and connections are often more different than similar regarding navigating graduate school and the professoriate. Additionally, given the different experiences and perspectives of African American and White faculty, there are often differences in how each group approaches the mentorship of African American students.

In a case study conducted across multiple sites, McCoy et al. (2015) found that White mentors operated from a colorblind perspective. Hence, White mentors believed that it was best to treat all mentees the same, which is problematic because the academy does not treat all graduate students the same. According to McCoy, the colorblind approach did not afford African American students equal access to socialization and career opportunities compared to their White counterparts. Furthermore, African American graduate students often received fewer teaching and research assistantships and less engagement with faculty. This trend is often rationalized by a lack of fit between the student's research interests and the research interests of the available faculty mentors, but this trend is often moderated by established differences in research agendas across different racial groups especially within the social sciences. Nonetheless, mentoring African American students requires guidance based on the unique nature of their experiences and needs (Alvarez et al., 2009). Mentors must be aware of all of the dynamics African American graduate students face as they navigate the academy as scholars and faculty. Mentoring, networking, and collaborative peer relationships are vital aspects of the socialization process and general success of African American graduate students (McCoy et al., 2015). These three relationship types are often enhanced through ethnic matching.

African Americans often face challenges and considerations related to scholarship, teaching, and service due to their racial background that require unique mentoring considerations. African American graduate students require mentorship because there are enormous challenges posed by the differences between the culture of African American students' communities of origin and the culture of many of the universities they attend (Alvarez & Blume, 2009). For instance, African American students regularly face systemic racism, discrimination, and microaggressions (Brunsma et al., 2017). They are affronted with the brunt of isolation and neglect within their respective departments (Gay, 2004). Racial hostility affronts Black students, and they face repeated challenges in search of a space to belong in academic and professional disciplines where few people look like them (Griffin & Reddick, 2011, Hinton et al., 2009). Thus, African American graduate students require guidance on the most effective means to navigate the professoriate from other African American faculty who have walked in their shoes.

For instance, African American faculty are often assigned more committee responsibilities and tend to take on more responsibility in advising due to what is commonly referred to as the "Black Tax" (Griffin et al., 2011; Griffin et al., 2013). Essentially, African American faculty members receive additional service responsibilities within colleges and universities (e.g., student advising, faculty searches, or diversity audits) due to their racial background; however, the same expectations are not placed on their White faculty peers (Louis et al., 2016). Ethnically matched mentorship can help African American graduate students to develop creative and nonpunitive ways to avoid or manage these added responsibilities by leveraging the experience, knowledge, and connections of African American faculty mentors.

Faculty mentor interactions are critical to fostering African American students' success in graduate programs. Unfortunately, African American students may not always find a mentor of the same race. The paired mentor should be culturally appropriate, responsive, and intentional in offering a counterspace or alternative to African American students' negative experiences, images, or perspectives (Milner et al., 2002). A culturally responsive approach to African American graduate student mentorship is ideal because most academic fields lack sufficient African American faculty to support ethnically matched mentoring programs for graduate students, but social media provides a means to connect African American scholars and graduate students from different colleges and universities through mentoring networks.

HOW DOES SOCIAL MEDIA BRIDGE THE RACIAL MENTORING DIVIDE?

The use of technology and social media to bridge the mentoring divide faced by African American students has become more prevalent in recent years. Issues of race, gender, and culture have inspired African American students, whose shared experiences have proved challenging in the academy, to access social media networks for support and greater visibility of ethnically matched mentors who make impactful connections with mentees on issues of relevance, collective experiences, and work-life-balance (Steele & Korn, 2014). Mentoring, networking, and collaborative peer relationships have demonstrated their vital importance to the socialization process and general success of African American graduate students. Thus, many African American students have turned to social media networks for shared experiences based on race, culture, and gender to support their graduate programs.

Social media mentoring networks help connect people by eliminating the location constraints of traditional face-to-face mentoring (Montgomery, 2018). This is especially important for African American students and faculty who derive strength and guidance from mentoring relationships (DeWalt, 2004; Griffin & Reddick, 2011; Milner, 2004). With the invention of the Internet, e-mentoring grew out of traditional mentoring and became popular in 1993 for young professionals across numerous industries and disciplines (Neely et al., 2017). It is important to note that early e-mentoring lacked the video conferencing capabilities of today, but rather written communication through email and follow-up phone calls were the norm. Today, e-mentoring retains the benefits of face-to-face interaction by utilizing video chat services, such as FaceTime, Google Hangouts, Skype, and video chat through Facebook, etc. (Steele & Korn, 2014; Agosto et al., 2016).

In recent years, the internet has added a more personal touch to the mentoring process (Crisp & Cruz, 2009), and social media platforms, such as Facebook and Twitter, are ideal networks to provide an informal community of support (Steele & Korn, 2014) for graduate students. These platforms are useful in fostering and facilitating engagement to support students from underrepresented groups in higher education and promote equity, advocacy, inclusion, and personal agency (Montgomery, 2018). However, all social media platforms are not created equal. Instead, each platform serves a unique primary function and often attracts a specific type of user seeking the platform's services.

For instance, Facebook is advertised as a technology; Twitter is packaged as a communication service platform; and YouTube is an information "distribution platform" (D'Onfro, 2016; Frier et al., 2016; YouTube, n.d.). Data from the Pew Research Center indicate that Facebook remains the most popular social media outlet, while Twitter remains the least popular (Greenwood, Perrin, & Duggan, 2016). Of the three major players in the social media field, Facebook's popularity is due primarily to the multiple functions that Facebook affords users. The ability to send and receive files, communicate with various people worldwide and build networks based on similar interests is among the affordances that make Facebook an ideal mentoring platform. Hence, Facebook is the home of numerous social media networks dedicated to the academic professional mentoring of African Americans. One extremely successful Facebook mentoring network is R.A.C.E. Mentoring.

R. A. C. E. MENTORING SOCIAL MEDIA NETWORK

R.A.C.E. (Research, Advocacy, Collaboration, Empowerment) Mentoring is an initiative and program co-founded by Drs. Donna Y. Ford, Michelle Trotman Scott, and Malik S. Henfield in 2013. R.A.C.E. Mentoring (RM) is a virtual mentoring community that plays a vital role in the scholarship of students and scholars of color through virtual mentoring on the social media platform, Facebook. It provides a "community of care" (Jones, 2017, p. 79) where individuals can express their needs without fear of judgement and receive advice from multiple professionals, which is recognized as one of the key features of RM. Wingfield (2017) reflected on how RM helped negotiate the multiple identities she experienced and asserted that social media represented a "safe harbor" of support as a counter to the racism and sexism she and other African American women experienced at PWIs (p. 13). Today, RM supports hundreds of scholars across the nation.

At the center of RM is a sense of community developed by connecting a network of people of color with some shared and divergent interests through the main hub and subsequent subgroups. RM subgroups are indicated in the diagram below and were first published in the 2016 RM book. The subgroups include: (1) RM Main, (2) RM scholarship, (3) RM Neo Writing Bootcamp, (4) RM Teaching and Advising, (5) RM Leadership, (6) RM Families and Communities, (7) RM Undergraduate and Graduate scholars, and (8) RM Health and Spirituality.

As presented in figure 11.1, the hub is RM Main. The network is maintained and expanded as members collaborate, co-publish, co-present, seek and share advice, and post job opportunities, as well as conference, publishing, and grant opportunities. To foster collaboration, members are encouraged to join RM subgroups of interests and required to contribute to 1–2 subgroups at least monthly with new/original posts or responses to posts by others. This obligation ensures that all members remain active, which maximizes the quality of interactions within RM.

Scholars from various education-related disciplines founded RM; thus, it remains mostly representative of education fields. Improving representation in education is a core value of RM. RM's organizational structure includes groups dedicated to teaching, scholarship, and the professoriate in general.

Figure 11.1 Diagram of R.A.C.E. Mentoring Subgroups

These foci allow the organization's mentoring abilities to be streamlined by enabling mentors to curate content based on their experiences and expertise and add this content to the most appropriate RM network section. Through peer-to-peer networking and numerous virtual activities, RM continues to inform scholars of color in the academy.

RM was founded to address three primary objectives related to equity and diversity in higher education. The first objective of RM is to provide mentoring to faculty and doctoral/graduate students of color. This is often considered the primary function of the group as it is the most pronounced. The group supports approximately five hundred members across networks of faculty and students of color from multiple colleges and universities. Mentoring activities include manuscript review, personal career counseling, webinars (at a small fee), as well as daily advice blogs. The second objective of RM is to increase the representation of faculty of color on campuses and within the tenure pool. To achieve this goal, RM takes advantage of a critical mass of tenured faculty of color from different colleges and universities to provide inroads for junior faculty and graduate students seeking employment. The third and final objective of RM is to promote collaboration among academics in all educational settings (e.g., P-12, higher education, nonprofits, etc.) and at all types of colleges and universities (e.g., HBCU and PWI, private, public, and online). This objective is essential to the synergy necessary for RM to thrive as a virtual mentoring community. Essentially, RM provides a conduit between different educational institutions that typically exist in silos. This is necessary because, unlike their peers, many African American graduate students lack opportunities to explore various colleges and universities before attending or seeking employment.

Since its inception, RM has been influential in the graduation, employment, tenure, and promotion of hundreds of African Americans within the academy. According to the organization's leadership, RM's success has primarily been attributed to the family dynamic that the organization fosters through what Dr. Ladson-Billings refers to as a "warm demander" approach to mentorship and motivation. Essentially, because RM is composed of scholars at every level within the professoriate (graduate students to distinguished full professors), there is a more than sufficient supply of aspirational mentors to support multiple career trajectories. However, more importantly, these mentors hold RM members and themselves accountable for their mutual success and RM's success by *warmly demanding* excellence from all of its members.

RECOMMENDATIONS FOR CULTURALLY
RESPONSIVE MENTORING

Through our participation in R.A.C.E. Mentoring, we have learned a great deal about the power of mentorship to support the growth and development of African American graduate students. Based on our shared experiences we provide the following three recommendations.

1. *Successful mentorship requires that both the mentor and the mentee contribute to the wealth of knowledge.* Mentorship is a relationship, thus it is only as good as the contributions provided by the mentor as well as the mentee. Institutional knowledge is the currency of the academy; thus, it is guarded by those in power. The traditions and policies of higher education are often kept foreign to African American faculty and graduate students, thus when we gain access to this knowledge it is important to share it with our network and sphere of influence. This means that as the mentor gains new insights they should share those insights, and likewise as the mentee gains new insights they should do the same. Within R.A.C.E. Mentoring, the reciprocal exchange of knowledge and opportunities is an expectation not only for faculty, but for graduate student participants as well.

2. *Multiple mentors provide mentees richer mentorship by offering the benefits of the combined experiences of more than one mentor.* The experiences of all African American faculty are not the same, and often differ based on discipline, college/university, and gender. Thus, it is important to develop a network of multiple faculty mentors. R.A.C.E. Mentoring facilitates these interactions by connecting scholars and graduate students from across the nation. Moreover, the development of these relationships is organic and often develops as the result of faculty responses to graduate student posts within the network's Facebook page. Hence graduate students receive advice from multiple sources instantly and then choose to pursue further mentorship as they deem necessary.

3. *Mentorship is enhanced by the level of connections and opportunities that a mentor can afford a mentee.* At the core of effective mentorship is the ability of the mentor to afford the mentee opportunities that the mentee would not have access to otherwise. Access to these opportunities is especially important for African American graduate students. Thus, effective mentors are well connected within broader networks and thus can broker opportunities and experiences for mentees. However, it is up to the mentee to make the best of these opportunities and ensure

that the mentor's network and connections remain intact. R.A.C.E. Mentoring is home to world-renown scholars, department chairs, deans, and other academic administrators, thus the connections to opportunities and experiences are endless for graduate students. However, trust and shared expectations of excellence must be maintained to sustain the success of the network for future generations of scholars.

CONCLUSION

Mentoring is one of the most salient factors related to success, thus the effects of mentoring are well-documented within academia and other settings (Kanten, 2017; Lorenzett et al., 2019). Yet, access to ethnically matched mentoring remains a challenge for African American students and professionals. In the present chapter, we focused on higher education, where mentoring is often restricted or limited by the availability of suitable or willing mentors. We argued that the documented experiences of African American faculty and students at Predominantly White Institutions reflect instances of prejudice, racism, and isolation from the campus and community (Ford et al., 2017; Griffin & Reddick, 2011; Thompson & Louque, 2005), which warrants the need for ethnically matched mentorship networks. However, the absence of a critical mass of African American faculty severely limits ethnically matched mentorship opportunities for African American graduate students. Consequently, we argued that social media and specifically Facebook provides an effective means to support mentorship between African American faculty and graduate students. Using R.A.C.E. Mentoring as an exemplar we provided several examples of how to utilize social media to support ethnically matched mentoring. In conclusion, we hope that this chapter expands the possibilities of social media as a means to mentor and develop the next generation of African American scholars.

REFERENCES

Agosto, V., Karanxha, Z., Unterreiner, A., Cobb-Roberts, D., Esnard, T., Wu, K., & Beck, M. (2016). Running bamboo: A mentoring network of women intending to thrive in academia. *NASPA Journal about Women in Higher Education*, *9*, 74–89.

Alvarez, A. N., Blume, A. W., Cervantes, J. M., & Thomas, L. R. Tapping the wisdom tradition. Essential elements to mentoring students of color. *Professional Psychology Research and Practice*, *40*(2), 181–188. https://doi.org/10.1037/a0012256.

Brunsma, D. L., Embrick, D. G., and Shin, J. H. (2017). Graduate students of color: Race, racism, and mentoring in the White waters of academia. *Sociology of Race and Ethnicity, 3*(1), 1–13. https://doi.org/10.1177/2332649216681565.

Carpenter, J. P., and Linton, J. N. (2018). Educators' perspectives on the impact of Edcamp unconference professional learning. *Teaching and Teacher Education, 73*, 56–69. https://doi.org/10/1016/j.tate.2018.03.014.

Crisp, G. & Cruz, I. (2009). Mentoring college students: A critical review of the literature between 1990 and 2007. *Research in Higher Education, 50*, 525–545. https://doi.org/10.1007/s11162–009–9130–2.

DeWalt, C. S. (2004), "In the midst of a maze: a need for mentoring," in Cleveland, D. (Ed.), *A Long Way to Go: Conversations About Race by African American Faculty and Graduate Students* (pp. 41–46). New York: Peter Lang.

D'Onfro, J. (2016, August 30). Facebook is telling the world it's not a media company, but it might be too late. *Business Insider*. Retrieved from http://www.businessinsider.com.au/mark-zuckerberg-on-facebook-being-a-media-company-2016–8.

Ford, D. Y., Trotman Scott, M., Goings, R. B., Wingfield, T. T., & Henfield, M. S. (2017). *R.A.C.E. mentoring through social media: Black and Hispanic scholars share their journey in the academy.* Charlotte, NC: Information Age Publishing.

Fountain, J., & Newcomer, K. E. (2016). Developing and sustaining effective faculty mentoring programs. *Journal of Public Affairs Education, 22*(4), 483–506. https://doi.org/10.1080/15236803.2016.12002262.

Gillespie, T. (2015). Platforms intervene. *Social media + Society, 1*(1). doi:10.1177/2056305115580479.

Greenwood, S., Perrin, A., & Duggan, M. (2016). Social media update 2016. *Pew Research Center, 11*(2). Retrieved from http://downtowndubuque.org/wp-content/uploads/2017/01/Social-Media-Update-2016.pdf.

Green, A., & Scott, L. (Eds.). (2003). *Journey to the PhD: How to navigate the process as African Americans.* Sterling, VA: Stylus.

Griffin, K. A., Bennett, J. C., & Harris, J. (2011). Analyzing gender differences in Black faculty marginalization through a sequential mixed-methods design. *New directions for institutional research, 151*, 45–61. https://doi.org/10.1002/ir.398.

Griffin, K. A., Bennett, J. C., & Harris, J. (2013). Marginalizing merit?: Gender differences in Black faculty D/discourses on tenure, advancement, and professional success. *The Review of Higher Education, 36*(4), 489–512. https://doi.org/10.1353/rhe.2013.0040.

Griffin, K. A., Perez, D., II, Holmes, A. P. E., & Mayo, C. E. P. (2010). Investing in the future: The importance of faculty mentoring in development of students of color in STEM. *New Directions for Institutional Research, 148*, 95–103, https://dx.doi.org/10.1002/ir.365.

Griffin, K. A., & Reddick, R. J. (2011). Surveillance and sacrifice: Gender differences in the mentoring patterns of Black professors at predominantly White research universities. *American Educational Research Journal, 48*, 1032–1057, https://dx.doi.org/10.3102/0002831211405025.

Haycock, K., Lynch, M. & Engle, J. (2010). *Opportunity Adrift: Our Flagship Universities are Straying from Their Public Mission.* Washington, DC: Education Trust.

Jones, C. A. (2017). I once was lost . . . But now I'm embracing social media guidance. In D.Y. Ford (pp. 77–84). *R.A.C.E. Mentoring Through Social Media: Black and Hispanic Scholars Share Their Journey in the Academy.*

Kanten, S. (2017). The Effects of Mentoring Functions on Career Adaptabilities and Career Self-Efficacy: the Role of Career Optimism. *European Journal of Multidisciplinary Studies, 2*(7), 259–272. http://dx.doi.org/10.26417/ejms.v6i2.

Kram, K. E. (1988). *Mentoring at work: Developmental relationships in organizational life.* Lanham, MD: University Press of America, Inc.

Lenhart, A. (2015). Teen, social media, and technology overview 2015. *Pew Research Center.* Retrieved from http://www.pewinternet.org/2015/04/09/teens-social-media-technology-2015.

Lorenzetti, D. L., Shipton, L., Nowell, L., Jacobsen, M., Lorenzetti, L., Clancy, T., & Paolucci, E. O. (2019). A systematic review of graduate student peer mentorship in academia. *Mentoring & Tutoring: Partnership in Learning, 27*(5), 549–576. https://doi.org/10.1080/13611267.2019.1686694.

Louis, D. A., Rawls, G. J., Jackson-Smith, D., Chambers, G. A., Phillips, L. L., & Louis, S. L. (2016). Listening to Our Voices: Experiences of Black Faculty at Predominantly White Research Universities With Microaggression. *Journal of Black Studies, 47*(5), 454–474. http://doi.org/10.1177/0021934716632983.

McCoy, D. L., Winkle-Wagner, R., & Luedke, C. L. (2015). Colorblind Mentoring? Exploring White Faculty Mentoring of Students of Color. *Journal of Diversity in Higher Education, 8*(4), 225–242.

Milner, H. R. (2004). "African American graduate students' experiences: a critical analysis of recent research," in Cleveland, D. (Ed.), *A Long Way to Go: Conversations About Race by African American Faculty and Graduate Students* (pp. 19–31). New York: Peter Lang.

Milner, H. R., Husband, T., and Jackson, M. P. (2002). Voices of persistence and self-efficacy: African American graduate students and professors who affirm them. *Journal of Critical Inquiry into Curriculum and Instructions, 4*, 33–39.

Neely, A. R., Cotton, J., & Neely, A. D. (2017). E-mentoring: A model and review of the literature. *AIS Transactions on Human-Computer Interaction, 9*(3), 220–242. https://aisel.aisnet.org/cgi/viewcontent.cgi?article=1101&context=thci.

Steele, C. K. & Korn, J. (2016). Mentors and Sister Friends: The Intersection of Race, Multiplicity, and Holism with Online Social Media, In S. Brown Givens (Ed.) *Critical examinations of women of color navigating mentoring relationships.*

Snyder, T. D., de Brey, C., and Dillow, S. A. (2019). *Digest of Education Statistics 2018* (NCES 2020–009). National Center for Education Statistics, Institute of Education Sciences, U.S. Department of Education. Washington, DC.

Wingfield, T. T. (2017). Finding my voice: The use of social media to counter racism and sexism in the Academy, In Ford, D. Y., Scott, M. T, Goings, R. B., Wingfield, T. T., & Henfield, M. S. (Eds.), *R.A.C.E. Mentoring through social media: Black and Hispanic Scholars share their journey in the academy* (pp. 13–24). Information Age Publishing.

YouTube. (n.d.). *About YouTube—YouTube*. Retrieved from https://www.youtube.com/yt/about/.

NOTE

1. Racial and ethnic groups are designated by proper nouns and are capitalized. Therefore, we use of "Black" and "White" instead of black and white (colors) when referring to human racial and ethnic groups.

PART VI

Mentoring in Practice

Chapter Twelve

Black Students Have the Last Word

How White Faculty Can Sustain Black Lives in the University

Mekiael Auguste, Herby B. Jolimeau,
Christelle Lauture, and Melissa Winchell

We are three Black undergraduate students at a predominantly white institution (PWI). This book has featured the work of academics to disrupt the reckless mentoring practices of white[1] faculty and to reimagine cross-racial mentoring to sustain Black lives. Yet no book about Black college students would be complete without us and our stories—in our own words, of our own experiences, and as a forum for our wisdom. Thus, we claim the final word of this volume, a final chapter which centers our narratives of cross-racial mentoring.

The publishing of Black students' narratives has its place not just in this volume, but in the wider literature. Some studies explain white faculty's experiences of cross-racial mentorship (Reddick & Pritchett, 2015), while others examine specific mentoring programs for Black students (Green et al., 2017; Hall, 2015). And our experiences are not forgotten—many studies analyze what we encounter as Black students in universities (Davis, 2007; Harper & Davis, 2012; Pope, 2002; Strayhorn & Terrell, 2007). As Black students, we are grateful for these researchers' attention to our lives; in writing this chapter, we know these are our research predecessors. What we hope to contribute to these foundational works are our own narratives of effective cross-racial mentoring, perspectives both individual and collective, insight only we can bring to the research about sustaining Black lives in the academy.

All three of us were secondary education students at a four-year public university in the northeast of the United States. We attended a PWI; in the spring of 2020, just 27 percent of our 8,857 undergraduate students were students of color. The faculty were even less racially diverse; during the same semester, just 19 percent of full-time faculty were faculty of color. And the secondary education major of which we were all enrolled is predominately white. While 27 percent of the student body are students of color, in the secondary education department, just 12 percent of our classmates identified as BIPOC.[2] In the 2018–2019 academic year our major included just eleven Black students (out of 570 in the secondary education program). In summary, we were three Black students in the least diverse college, in one of the least diverse majors at our PWI.

We each contributed a narrative to this chapter, which Dr. Melissa Winchell, our former professor and co-author (and a co-editor of this volume), helped to frame and analyze. We validated the analyses we each contributed and provided revisions and suggestions to this writing so that the conclusions of the chapter accurately reflect our lived experiences. We had a lot of dialogue about our positionalities, and in particular, the power Dr. Winchell holds as our former professor, a white academic, and the one who will benefit most from the publishing of this chapter. When we noticed the dynamics of white power and privilege, we called them out and reworked our conversations and this chapter to center our Black voices and experiences.

Our chapter calls the reader of this volume to learn from the lived experiences of Black students. This book began with the cross-racial juxtaposition of three editors' mentoring experiences when they were students. The book will end here, with the layering of our three mentoring experiences as Black undergraduates. As such, this chapter represents our opportunity to have the final word about what reimagining cross-racial mentorship can and should be.

LITERATURE REVIEW: CROSS-RACIAL MENTORING, COUNTERSTORYTELLING, AND RADICAL LISTENING

The literature provides multiple descriptions of Black students' experiences in predominantly white universities; that Black students experience PWIs as racially inequitable is well-established in the literature (Barker, 2007; Conyers, 2009; Davis, 2007; Green et al., 2017; Grier-Reed, 2013; Griffith et al., 2019; Reddick & Young, 2012; Torres & Massey, 2012). According to Reddick and Young (2012), multiple studies suggest that Black college students fare worse at predominantly white universities than their white peers due to the white supremacist ideologies, biases, and practices of these institutions (Barker, 2007; Grant & Ghee, 2015; Griffith et al., 2019; McCormick,

1997; Strayhorn & Terrell, 2007). For example, Guiffrida (2005) describes Black students' frustrations with faculty who effusively and needlessly single them out for praise in the classroom, or who praise them for traits (like speaking articulately) that reveal white faculty's stereotypes (i.e., that Black students are not articulate). In addition, homogenization—the assumption that all Black students are the same—is a pervasive problem for Black students at PWIs; Black students find their identities flattened and their cultures presumed and overgeneralized (Green et al., 2017; Guiffrida, 2005). Black students also describe the difficulties some white faculty have with telling them apart from other Black students; this misnaming of students is a form of spirit-murdering (Williams, 1987; as cited in Love, 2016, p. 22). As this book has established, white supremacy in higher education yields multiple, negative outcomes for Black students, impacting their achievement, university engagement, health, and self-efficacy (Brittain et al., 2009; Defreitas & Bravo, 2012; Duren Green et al., 2017; Reddick & Young, 2012).

The literature provides white faculty with guidance for effective cross-racial mentoring, even within PWIs. In fact, Ishiyama (2007) indicates that Black students at PWIs seek more personal forms of mentoring than their white classmates and that this is likely due to their increased need for social belonging given their PWI context. Guiffrida (2005) joins the Black feminist tradition by naming this highly personal way of mentoring as "othermothering" (p. 716). Black teachers (both female-and male-identifying) often hold expansive roles in the lives of their Black students, taking on mothering roles in the community such as visiting homes, pushing students to succeed, collaborating with families, teaching African American traditions, and even tutoring parents (Guiffrida, 2005).

Counterstorytelling

Black university students and our experiences with racism in higher education have mobilized this body of research. These studies represent our experiences and perspectives in multiple ways, especially via statistics, case study approaches, surveys, and interviews. Our goal with this chapter is to add to this growing body of work an additional, powerful representation of Black college student experience—counterstorytelling. Counterstorytelling, a foundational tenet of critical race theory and practice, is "a method of telling the stories of those people whose experiences are not often told" (Bell, 1987; Solórzano & Yosso, 2002, p. 32). In counterstorytelling, the perspective that is centered is the minoritized one. It is not a response to a majority perspective (though it can be), but it is a reifying of the community, a way to reaffirm the solidarity of the experience of minoritized communities, and a methodology that provides a new reality for reimagining an aspect of educational practice

(Solórzano & Yosso, 2002). For us, counterstorytelling is an affirmation of the wealth of the Black college student communities as wise, resistant, and aspirational (Yosso, 2005).

Counterstorytelling is important to the literature on crossracial mentoring because there are too few narratives from Black college students about how crossracial mentorship works and how it can be successful. The most useful to our work proved to be the works of Johnson-Bailey and Cervero (2002, 2004). Their description of their cross-racial mentorship as historically and socially fraught provides an apt frame for the counterstories will tell here. As Johnson-Bailey and Cervero (2002) explain:

> . . . in cross-cultural mentoring what should be a simple matter of negotiation between two persons becomes an arbitration between historical legacies, contemporary racial tensions, and societal protocols. A cross-cultural mentoring relationship is an affiliation between unequals who are conducting their relationship on a hostile American stage, with a societal script contrived to undermine the success of the partnership. (p. 18)

In fact, given our many negative experiences with white faculty, it seems to us that finding white faculty actively engaged in disrupting the "societal script" and disarming white "hostility" makes our stories worth telling. And while Johnson-Bailey and Cervero's mentoring relationship has now progressed to a relationship between two colleagues (and our relationship with our faculty mentors has not), we, too, experienced successful cross-racial mentorships, despite society's historical and current insistence that such relationships will fail.

In addition, counterstorytelling is a powerful addition to the literature on cross-racial mentorship because it seeks to lend another tool for decolonizing the so-called "achievement gap" paradigm that centers white experiences as normative and ideal. Given that the master narrative on achievement has been the white lie of meritocracy, counterstorytelling reclaims the narrative of Black excellence. As del Carmen Salazar and Rios (2016) explain: "There is no greater way to colonize a people then to render them silent" (p. 3). Indeed, the narrative of the achievement gap (fueled by measures of success that privilege intergenerational white power, wealth, and property ownership) prefers to write *about* us, *without* us. We find our failings in institutions of higher learning described again and again without our lived realities represented therein. Counterstorytelling amplifies our voices and refuses the narratives that have historically rendered us silent. *We* are the authors, *we* are the storytellers, and *we* are the teachers. Centering us—three Black undergraduate students at a large public university—as teachers of white faculty is a radical approach.

Radical Listening

While this chapter is about us and our experiences, it is also co-authored with our white professor and intended, in large part, for an audience of white faculty and higher education professionals who want to do better in their work with Black college students. Counterstorytelling explains our positionality as Black students, but it does not describe the positionality of Dr. Winchell nor our white audience. For that, we turn to Tobin's concept of radical listening, which he describes as "understand[ing] others' texts in terms of their standpoints and axiological commitments" (Tobin, 2009, p. 505). Radical listening involves giving attention to the historical situatedness—for the purposes of this chapter, the racial-historical situatedness—of our narratives and understanding our counterstories as having multiple, rather than authorial or canonical, meanings. In practice, this means that Dr. Winchell listened to our conversations about our experiences as Black students at a PWI and read our narratives as a listener. As such, she is the last author of this chapter and an unrepresented narrator within it; her work in our co-authorship has been to give us access to this academic space and to allow us to represent our experiences as complexly and thoroughly as we are able. In the same way, we hope our white readers will make space for new meanings, ideas, and paradigms without needing to judge, fix, nor reconstruct them. Our invitation to white faculty is direct and profound: listen to us as we share our counterstories.

We invite white faculty to consider us subject-matter experts on cross-racial mentorship. As Kincheloe explains, our readers can:

> . . . [listen] to people who [have] been deemed failures by the larger society or by the schools they attended. Such individuals . . . often possess some of the most compelling insights into what is actually happening, into how people are seriously harmed by institutions ostensibly constructed to help them improve their lives (Kincheloe, 2008, p. viii, as qtd. in Tobin, 2009).

We know firsthand how white supremacy plays out in mentorships at the academy; we hope our experiences and our expertise will make our universities spaces that celebrate, respect, and sustain all the Black lives that come after us.

BACKGROUND

As we have established, we all were Black students at a predominantly white public university in the northeast; we were secondary education majors. We each have taken one or more education courses taught by Dr. Winchell. One of us remained in the major, while two left the education major for other education-related programs. Two of us graduated in May of 2020; the other graduated in May 2021. As the literature would suggest, all three of us have had negative experiences with white faculty. But we also have had some positive experiences with white faculty and credit these positive mentoring relationships as one of the factors that have helped us to feel a sense of belonging within our predominantly white university. In this chapter, we want to demonstrate the qualities and paradigms of white faculty who have served as cross-racial mentors to us in the hopes that, by highlighting these paradigms, we can help white faculty to reimagine their mentoring of Black college students and enact the kinds of antiracist behaviors that allow those mentorships to flourish.

Dr. Winchell invited us to write this chapter together. While some of us have not been in her classroom for over two years, each of us maintained contact with her, mostly via email. And we each knew Dr. Winchell outside of our shared classroom experiences with her. Two of us were part of a panel Dr. Winchell moderated on increasing racial consciousness in teacher education; all three have visited Dr. Winchell's office hours to talk about issues beyond our coursework. One of us was a student consultant in a faculty teaching center where Dr. Winchell served; another of us co-taught with Dr. Winchell a roomful of high school students interested in pursuing careers in teaching. The three of us know one another, but we do not all share the same social circles and so we learned more about one another in the authoring of this chapter.

Positionality: Who We Are

I (Herby) proudly identify as Haitian Black. I am a bit older than the typical undergraduate. Like most of my classmates, I chose the university so I could commute. In fact, about 70 percent of students who attend my PWI are commuting students. The location allows me to live at home and continue working as a mentor to youth of color in a small gateway city that neighbors the university. I left the secondary education major after realizing I wanted to be involved in the lives of students as a counselor and mentor rather than as a teacher in a traditional classroom. I graduated in 2020 as an English major and plan to pursue graduate studies related to counseling.

I (Christelle) am a Black Haitian. I chose the university because it would allow me to leave home while remaining near my community; I lived on campus in the residence halls for all four of my years as an undergraduate. I was an English major who double-majored in secondary education for a time, however, I eventually left the secondary education program. I was torn between wanting to be a teacher of color (which I know is needed) and pursuing an education career in less traditional ways. I graduated in 2020 as an English and graphic design major; I hope to work in higher education either as an academic or as a faculty developer.

I (Meka) identify as biracial and Black. My father is Haitian, and my mother is a white North American. I recently finished my degrees in English and secondary education; I chose my university for its reputable education program. I am a nontraditional college student; I am a first-generation student who came to the university a few years after I finished high school. I have two children, I am a single mom, and I work full-time as an English teacher at a public charter school. I graduated in May 2021.

COUNTERSTORIES OF SUSTAINING CROSSRACIAL MENTORING

In the following section, we will present our three counterstories. Each of our narratives begins with some context by briefly discussing our own experiences with harmful, reckless cross-racial mentoring. In some cases, we included some experiences from earlier in our school careers, when we felt this was salient to our stories. Then each narrative details an effective experience with cross-racial mentoring at our PWI. We offer these positive stories of mentoring to disrupt deficit-based narratives of our schooling, to offer hope to both Black students and white faculty that cross-racial mentoring is possible, and to provide practices white faculty can use to develop the kinds of cross-racial mentoring that have been meaningful to us.

Herby's Narrative: High Expectations and Rigor in Cross-racial Mentoring

As an English major at my PWI, I am usually the only Black male in my English classes. And throughout my college career, I have been taught by just one faculty member of color. I have often felt out of place, like I am spending my time with white people studying white people's writing. I have wondered more than once whether I should be around my own people and spend more of my time studying the literature, issues, and experiences that are important to them.

My sense of otherness has been exasperated by my experiences of faculty expectations of me. As the singular student of color in most of my classes, I am particularly aware of the different levels of expectations my white professors hold for white students versus Black students. In classes where I am the only student of color, white professors want to give me passing grades. They tend to be very impressed by anything I do. But in my classes, I want to exceed expectations—not their low expectations, but real, college-level expectations of dedicated and committed students. So often I have wanted to tell my white professors not to pass so much judgement on me and to stop expecting so much less of me than they do from my white peers.

But I have come across several professors who have provided me with words of encouragement and played an integral role in shaping how I conduct myself as a student. Throughout much of my life, I did not seek a school mentor of any kind, mainly because I did not see the benefit in it. At the PWI I attended, however, I had a moment that made me more open-minded, willing to take advice from others, and receptive to criticism. In other words, I became willing to have a mentor. A white, middle-aged male named Professor Paulsen[3], who taught non-Western English Literature in my first semester of my undergraduate studies, had an undeniably positive effect on me in a multitude of ways. His mentoring shaped the student I have become.

I can recall our first assignment; it was to read Chinua Achebe's *Things Fall Apart* and write an analysis paper about it. The assignment seemed simple enough, and I believed I did not need help with it; upon completion when I turned it in, I felt confident in my work. I expected a decent grade for the essay, but to my surprise I received the exact opposite. The essay was littered with what I deemed at the time negative comments, grammar edits, and suggestions on how to improve. My initial reaction was anger, frustration, and some disappointment in myself, which led to an email conversation with Professor Paulsen expressing my displeasure with my grade. In our conversation about my essay, I remember he was extremely straightforward and did not attempt to sugarcoat his response. What stood out most though was how he encouraged me and told me that I could do better work and provided me with the necessary guidance to show improvement.

Too often, professors in my experience have tended to pass students for simply doing the work rather than helping the student to do it the right way. I will never forget how hard I worked on my revision of that essay because I got the appropriate assistance to do better and had established a solid sense of rapport with my professor. Eventually, I realized that Professor Paulsen was not trying to ridicule me nor my work, but that he wanted me to be knowledgeable and continuously perfect my craft. It was my first experience of a teacher expecting more out of me and it raised my own expectations of my work as a result. It was a much-needed confidence boost. From that moment, I knew that I could excel in my area of study.

From my perspective as a Black male student, I have seen firsthand my Black peer classmates become disinterested or unmotivated in class because of their relationship with a professor. Whether it be related to a poorly graded assignment or a disciplinary issue, Black students take it personally when these types of issues occur with a white professor. Sometimes, a Black student may feel that a white professor already has a preconceived and negative notion about them and their abilities. In addition, they worry their academic skills are behind their white classmates after years of a lack of meaningful feedback from teachers. Worse, they feel they are left on their own to catch up to their white peers. For example, a white student hands in an essay to a white professor. The professor grades it, adds their edit marks, and leaves meaningful comments to encourage improvement. In comparison, a Black student hands in an essay for the same assignment; the teacher grades it more leniently, leaving fewer comments and minimal suggestions on where to improve. The teacher essentially lets the Black student slide by.

White professors sometimes—whether consciously or unconsciously—have a habit of expecting more from their white students and pushing them to do better. Some white professors expect the bare minimum from Black students, and this is reflected in the professor's grading. To improve their bias and its effects on their Black college students, white professors need to work hard to create mutual respect with their Black students. Professors should show a Black student the same amount of respect they give to a white student when grading an assignment. They need to eliminate the negative stigma of Black students not trying as hard or putting in as much effort as their white classmates. By establishing a mentor role in a Black student's education, a white professor makes it clear that they want the student to succeed and that they are willing to guide and assist the student whenever necessary.

All in all, from my own experiences of being mentored and now as a mentor to children in my community, I know that mentoring can benefit everyone in the relationship. But the mentoring must be well-received by the Black mentee. From my own work experience, I have seen white mentors try too hard to relate to their mentees of color by dressing more casually than they would otherwise, talking with more slang (or worse, their imitation of Black English), and generally trying too hard to fit in with their mentees. One of the main things white faculty need to know to improve being a mentor to Black students is to be who they are. If white faculty approach relationships with Black college students in ways that are real and honest, their students will appreciate the honesty and are likely to be more receptive towards them. And receptivity is more than half the battle in mentoring.

Christelle's Narrative: Resisting Homogenization in Cross-racial Mentoring

Whiteness—its supremacy and its normativity in the university—has certainly impacted my experience as a Black student in a PWI. For example, I have frequently encountered white professors who make assumptions about my socioeconomic status because of my race. I have had educators ask me if I need freebies—free clothes, free books, free food. They think I am poor because I am Black. But I am not poor, and I find these stereotypes and low expectations a form of educational microaggression. They do harm to me and to students like me because they seek to position me and my Black classmates as suffering, Black people in need of white saving.

My excellence—as a student and a scholar—is likewise obscured when I seek to study topics about which most white professors know nothing. For example, as I pursued undergraduate research around African American English (AAE) and other Black linguistic discourses, many white faculty were overly impressed with my work because the field was completely unknown to them. This experience is certainly different from my white peers, whose forms of research are usually white-centric and therefore, an epistemology white faculty have studied. White college students therefore are privileged by this shared epistemology; white students receive more incisive feedback about their scholarship from white faculty and benefit from the capital their white faculty hold within white research communities. These unfair advantages speak to the lack of faculty of color at the PWI as well as white faculty's resistance to learn about topics of interest to Black college students. Further, white faculty accolades of Black scholarship are often, in my experience, racist; these accolades are akin to the historical infantilizing of Black people, such that our excellence receives degrading pats on the head.

Despite the many racially contested relationships I experienced with white faculty, a white faculty mentor proved to be one of the most transformational relationships of my PWI experience. From a young age, I always sought wisdom from people wiser than me, whether that be in my personal life, or through philosophers, musicians, or authors. In some way I was always seeking a life guide. When I came to college, I continued to seek wisdom in the form of professors, faculty, and upperclassmen. But when it came to being mentored as a college student, I had strict criteria. Most importantly, I wanted to actually like my mentor and know that they value what I offered as much as I value them.

I thought at first that these criteria were basic and would open the door for a traditional faculty-student, mentor-mentee relationship. What I found instead was a mentoring relationship more multifaceted and vibrant. I have been lucky to find a mentor from the early days of my undergraduate career; I was mentored by an administrator at the university for over two years.

As someone with multiple, intersectional identities, I had been encouraged to find mentors with experiences and identities similar to my own. People suggested I try to find a queer mentor, a female mentor, a Black mentor, a first-generation mentor—any combination to which they assumed I would best relate. What I found instead was a white-passing, cis male, non-first-generation mentor who encountered me as a person before any of my identities.

In lesbian feminist author Pat Parker's poem, *For the White Person who Wants to Know How to Be My Friend,* Parker writes: "First . . . forget that I'm Black,/Second you must never forget that I'm Black." In my experience, cross-racial mentoring actualizes these ideas. I am Black. Blackness is an inextricable quality of mine; my race will always be a part of how I am received and how I understand and move in this world. There are decisions I make in my life where I must consider that I am Black, and many settings and circumstances in which I am reminded that I am Black. But before I am Black, I am me. I see me as me; I make decisions and move through my own life as me, not as a categorically Black person. So in mentorship, I sought guidance for *me*, in a relationship where *I*, not my Blackness, was valued. In a mentorship in which two people wholly value the other and not merely the characteristics of one another, they both flourish and the mentoring relationship can grow.

When I encounter a white person, I do not first consider their identities, except for how their identities might react to my own. This is an inescapable awareness that puts me on the defense, ready for whatever unpleasant encounter I may have to receive. But behind this defensiveness, I am also able to see a person that I am making an encounter with, who I will try to get to know as such. This was my approach when I first met my mentor—I was both defensive and open-minded. My mentor, too, was open-minded about me and sought to know me as an individual. I met him as Christelle—he was not just a straight, white, educated man meeting a queer, Black, undergraduate student. We met as individuals.

As I finished my undergraduate experience, my mentor and I began to talk about our mentorship as a friendship. We discussed the qualities that made our cross-racial mentoring successful. He described my confidence, my passion, my contemplativeness, and my assuredness as some of the qualities that suited the needs that we have as people, allowing for our mutual growth. In my white mentor, I experienced belonging and growth because of his deep listening, his candor, his reflectiveness, his support, his advocacy, and above all, his willingness and desire to see, understand, and value me. He did not flatten my identity; he did not see me as a representative of Black people or queer people or undergraduate students. He knew me within and beyond those identities. He mentored me as a queer Black student, yes, but also, as me.

Meka's Narrative: Fearless Vulnerability and Inclusivity in Crossracial Mentoring

Throughout my school career, many of my experiences with white educators have been negative. Since I was young, white teachers have asked me uncomfortable questions about my ethnicity, hair type, religion, and languages. Worse, I have often been singled out in classroom discussions to speak as a representative of all Black points of view or experiences. In high school, a white English teacher offered me a free prom ticket, incorrectly assuming, based on my race and an essay I had written about a family member's incarceration, that I was poor and could not afford one. At my PWI, I have taken classes with just two faculty of color, and my experiences with white faculty have not all been positive. I am a single mom to two children; raising my children, working full-time as a teacher, and finishing my undergraduate studies has been challenging. Still, I expect my professors to hold high standards for me and to support me as I reach those standards. But this has not always been my experience. In one memorable instance, I asked a white professor for an extension on a paper and instead, the professor offered to change the requirements of the paper entirely. In my experience as a Black college student, I understood this offer to be biased; the professor was dumbing down the assignment rather than responding to my actual request for an extension. I did not need an easier assignment; I needed time to produce my best work.

But my experiences at a PWI have included positive experiences, too. I am a first-generation college student, so navigating the college experience was intimidating at first. I was quiet, shy, and I could not shake the feeling of not being good enough. Most of my classmates were younger than me, fresh out of their senior year of high school, whereas I had graduated three years prior, and my grasp on certain subjects did not seem sufficient when measured alongside my peers. It was within an introductory course to my major in education during my second year that I found my first mentor.

It was my first day of class in a course in education; the professor was white, as were most of the students in the class. On the first day of classes, many professors have their students do a get-to-know-each-other activity. This class proved to be no different, except the professor did something I was not expecting. Before having us introduce ourselves to each other, she stood in front of the class and presented a slideshow introducing herself to us. Within that slideshow she revealed personal information about her family, their milestones, her career, and her passions. Normally, I spend my first day of class with my head down in my notebook doodling, but on this day, and for the days to follow, I was fully engaged. And honestly, I was shocked. I could not believe she was standing in front of a room full of strangers and being so vulnerable. For example, in explaining to us how she had become a professor at our university, she shared a bit of her life story, which included truly painful and difficult obstacles; she told us she wanted us to know that we were each stronger than we thought, and more able to navigate our semester than we might yet know. I thought to myself, *Wow, she's amazing . . . she's fearless . . . she's absolutely amazingly fearless!* It was what happened next that moved me out of my shy reservedness and made me a part of a classroom community: when it came time for the class to talk in small groups about themselves, my classmates began talking in personal and genuine ways, and I found it in myself to do the same. I was speaking and living my truth for the first time in a university classroom, and I felt so unapologetically free.

I was, and still am, very open with this professor about my college career, personal life, and aspirations. In the years since I took the course, this professor has reached out to me more than once. She checks in to see how I am doing. She asks about my children and has even invited the three of us to come and swim in her backyard pool. When the pandemic began, she included me in an ongoing support group for parents. During one of these, she was leading a workshop on resilience; she cried as she shared her family's struggles during the pandemic. And she has kept in touch with me via text to find out how my family and I were doing. I feel comfortable talking with her. Her mentorship—as a professor and a mother—has been the most vulnerable and genuine I have experienced at the PWI. I never feel like I am less-than in her presence, and if she is listening, I know I am being heard. I do not know another white faculty member as I know her, and I am not known to this extent by any other faculty, either. The vulnerability and this sense of being included and valued—not because I am Black, but also inclusive of my Blackness and my experiences as a biracial person, mother, and student—is a feeling I have never experienced with any previous white educator.

A lot of professors will write in their syllabi that their classrooms foster inclusivity. But there is difference between talking the talk and walking the walk. My mentor walks the walk. And Black students like me need white faculty who demonstrate that despite our differences, we are equally as deserving—of mentorship, of belonging, of human connection, of care—in this lifetime. My white mentor did just that. She was vulnerable, making her not only approachable, but personable. Being able to witness her in all aspects of her life, as fully herself and fully human, reminded me that even though she is a professor, she is still a person. And even though she is white does not mean she will not understand me. I know she will be my advocate, mentor, and support, long after I leave the classrooms of our PWI.

COMMONALITIES IN OUR COUNTERSTORIES

Our narratives highlight some common negative experiences at a PWI and with white faculty in particular. All three of us have experienced being treated differently than our white peers; we were often singled out (usually as called-upon representatives for the Black experience) and overlooked (usually as excellent students and scholars). In the layering of these negative experiences, we find that Black lives matter for all the wrong reasons in classrooms taught by white faculty: being a student while Black is overly noticed without being appropriately addressed. For Black students like us, this kind of mattering—a hypervisible erasure—is a daunting and harmful experience. It is little wonder to us that so many Black classmates we know choose not to remain at PWIs or leave higher education all together.

But our stories of white faculty mentoring are also meant to show that white faculty can mentor Black students. Our experiences demonstrate that within a PWI, there are white faculty who know how to develop meaningful mentoring relationships with Black students; certainly, these white faculty can and should provide mentoring wisdom for their colleagues. More importantly, however, our counterstories demonstrate that Black students are not just the objects of the mentoring relationship; we are also its subjects. That is, we bring to mentoring years of experience with white educators and insight into how cross-racial mentoring can be reimagined. Thus, the practice of cross-racial mentorship must provide space for the Black student's dialectical positionality as both a guide into and through racially contested spaces, and a person needing guidance into and through academic spaces still saturated with white supremacy.

RECOMMENDATIONS FOR CULTURALLY RESPONSIVE MENTORING

In this concluding section, then, we aim to discuss three themes from our counterstories. Each of these themes will highlight responsive practices white faculty can use to disrupt the kinds of reckless, harmful mentoring many white faculty too often inflict on their Black students. In particular, the three practices we will discuss include: 1) authenticity and vulnerability, 2) high expectations, and 3) individuality.

Disrupting Reckless Mentoring with Authenticity and Vulnerability

All three of the counterstories identified authenticity as a critical component of our mentoring relationships with white faculty. Christelle wrote that her most important criteria was likeability; Herbie defined what makes a white mentor unlikeable by writing about the white mentors he has seen who "try too hard" to relate to Black students. As he indicates, white faculty do not need to change the way they talk or dress to connect with Black students. In fact, as Meka explains, white faculty do best when they are genuinely themselves and when they are willing to be vulnerable—to be both professor and human—in their relationships with their mentees.

Our experiences reflect the literature on the personal forms of mentoring most meaningful to Black college students more broadly. As explained in the first chapter of this volume, this kind of highly personalized, expansive approach to the academic mentor's role disrupts white boundary-setting and white binaries of professional and personal. White faculty need to acknowledge their whiteness and be vulnerable with their students as they learn antiracism and cultural humility. Further, Guffrida's (2005) description of mentoring as othermothering is often not valued in institutions. How and in what ways faculty can embrace the highly personalized approaches to mentoring Black students will require institution-wide conversation and change. In the meantime, white faculty need to know that Black students like us want our mentors to bring their whole, genuine selves to our relationships with them. We value your vulnerability, as Meka explained, and your friendship-mentorship, as Christelle experienced with her mentor.

In practice, this means that white faculty need to share about their lives; not because their lives are more interesting than ours or warrant more attention, but because doing so indicates to us that you are willing to have a reciprocal relationship with us. As Black students, we are always vulnerable—to microaggression, to harm in the classroom, to trauma from the day's news, to the pain of faculty silence and neutrality. We have a right, given our vulnerabilities as minoritized students at a PWI, to have a reasonable expectation of vulnerability from our white faculty.

In addition, authenticity for us also means that our white faculty speak up in the classroom when injustice occurs on a local or national scale. We have sat through too many already-planned, divorced-from-the-headlines lectures in the days following events like a political election, a murder of a Black person by police, or the attack on our Capitol by white men waving Confederate flags. Being vulnerable in these moments means breaking white silence and creating a space in a classroom for dialogue; it means allowing for discomfort—even your own—while we, your students, seek to understand how better to live in a world intent on undermining human rights. Your authenticity is not just about your life with your partner or your dog, your vulnerability is not just about how you navigated your own imposter syndrome to succeed in the academy. Your authenticity is also your willingness to acknowledge that you, too, are affected by events that seek to murder the minds, spirits, and bodies of all who are not white. We need you to speak, we need you to hold space for discomfort in your classroom, and we need you to reduce harm during these discussions by immediately interrupting and addressing our classmates who make racist (or other such harmful) remarks.

Disrupting Reckless Mentoring with High Expectations

In addition, our counterstories demonstrate the intersections of faculty expectations in our experiences in the classroom, our learning, and our relationship with our professor. Herby explains this thoroughly in his story of his English professor returning his paper with multiple comments for revision, as does Meka when she writes about approaching a professor for an extension on an assignment. Each of us has multiple experiences like this—stories in which well-meaning white professors lowered their expectations attempting to help us, their Black students.

While we understand the intent of these white professors, good intentions can still be colorblind, biased, and even discriminatory. In lowering their expectations, white faculty are not communicating that they are goodhearted; rather, they are communicating to Black students that Black students are not expected to, nor can they, meet expectations. Such offers are ignorant of the histories of race relations in the United States and the ongoing struggles in our society for Black people to claim their excellence in ways that white people will acknowledge, let alone accept. As Black students, we are savvier about the contested spaces of American race relations; as a result, we experience white faculty, even well-intentioned white faculty, as racist when they make allowances for us that they do not make for their white students.

Maintaining high expectations for Black students requires intentional, committed practices that draw attention to the insidious ways unconscious bias can alter white faculty policies and practices in the classroom. For example, white faculty can use anonymous grading through their online classroom systems or by asking students not to put their names on the front of their papers. In addition, white faculty should be clear about their policies for issues like absenteeism and late work. Even if white faculty have flexible practices (for example, one faculty member we know will grant their students an extension if it is requested prior to the deadline), the practices should be stated clearly and in writing in the syllabus and/or other course materials. This strategy holds the white professor accountable to implementing the same practice with all students, regardless of the student's race, and prevents white faculty from using limiting, low-expectation policies for Black students.

Disrupting Reckless Mentoring with Individualization

The most pervasive theme of all our counterstories is that we want to be treated as individuals. Christelle clearly states this when she quotes poet Pat Parker to forget—and never forget—her Blackness. For Christelle, this means that a white mentor can acknowledge her Blackness even while looking beyond it. Further, it means that white faculty do not stereotype Black students by treating us as low-income, assuming we are first-generation college students, or expecting us to think, speak, or behave as representatives of our race.

Yet, our insistence on individualization creates a tension for white faculty. On the one hand, white faculty who are not doing the work of antiracism might misunderstand us to mean that we want them to be colorblind. We are aware of white faculty at our PWI who are unable, for example, to talk about their own whiteness, let alone to name their students' races. White faculty are prone, given the history of white supremacy and white silence in the United States, to use any excuse to avoid race talk with students. This avoidance tactic is a major impediment to cross-racial mentoring. However, our insistence that we be treated as individuals is not an excuse to ignore race; our Blackness matters, and it matters unequivocally. In fact, one of the best ways white faculty can signal to their Black students that they are learning to both understand race and to treat their Black students as individuals is by engaging in race talk in and out of the classroom.

In practice, this means that white faculty must talk about race at every opportunity in the classroom. When introducing a new reading, for example, the faculty member can simply state the author's race. White faculty can inform their students of antiracist scholars relevant to their discipline, inform students of antiracist events and lectures on campus, and use antiracist images and language in their syllabi and course materials. In addition, representation matters; white faculty who want to be effective cross-racial mentors must represent BIPOC excellence in their curriculum, their syllabi, their required and recommended reading lists, their course websites, their offices, and in any place in which they interact with us. We know white faculty who perform race consciousness in the classroom—they talk about it a lot—but when we look at their course website, all of the images are of white people and nearly all of the readings by white researchers and scholars.

In addition, white faculty must treat their Black students as individuals. They must learn our names and use them correctly. They must find ways to learn about us; for example, many effective white professors we know provide their students with online surveys through which we tell them more about ourselves. The best white faculty we know do not just read these surveys; they use them to generate an individualized conversation with each of their students over the course of a semester. Also, white faculty treat us as individuals when they understand us as having the full range of human experiences. Christelle experienced this in a powerful way when one of her white professors sent her an email after class. In it, the white professor said they noticed Christelle's unusual silence during class; the white faculty member simply wanted to check in and see how Christelle was doing. The professor noted that they did not expect Christelle to respond and that Christelle was not under any obligation to divulge any personal details of their life; the email message was that the professor wanted Christelle to know she was seen and cared for. This kind of attention to our individual experiences—without assumption via an open, curious, and caring inquiry—is precisely the kind of individual attention our white peers regularly receive. It is the kind of attention we deserve.

CONCLUSION

As an addition to the literature on the Black student experience at predominantly white institutions, we shared here our counterstories to identify cross-racial mentorships that made a difference in our PWI experience. Our experiences suggest three themes that can improve white faculty's mentoring of Black students. Still, we want to acknowledge that each theme also represents a particular tension for white faculty, and we want to invite white faculty to become comfortable with the discomfort of those tensions. Our first theme of authenticity and vulnerability invites white faculty into the tension of being themselves while also growing their identities as antiracists. This tension asks, *How can white faculty be both completely themselves and a learner of pedagogies that disrupt white silence and white violence?* It also asks, *How can white faculty acknowledge their whiteness and white privilege and learn to decenter it in the classroom and in their relationships with Black students?* Our second theme of high expectations invites white faculty into the tension of maintaining high standards while supporting all students to meet them. This tension asks, *How do white faculty maintain their expectations for student learning while supporting Black success in ways that are equitable to their support of white students?* And finally, our third theme of individualization invites white faculty into the tension of being both race conscious and person-centered. This tension asks, *How do white faculty forget race, and never forget race, in their relationships with Black students?*

These tensions are uncomfortable for white faculty, we know. But if white faculty are serious about the work of cross-racial mentoring—and we hope that they are—living within these tensions is a practice of discomfort and growth with which faculty must daily engage. Given our stories of how cross-racial mentoring impacted our college experiences for the better, we hope that white faculty will wholeheartedly embrace the disruptive and joyous work of sustaining Black lives like ours within the a higher education system that otherwise ignores, excludes, and extinguishes us.

REFERENCES

Barker, M. J. (2007). Cross-cultural mentoring in institutional contexts. *Negro Educational Review*, *58*(1/2), 85. http://www.oma.osu.edu/vice_provost/ner/index. html.

Bell, D. (1987). *And we are not saved: The elusive quest for racial justice*. Basis Books. Brittain, A. S., Sy, S. R., & Stokes, J. E. (2009). Mentoring: Implications for African-American college students. *Western Journal of Black Studies, 33*, 87–97.

Conyers, A. (2009). Dual deviants: The balancing act of Black graduate students. *Challenge (1077193X)*, *15*(1).

Davis, D. (2007). Access to academe: The importance of mentoring to Black students. *Negro Educational Review, 58*(3/4), 217–231.

Defreitas, S. C., & Bravo, A. (2012). The influence of involvement with faculty and mentoring on the self-efficacy and academic achievement of African-American and Latino college students. *Journal of the Scholarship of Teaching and Learning, 12*(4), 1–11.

del Carmen Salazar, M. & Rios, F. (2016). Just scholarship! Publishing academic research with a social justice focus. *Multicultural Perspectives*, *18*(1), 3–11. https:// doi.org/ 10.1080/15210960.2016.1127073.

Grant, C., & Ghee, S. (2015). Mentoring 101: Advancing African-American women faculty and doctoral student success in predominantly white institutions. *International Journal of Qualitative Studies in Education (QSE), 28*(7), 759–785. https://doi.org/ 10.1080/09518398.2015.1036951.

Green, T. D., Ammah, B. B., Butler-Byrd, N., Brandon, R., McIntosh, A. (2017). African-American Mentoring Program (AAMP): Addressing the cracks in the graduate education pipeline. *Mentoring & Tutoring: Partnership in Learning, 25*(5), 528–547. https://doi.org /10.1080/13611267.2017.1415807.

Grier-Reed, T. (2013). The African American student network: An informal networking group as a therapeutic intervention for Black college students on a predominantly white campus. *Journal of Black Psychology*, *39*(2), 169–184. https://doi. org/10.1177/0095798413478696.

Griffith, A. N., Hurd, N. M., & Hussain, S. B. (2019). "I didn't come to school for this": A qualitative examination of experiences with race-related stressors and coping responses among Black students attending a predominantly white institution. *Journal of adolescent research*, *34*(2), 115–139. https://doi. org/10.1177/0743558417742983.

Guiffrida, D. A. (2005). Othermothering as a framework for understanding African-American students' definitions of student-centered faculty. *The Journal of Higher Education*, *76*(6), 701–723. https://doi.org/10.1080/00221546.2005.11 772305.

Hall, H. (2015). Food for thought: Using critical pedagogy in mentoring African American adolescent males. *The Black Scholar*, *45*(3), 39–53. https://doi. org/10.1080/ 00064246.2015.1049328.

Harper, S. R., & Davis III, C. H. (2012). They (Don't) care about education: A counternarrative on Black male students' responses to inequitable schooling. *Educational Foundations*, *26*, 103–120. https://doi.org/10.1086/705799.

Ishiyama, J. (2007). Expectations and perceptions of undergraduate research mentoring: Comparing first-generation, low-income white/Caucasian and African-American students. *College Student Journal*, *41*(3), 540–549.

Johnson-Bailey, J. and Cervero, R. M. (2002). Cross-cultural mentoring as a context for learning. *New Directions for Adult and Continuing Education*, *96*, 15–21. https://doi.org/ 10.1002/ace.75.

Kincheloe, J. L. (2008). *Knowledge and critical pedagogy: An introduction*. Springer.

Love, B. L. (2016). Anti-Black state violence, classroom edition: The spirit murdering of Black children. *Journal of Curriculum and Pedagogy*, *13*(1), 22–25. https://doi. org/ 10.1080/15505170.2016.1138258.

McCormick, T. (1997). An analysis of five pitfalls of traditional mentoring for people on the margins in higher education. In H. T. Frierson (Ed.), *Diversity in higher education: Mentoring and diversity in higher education* (Vol. I, pp. 187–202). JAI Press, Inc.

Pope, M. L. (2002). Community college mentoring: Minority student perception. *Community College Review*, *30*(3), 31–45. https://doi. org/10.1177/009155210203000303.

Reddick, R. J., & Pritchett, K. O. (2015). "I don't want to work in a world of whiteness": white faculty and their mentoring relationships with Black students. *Journal of Professoriate*, *8*(1), 54–84.

Reddick, R. J., & Young, M. D. (2012). Mentoring graduate students of color. In S. Fletcher & C. Mullen (Eds.), *The SAGE handbook of mentoring and coaching for education* (pp. 412–429). SAGE.

Solórzano, D. G., & Yosso, T. J. (2002). Critical race methodology: Counter-storytelling as an analytical framework for education research. *Qualitative inquiry*, *8*(1), 23–44. https://doi.org/10.1177/107780040200800103.

Strayhorn, T. L., & Terrell, M. C. (2007). Mentoring and satisfaction with college for Black students. *Negro Educational Review*, *58*, 69–83.

Tobin, K. (2009). Tuning into others' voices: radical listening, learning from difference, and escaping oppression. *Cult Stud of Sci Educ* 4, 505–511. https://doi. org/10.1007/s11422-009-9218-1.

Torres, K., & Massey, D. S. (2012). Fitting in: Segregation, social class, and the experiences of Black students at selective colleges and universities. *Race and social problems*, *4*(3–4), 171–192. https://doi.org/10.1007/s12552-012-9077-3.

Williams, P. (1987). Spirit murdering the messenger: The discourse of finger pointing as the law's response to racism. *University of Miami Law Review*, *42*(1), 127–158.

Yosso, T. J. (2005). Whose culture has capital? A critical race theory discussion of community cultural wealth. *Race ethnicity and education*, *8*(1), 69–91. https://doi. org/10.1080/ 1361332052000341006.

NOTES

1. We have chosen to use lowercase for "white" as a lexical call to all of us to dismantle anti-Blackness in the university.

2. Black, Indigenous, and People of Color (BIPOC).

3. Identifying names have been anonymized.

Index

275

About the Editors

Bettie Ray Butler, PhD, is an associate professor of urban education and the director of the MEd in urban education program at the University of North Carolina at Charlotte. Dr. Butler is also the associate editor for the *Journal of African American Women and Girls in Education* (JAAWGE), a research journal devoted to advancing scholarship and praxis. She currently serves as a content specialist for the National Technical Assistance Center on Transition: The Collaborative (NTACT:C) where she leads initiatives centered around culturally responsive practices. Dr. Butler earned her doctorate in curriculum and instruction with a focus on urban education and her master's in political science with a concentration in public policy/public administration and race and education at Texas A&M University (College Station, Texas). She has a BA from North Carolina Agricultural & Technical State University in political science and criminal justice with a minor in journalism and mass communications. She currently teaches both core and specialized courses in the curriculum and instruction PhD program at the University of North Carolina Charlotte. She has also taught undergraduate and master's level courses that center on equity and diversity in education and teacher preparation. Dr. Butler has nearly twenty years of scholarly experience in the area of social justice and education reform, as well as seventeen years of teaching and presenting on diversity in education using an interdisciplinary approach. Dr. Butler has facilitated numerous professional development workshops, led multiple national webinars, presented at international and national conferences, and published several peer-reviewed journal articles, book chapters, toolkits, and policy reports. Her publications have appeared in nationally recognized publishing outlets such as *Teachers College Press*, *Routledge*, *Peter Lang Publishers*, and *Emerald Group Publishing;* and her work featured in academic journals, such as, *Journal of Negro Education*, *The Urban Review*, *Theory into Practice*, *Multicultural Perspectives*, *Teachers College Record,* and *The Journal for Multicultural Education* (recipient of the 2019 Emerald Literati Award for Outstanding Paper/Article). Broadly, her larger interdisciplinary research interests focus on issues of culturally responsive practices (i.e., instruction, classroom management, leadership, advising/mentoring, and transition planning). More specifically, Dr. Butler's specialized area of interest is in restorative practices. Through this work she uses a restorative philosophy to improve school/institutional climate, reduce educational disparities and positively impact academic and socioemotional outcomes.

Abiola Farinde-Wu, PhD, is an assistant professor of urban education in the Department of Leadership in Education at the University of Massachusetts Boston, where she teaches doctoral students pursuing degrees in urban education. In her previous position, she was a visiting assistant professor in the Center for Urban Education at the University of Pittsburgh. Farinde-Wu's teaching and service focus on preparing urban preservice and inservice teachers for diverse student populations. Her research focuses on equitable educational opportunities for students of color. In particular, she is interested in research questions lying at the nexus of the school experiences of Black female students and their educational and life outcomes. Highlighting how racial, social, and cultural issues impact the educational opportunities and treatment of Black women and girls, she explores the policies, structures, and practices that influence the recruitment, matriculation, and retention of this particular group in urban schools and contexts. Her research interests are the educational experiences and outcomes of Black women and girls, diversifying the U.S. teacher workforce, and urban teacher education. In her scholarly work, she draws from critical theory frameworks. She has authored and co-authored numerous studies published in journals, including *Urban Review, Teachers College Record, Urban Education,* and *Teaching and Teacher Education.* In addition, she is the co-editor of *Black Female Teachers: Diversifying the United States' Teacher Workforce* (Emerald, 2017). Her professional activities include being on the editorial board of Urban Education and serving as an affiliated faculty member in The Urban Education Collaborative.

Melissa Winchell, EdD, is an associate professor of secondary education and chair of the accelerated post baccalaureate program at Bridgewater State University, where she teaches courses in secondary education pedagogy, curriculum, and assessment for undergraduate and graduate students at Bridgewater State University. A former urban high school teacher, urban district administrator, and urban community college professor, Melissa's research interests include antiracist and critical cultural competence. She has published multiple chapters, including as lead author for a chapter in *Freire's Intellectual Roots: Toward Historicity in Practice,* which won the Society of Education Professors Book Award for 2014. Her most recent chapters include

"No Place Like Home: Reconceptualizing Whiteness as Place | Space within Teacher Education" in *Critical Multicultural Perspectives on Whiteness: Voices from the Past and Present* (Lang, 2018) and a chapter on immersive teacher education experiences for confronting Other-ing within the forthcoming Peter Lang series volume, *Confronting Anti-Semitism on Campus*. Melissa's scholarship includes community activism within local, state, and national communities. She founded and leads a nonprofit, Inclusion Matters, and volunteers her time as an ally and community advocate with DESE's state-appointed Special Education Advisory Panel, Massachusetts Federation for Children with Special Needs, a local school council, and as a member of the state-appointed Citizen Advisory Board for a local Department of Developmental Services.

About the Contributors

Edwin Obilo Achola, PhD is an associate professor and co-project director specializing in special education in the Department of Advanced Studies in Education and Counseling at California State University, Long Beach. Achola helps train teachers to work more effectively with students with disabilities who come from diverse communities and also to help students transition from adolescence to adulthood.

Meka Auguste is an English and secondary education major at Bridgewater State University in Bridgewater, Massachusetts. She aspires to teach English at a diverse middle school and to become a children's book author. Mekiael has presented at university conferences on her own writing and the work of Edwidge Danticat. In 2016, she published an op-ed in a local publication, the *SouthCoast Today* newsletter, titled "Emotional Loss of a Living Addict Needs Attention."

Daniel E. Becton is a graduate student in the Program of Higher Education Leadership and a graduate research assistant in residence life at The University of Texas at Austin. Becton's research focuses on critical pedagogy, feminist theory, and arts-based research.

Jamiylah Butler, PhD graduated from The Ohio State University with a doctoral degree in counselor education. She is licensed as a professional counselor and certified as a professional school counselor in the state of Ohio. She is passionate about magnifying higher education access and attainment for all students, especially Black students. Dr. Butler is currently consulting, writing grants, and speaking in various communities. She currently serves on the African American concerns committee of the Florida Association of Multicultural Counseling and Development.

Issac M. Carter, PhD is a critical educator, organizer, and scholar. Over the course of his career, he has led many initiatives to support college access, retention and graduation of low-income, students of color, and other under-represented student populations. Dr. Carter possesses over twenty-five years of higher experience having served as chief student affairs officer, and chief housing office, as well as holding the rank of associate professor (tenured). His scholarship incorporates Critical Race Theory, intersectionality, and decolonizing methodologies. Dr. Carter teaches courses that critically examine higher education administration, organizational leadership, Black musicking, and coloniality. His curricular and pedagogical praxis continually connects knowledge production with the pursuit of justice in our communities. Much of his time with youth and young adults is dedicated to addressing the intersections of racial criminalization, LGBTQ rights, immigration, the prison industrial complex and gender justice. Dr. Carter's research includes "*Interfaith Engagement and Student Empowerment Among Latino/a and African American Students,*" *Journal of College and Character* 2019; No Ways Tired: The Journey of Professionals of Color in Student Affairs, "I am Not Your Negro," 2019; Black Bodies, Blue Ribbons, "The Jim Crow Effect on Federal Policy?" Sense-Brill, 2018. In addition, Dr. Carter is the co-editor of the upcoming volume, *Unhooking from Whiteness III.*

Delando L. Crooks is a graduate student in the Program of Higher Education Leadership and a graduate research assistant in the Heman Sweatt Center for Black Males at The University of Texas at Austin. Delando's research interest focuses on the successful transition of college athletes out of sports and Black male development and persistence at predominantly White institutions.

Alyssa Hadley Dunn, PhD is an associate professor of teacher education at Michigan State University. Her teaching and research focus on urban education and the sociocultural and political contexts of urban schools, especially issues of race, justice, and equity. In addition to publishing in journals such as *Teachers College Record, American Journal of Educational Research, Teaching and Teacher Education*, and *Urban Education*, she is currently working on her third book, based on interviews with teachers around the country, about how educators make pedagogical decisions on "days after" major events, tragedies, and instances of injustice. As a public scholar, Dr. Dunn's work has been featured on *CNN, NPR*, and *The Huffington Post*, and she is a past recipient of the Critical Educators for Social Justice Revolutionary Mentor Award from the American Educational Research Association. She is also the mother of two white sons who she is committed to raising as co-conspirators in the fight for racial justice.

Erinn F. Floyd, PhD is a gifted education, diversity, equity, inclusion, and social justice scholar who serves as director of training and partnership development for The Consortium for Inclusion of Underrepresented Racial Groups in Gifted Education (I-URGGE). Dr. Floyd serves as assistant professor at the University of Georgia and course lecturer at Texas State University-San Marcos. She is former director of professional learning for the National Association for Gifted Children (NAGC) and state director of gifted education for the Alabama Department of Education. She has over twenty-nine years of experience as a classroom teacher, gifted and school improvement specialist, gistrict gifted education coordinator, and assistant principal, and provided professional learning opportunities in Alabama, nationally, and internationally. Dr. Floyd is an inaugural recipient of the NAGC Dr. Mary Frasier Teacher Scholarship for Diverse Talent Development and serves on the Board of Trustees for her alma mater, The Alabama School of Fine Arts. She has authored and co-authored several publications, including *Poverty and the (Mis)Education of Black and Hispanic Gifted Students; Power Advocates: Families of Diverse Gifted Learners Taking a Seat at the Table; Black and Gifted in Rural America: Barriers and Facilitators to Accessing Gifted and Talented Education Programs; The Red Owl Collaborative: Leveraging Sisterhood and Social Justice;* and *Black, Gifted, and Living in the "Country": Searching for Equity and Excellence in Rural Gifted Education Programs.* Dr. Floyd is founder and CEO of Equity and Excellence in Education, LLC, which provides professional learning support to educators and virtual learning support to students in grades K-12. Dr. Floyd and her husband are the proud parents of two gifted children, a son (15) and a daughter (11).

Donna Y. Ford, PhD is a distinguished professor of education and human ecology and Kirwan Institute faculty affiliate at The Ohio State University's College of Education and Human Ecology. She is in the educational studies department, special education program. She returned to OSU in August 2019. Professor Ford earned her PhD in urban education (educational psychology) (1991), MEd (counseling) (1988), and BA in communications and Spanish (1984) from Cleveland State University. Professor Ford conducts research primarily in gifted education and multicultural/urban education. Specifically, her work focuses on: (1) the achievement gap; (2) recruiting and retaining culturally different students in gifted education; (3) multicultural curriculum and instruction; (4) culturally competent teacher training and development; (5) African American identity; and (6) African American family involvement. She consults with school districts, and educational and legal organizations on such topics as gifted education under-representation and Advanced Placement, multicultural/urban education and counseling, and closing the achievement gap. Professor Ford has written over three hundred articles and book chapters; she has made over two thousand presentations at professional conferences and organizations, and in school districts. She is the author/co-author of several books, including *Gumbo for the Soul: Liberating Memoirs and Stories to Inspire Females of Color* (2017); *Telling Our Stories: Culturally Different Adults Reflect on Growing Up in Single-Parent Families* (2017); *R.A.C.E. Mentoring Through Social Media: Black and Hispanic Scholars Share Their Journey in the Academy* (2017); *Recruiting and Retaining Culturally Different Students in Gifted Education* (2013), *Reversing Underachievement Among Gifted Black Students* (1996, 2010), *Multicultural Gifted Education* (1999, 2011), *Gifted and Advanced Black Students in School: An Anthology of Critical Works* (2011), *In Search of the Dream: Designing Schools and Classrooms that Work for High Potential Students from Diverse Cultural Backgrounds* (2004), *Diverse Learners with Exceptionalities: Culturally Responsive Teaching in the Inclusive Classroom* (2008), and *Teaching Culturally Diverse Gifted Students* (2005).

Horace R. Hall, PhD is associate professor at DePaul University in Chicago, Illinois. He is affiliated with DePaul's Department of Teacher Education and the Department of African and Black Diaspora Studies. In addition to his university work, Hall co-directs a youth activism program in Chicago called R.E.A.L. (Respect, Excellence, Attitude, and Leadership). Since 2000, R.E.A.L. has worked closely with youth and their families in challenging political and economic inequities prevalent within Black and Latinx Chicagoland communities.

Troy Harden, EdD is the director of Northeastern Illinois University's Master of Social Work Program, where he is also associate professor. He has over twenty-five years of experience serving and consulting in social service, educational and community settings. Dr. Harden has worked as a clinician, administrator, educator, activist and community practitioner concerning community issues in diverse settings.

Cleveland Hayes, PhD is the associate dean, academic affairs and professor of education foundations in the urban teacher education department at the school of education at Indiana University-Indianapolis. Dr. Hayes teaches elementary foundations of education, elementary science methods and qualitative research methods. Dr. Hayes's research interest includes the use of Critical Race Theory in education, historical and contemporary issues in Black education to include the school to prison pipeline, teaching and learning in the Latino community, Whiteness and the intersections of sexuality and race. Dr. Hayes is an active member of the American Education Research

Association (AERA) at the Division Level, SIG level and committee level. He is currently the co-program chair for Division G and has served as a section co-chair for Division K and a member of the special interest group executive committee. He was the 2019 president of the Critical Race Studies in Education Association (CRSEA). Dr. Hayes's research can be found in *Democracy and Education; Qualitative Studies in Education, and Gender and Education; Urban Review; and Power of Education.* In addition, he is the co-editor of the books titled: *Unhooking from Whiteness: The Key to Dismantling Racism in the United States* and *Unhooking from Whiteness: Resisting the Esprit de Corps.*

Tiffany N. Hughes is a graduate student in the program of higher education leadership and a graduate research assistant at The University of Texas at Austin. Tiffany's research interests focus on examining the experiences and amplifying the narratives of minoritized students across post-secondary institutions including those of Black medical students and Black women graduate students.

Herby B. Jolimeau is a psychology major at Bridgewater State in Bridgewater, MA. He plans to pursue graduate studies in education and become a guidance counselor. Herby has extensive experience in youth mentoring, including at an all-male residential facility for children ages 7–18, at an all-female residential facility, and as a volunteer youth mentor in his community.

Christelle Lauture is a computer design major at Bridgewater State in Bridgewater, MA. Christelle works in the Office of Teaching and Learning at the university and serves as a student mentor to faculty who seek to improve their teaching. Christelle has presented at national and international conferences, including at the Caribbean Studies Association Annual Conference in Colombia in May 2019. Her research interests include student-faculty partnerships, Creole oral language, and African American Vernacular English.

Timothy J. Lensmire, PhD is a professor in the Department of Curriculum and Instruction, University of Minnesota, where he teaches courses in literacy, critical pedagogy, and race. His early work focused on how the teaching of writing might contribute to education for radical democracy, and includes his books, *When Children Write* and *Powerful Writing/Responsible Teaching.* His current research seeks to build descriptions of, and theoretical insights about how whiteness and white racial identities play out in U.S. schools and society. Lensmire's writing on race and education includes articles in *Curriculum Inquiry, Educational Researcher, Harvard Educational Review,* and *Race Ethnicity and Education,* as well as his new book, *White folks: Race and identity in rural America.*

Brian D. Lozenski, PhD is an assistant professor of urban and multicultural education in the educational studies department at Macalester College in St. Paul, Minnesota. He received his doctorate from the University of Minnesota where he studied the cultural contexts of teaching and learning. His research explores the intersections of critical participatory action research, black intellectual traditions in education, and cultural sustainability in the education of youth of African descent. Prior to pursuing his PhD, Dr. Lozenski taught for over a decade in his hometown of Philadelphia, PA and then St. Paul, MN. As a teacher educator and researcher he has worked with other educators, parents, schools, and districts to develop perspectives and strategies that aspire toward social justice while illuminating the historical realities that have created current educational disparities. He has publications in educational research journals such as *Harvard Educational* Review, *Review of Research in Education,* and *Equity & Excellence in Education,* among others. Dr. Lozenski holds deep commitments to a community-engaged research framework where academic researchers follow the lead of community members and organizations to identify prevalent issues that can be addressed through an inquiry-based approach. In this effort he is affiliated with organizations such as the Network for the Development of Children of African Descent, the African Diaspora Consortium, the Education for Liberation Network, and the Twin Cities Solidarity Committee.

Lisa R. Merriweather, PhD is a professor of adult education at the University of North Carolina at Charlotte with a PHD in adult education from the University of Georgia, co-founder and co-editor of *Dialogues in Social Justice: An Adult Education Journal,* and aspiring writer of historical science fiction centering issues of race and racism. Employing the art of story and dialogic engagement, complete with creativity and innovativeness, emotionality and theorizing, and historical and contemporary cultural and political critique informed by Africana philosophy and Critical Race Theory, Lisa invites readers and interlocutors to a space of reflection through (re)presenting and (re)languaging racialized experiences. Her research interests include culturally liberative mentoring, critical race pedagogy, STEM doctoral mentoring, and race and racism in non/informal adult education.

Richard J. Reddick, EdD is an associate professor and associate dean for equity, community engagement, and outreach in the College of Education at The University of Texas at Austin, where he is affiliated with the Department of African and African Diaspora Studies. Reddick is also faculty co-chair of the Harvard Institute for Educational Management. Reddick's research focuses on the experiences of Black faculty and faculty of color at predominantly White institutions, and mentoring relationships between faculty and Black students.

Marjorie C. Shavers, PhD is department head of counseling, leadership, and special education at Missouri State University and is associate professor in counseling. Dr. Shavers is currently licensed as a licensed professional clinical counselor with supervision designation and a licensed professional school counselor in Ohio. She has worked as a counselor in an agency setting, a college counseling center, and a public school district. In her various roles, her work focused on diversity, advocacy, and racial trauma. Dr. Shavers's research agenda using Critical Race Theory, Critical Race Feminism, and Black Feminist Thought, combines her personal and professional experiences and is aimed at studying how educational experiences can impact the mental health and overall well-being of Black girls and women. In addition to her research in this area she has received over two million dollars in grant funding to explore this work and to train culturally competent behavioral health providers engaged in social justice and anti-racist work.

Christine Sleeter, PhD is a professor and education activist. She is professor emerita in the College of Education, California State University, Monterey Bay. She has helped hundreds of teachers become better teachers of the schools' culturally diverse students. She has also served as the vice president of Division K (Teaching and Teacher Education) of the American Educational Research Association, and as president of the National Association for Multicultural Education. Her work primarily focuses on multicultural education, preparation of teachers for culturally diverse schools, and antiracism Considered an expert in her field, Dr. Sleeter is a much sought-after speaker and is the author of more than twenty-two books and eighty blog posts. She has been honored for her work as the recipient of the American Educational Research Association Social Justice Award, the Division K Teaching and Teacher Education Legacy Award, the CSU Monterey Bay President's Medal, the Chapman University Paulo Freire Education Project Social Justice Award, the American Educational Research Association Special Interest Group Multicultural and Multiethnic Education Lifetime Achievement Award, and the National Association for Multicultural Education Exceptional Service Award.

Terrell L. Strayhorn, PhD is provost and senior vice president, academic affairs and professor of urban education in the Evelyn Reid Syphax School of Education at Virginia Union University, where he serves as director for the center for the study of HBCUs. He is a faculty affiliate at Rutgers University's Center for Minority Serving Institutions (MSIs) and several other national research institutes. An internationally recognized education equity expert, Strayhorn's research commitments center on the social psychological determinants of student success for minoritized and other vulnerable populations. His pioneering research on college students' sense of belonging has informed state policy reform, transformed campus/school practices, and advanced theory and intervention testing. Dr. Strayhorn is the author of ten books and over one hundred chapters, articles, and scientific reports on issues of access, equity, diversity, mentoring, and student learning. He's a member of several journal editorial boards and national advisories for NSF AGEP, Thurgood Marshall College Fund, Children's Defense Fund Freedom School Board, and AAUP Scholars of Color.

M. Yvonne Taylor is a doctoral student in the Program of Higher Education Leadership and assistant professor of instruction for the diversity, equity and inclusion concentration in the College of Natural Sciences at The University of Texas at Austin. Her research interests include the experiences of underrepresented identities on predominantly white campuses, the role of narrative in organizational change, and the recognition and inclusion of staff in DEI change efforts and narratives.

Torie Weiston-Serdan, PhD is a scholar and practitioner with over thirteen years of teaching and youth programming experience. Her research examines how marginalized and minoritized youth are served by mentoring and youth development programs. An emerging leader in the youth mentoring field, she wrote *Critical Mentoring: A Practical Guide*, which has become the handbook for culturally sustaining youth work in the discipline. Outside of teaching and research, Weiston-Serdan runs the Youth Mentoring Action Network, a non-profit dedicated to leveraging justice and equity mentoring. Through her community-based work, she mentors Inland Empire youth through high school into college and careers. She also works extensively with other community-based organizations in support of their youth advocacy efforts, specializing in training mentors to work with diverse youth populations: i.e., Black, Latinx, LGBTQQ, first-generation college students and low-income youth. As a scholar, she examines how marginalized and minoritized youth are served by mentoring and youth development programs. Weiston-Serdan currently serves on the Big Brothers Big Sisters LGBTQ National Advisory Council and the Research Board of the National Mentoring Resource Center. is a scholar and practitioner with over fifteen years of teaching and youth programming experience. Passionate about young people and armed with a firm understanding of educational institutions, Dr. Weiston-Serdan is a strong education and community leader who is using her voice to advocate for youth voice. She has given several talks on education and mentoring, including a TedTalk and has published think pieces on mentoring, education and teaching. Dr. Weiston-Serdan currently serves on the LGBTQ National Advisory Council and as a researcher for the California Mentoring Partnership Research Committee.

Jemimah L. Young, PhD is an associate professor, academic program chair, and presidential impact fellow in the department of teaching, learning, and culture at Texas A&M University. Dr. Young's multicultural and urban education research specialization investigates the academic outcomes of historically marginalized and minoritized populations, with a particular emphasis on Black women and girls. She has over one hundred scholarly publications. In addition, she teaches classes at both the undergraduate and graduate level related to culture, identity, diversity, social justice, foundations in education, and research methodology. In addition to her faculty role, Dr. Young has taught in K-12 schools and has served as a consultant in schools across the U.S. Dr. Young currently serves the program chair for the AERA Critical Examinations of Race, Class, and Gender SIG and editor of the *Journal of African American Women and Girls in Education.*